KT-406-707

HEALTH, WELL-BEING AND OLDER PEOPLE

Jan Reed, David Stanley and Charlotte Clarke

'NIVERSITY

The POLICY

P~P

PRESS

First published in Great Britain in March 2004 by

The Policy Press
University of Bristol
Fourth Floor
Beacon House
Queen's Road
Bristol BS8 1QU
UK

Tel +44 (0)117 331 4054
Fax +44 (0)117 331 4093
e-mail tpp-info@bristol.ac.uk
www.policypress.org.uk

© Jan Reed, David Stanley and Charlotte Clark 2004
Index © Jane Horton 2004

British Library Cataloguing in Publication Data
A catalogue record for this book is available from the British Library.

Library of Congress Cataloging-in-Publication Data
A catalog record for this book has been requested.

ISBN 1 86134 421 X paperback

A hardcover version of this book is also available

Jan Reed and **David Stanley** are Directors of the Centre for Care of Older People, Northumbria University. **Charlotte Clarke** is Professor of Nursing Practice Development Research, School of Health, Community and Education Studies, Northumbria University. **Glenda Cook**, author of Chapter Eight, is a Senior Lecturer in the School of Health, Community and Education Studies, Northumbria University.

The right of **Jan Reed**, **David Stanley** and **Charlotte Clarke** to be identified as authors of this work has been asserted by them in accordance with the 1988 Copyright, Designs and Patents Act.

Cover design by Qube Design Associates, Bristol.
Front cover: photograph supplied by kind permission of Martin Parr at Magnum.
Printed and bound in Great Britain by Hobbs the Printers Ltd, Southampton.

Contents

Foreword   vi

Acknowledgements   vi

Introduction: **The knowledge basis for working with older people**   I

    Evidence-based practice: the measure and mark of   3
professional practice

    Knowledge topics   6

    Locus of expertise   7

    Knowledge chains   7

    Where older people's knowledge fits in this book   9

    Conclusion   I2

one   **Ideas and models of growing older**   I5

    Introduction   I5

    Theories of ageing   I8

    Policy implications   20

    The social 'problem' of older people   22

    Conclusion   26

two   **Attitudes and images**   3I

    Introduction   3I

    Ageism and stereotypes of older people   33

    Cultural and societal factors that shape views and expectations of   35
older people

    Older age stereotypes acting alongside other stereotypes of gender,   36
ethnicity, class and sexuality

    Older people's experiences of ageism   37

    Exploring ageism and attitudes   39

    Empowerment   42

    Implications for change   42

three   **The body growing older**   47

    Introduction   47

    Biomedical models of physical ageing processes   49

    Intrinsic ageing theories   5I

    Extrinsic ageing theories   52

    Disposable soma theory   53

    Longevity and health in older age   53

    Self-assessed health   55

    Managing and responding to ill-health   56

	Older people's views of health	57
	Implications for quality of life and successful ageing	59
	Conclusion	61
four	**The lived environment**	67
	Introduction	67
	Housing	67
	The community environment, pedestrians and transport	74
	Conclusion	77
five	**Memory: self, relationship and society**	79
	Introduction	79
	Cognition, dementia and functional ability	80
	Cognitive disability	81
	The importance of cognition and relationships	82
	Care beyond cognition	87
	The evolution of memory loss	88
six	**Older people, sexuality and intimacy**	95
	Introduction	95
	Sexuality and the quality of life across ages	97
	Images of older people and sexuality	97
	Distaste	99
	Changes in attitudes	100
	Sexual activity	101
	Physical changes over time	102
	Psychological factors	102
	Social contexts	103
	Sexuality and intimacy: the views of older people	103
	Professional support	106
seven	**Living in families and communities**	111
	Older people and their families	115
	Friendship and socialising	119
	Activities	122
eight	**Money and financial resources in later life**	127
	Glenda Cook	
	Introduction	128
	Key issues that concern older people regarding money	129
	The impact of income on the quality of later life	130
	A time to spend money that has accrued throughout life	130
	Income: only one of many resources	131
	Harsh times: life on a low income	132

	Poor benefit take-up	134
	Inappropriate housing leading to liquidity problems	136
	Financial literacy	137
	Money, disability, ill-health and frailty	139
	Direct payments and brokerage schemes	140
	A national asset: older people's contribution to society	141
	Conclusion	143
nine	**Safety and risk**	149
	Introduction	149
	Safety and living	150
	Safety, risk and professional practice	152
	Risk taking and risk management	156
	Organisational risk management	162
	Conclusion	164
ten	**Services, satisfaction and service-user involvement**	169
	Introduction	169
	The policy context	170
	Satisfaction with the services	171
	Satisfaction and service users	172
	Conclusion	182
eleven	**Issues for discussion and practice**	187
	Personhood	188
	Sharing and exercising power	189
	Justice and equity	190
	Practice	191
	Policy	192
	Research	192
	Final comments	193
	Index	195

Foreword

It is difficult now to believe that it was almost seven years ago that the authors of *Health, wellbeing and older people* began asking groups of older people about the issues most important to them in their daily lives. It was an attractive proposition – that they would focus their book on issues raised by us. Older people in Newcastle are sometimes involved as passive subjects of university researchers, and are 'consulted' as users of services. This approach seems refreshingly different.

The authors have drawn freely on material from reports, discussions, drama group scripts and performances, to illustrate each section. But now we can see older people's concerns in relation to the authors' discussion of findings from academic research, their analysis of policies, and their assessment of professional practice and attitudes. Older people's knowledge may be experiential rather than scientific but still has value. Providing a context adds strength to our efforts, as individuals or groups, to change the stereotypes of older people, to overcome ageism in society and in services, and to demonstrate that older people are not just a problem but can contribute to solutions.

There are many messages here for practitioners and policy makers. Each chapter has key points at the beginning, and exercises at the end, which provide a way of relating the issues highlighted to everyday professional practice. So there is something here for everyone with an interest in the processes of ageing, to increase our understanding as practitioners, as teachers, as researchers and as older people. In other words, a good read for everyone!

Vera Bolter, January 2004

Acknowledgements

The authors are grateful to the following:

Vera Bolter, Billie Cummings, Eileen DeVoy, Sheila Manley, Eddie Mottram (Action for health –Senior Citizens in Newcastle)
Barbara Douglas (Better Life in Later Life, Newcastle)
Stella Swinburne (Going Home from Hospital project group and Sexuality in Later Life group)
Robert Weiner (Liaison Officer, North East Pre-retirement Association)
Alan Curry (Age Concern, Newcastle)
Peter Fulton (Older Person's Champion, South Tees Hospitals NHS Trust)
Sheila Rooney (Social Policy Coordinator, Washington Citizens' Advice Bureau)
Sue Childs (Information Management Research Institute, Northumbria University)

The knowledge basis for working with older people

Contents

Evidence-based practice: the measure and mark of professional practice   3
Knowledge topics   6
Locus of expertise   7
Knowledge chains   7
Where older people's knowledge fits in this book   9
Conclusion   12

Key points

- The experiences and views of older people can be marginalised in the development of professional and academic practice.
- There are different forms of knowledge that can contribute to evidence-based practice.
- The basis of this book is discussions with older people about their experiences and views.

This book has taken a long time to develop from an idea to publication – about seven years. Part of this delay was due to the usual everyday problems of getting anything done in a busy world, but other reasons for the delay point to a more enduring issue – the way in which older people can be excluded from debates about the services and support they receive.

The history of this book can be summed up quite quickly – it is not a very complicated story. For some years we had been working with groups of older people who were energetic, interesting, inspiring and insightful. Some of this had been as social work and nursing practitioners, but in later years this had been as lecturers and researchers based in a university. Over time we had built up experience in many different types of activity with many different older people. This could be quite formal, such as interviewing older people as part of research projects, where interview agendas were restricted to a specific focus, or it could be less formal, as we began to participate in workshops, discussion groups and committees with older people. It must be said that the informal conversations that we had with older people tended to be more interesting than some of the structured interviews that we did – partly because in these interviews we felt as if we were imposing our ideas of what was important, rather than listening to older people's priorities. The workshops and other activities, however, allowed for much more exploration of experiences and wishes, not driven by research questions that had come from academic debates.

Capturing and communicating these discussions seemed a natural next step. We had invited some groups of older people to contribute to teaching sessions, and these had always been successful, with students finding that the sessions were useful in grounding their ideas and practice in the real-life experiences of older people. We had also begun to adopt a more participative way of doing our research, with older people involved in writing proposals, collecting data, acting as advisors and writing papers and reports. It seemed that these experiences could be usefully shared with others who were working with older people.

We developed a book proposal with groups of older people, asking them to suggest issues that they thought were key to their well-being, rather than simply follow the ideas of policy makers and educationalists about what was important. Having developed the proposal, we then sent it off to publishers. Every time, the proposal would be returned, rejected. The comments that we got back were mixed. Some reviewers complimented us on our ideas, saying that the book was much needed. Others commented on the 'academic rigour' of the proposal, feeling that the material from the older people might not be of a very high standard and, paradoxically, if it was of a high standard, then it would be from older people who were not 'typical' and therefore the book would be misleading.

The comments from the publishers expressed equally mixed views, but often ended with the conclusion that it was difficult to place such a book, which was not a straightforward academic text but wasn't a self-help book for older people either. It seemed that we were caught in a trap between the traditional academic discussion of issues, which we had become increasingly uncomfortable with, and the accessible but colloquial advice book. The problem seemed to be the contribution from older people, with many reviewers being unsure of what the book would look like and how this material would be presented and used.

Eventually, with advice and support from a freelance editor, the proposal was accepted, and the book was written. The problems that we had, however, are important when thinking about the way in which the voices of older people are marginalised. If we treat their views and experiences simply as interesting phenomena to be researched, we make them less important than if we treat them as the starting point and arbiter for debate and discussion. By feeling uncomfortable about the way material from older people would be 'used' in this book, and by worrying over what category the book would belong to, the reviewers were echoing a widespread view of what is suitable knowledge for practitioners and researchers, and what is not.

These views, of course, have to be placed in the context of debates about what constitutes appropriate knowledge, both for practice and for academic debate.

In the following sections we outline some of these debates, starting with the current calls for practice to be 'evidence based'. From this we go on to discuss what forms this evidence may take. The whole debate has implicit concerns with power – for whoever defines and identifies 'good' evidence has control over what is regarded as knowledge – and so our discussion moves on to this. Returning to this book, we then consider how these debates help to place it in the context of debates about types of knowledge, and how this book might be useful to those working with older people in a variety of different ways.

Evidence-based practice: the measure and mark of professional practice

One of the frequently used phrases in health and social care debates is 'evidence-based care'. In contrast to other bases for care – such as custom and practice, professional preference or opinion – evidence-based care is advocated as a more sound and scientific foundation for taking action. The evidence-based care movement fits in, therefore, with a range of other modernisation drives to improve services and practice, moving away from tradition-based justifications for action. Saying that you do something 'because it has always been done this way', then, is not enough – there has to be a scientific rationale. Delivering care in a way that is evidence based has become critical in contemporary health and social care practice as practice becomes increasingly open to scrutiny. One central feature of the evidence-based practice approach is that it is described as a logical decision-making process in which as much of the proposed intervention is informed by good quality research as is possible. The judgement about the quality of the research base, is, of course, an area of dispute, with some restricting this to the 'gold standard' of the randomised controlled trial, and others including a range of research approaches, including qualitative and less structured methods.

Evidence-based practice, then, is a goal set for practitioners, but there are still some disputes about what is meant by evidence. One way of summing up the types of knowledge used as evidence is to label them 'scientific knowledge', 'intuitive/experiential knowledge' and 'moral/ethical knowledge'. We have used these terms in the following discussion of the nature of these types of knowledge.

Scientific knowledge

Scientific knowledge is the form of knowledge with the highest public profile, and which perhaps attracts the most approval. There are two forms of 'scientific' knowledge. The most common form is depersonalised and decontextualised 'traditional' science (Reed and Procter, 1995). It is knowledge that is generated by someone else, somewhere else and communicated to the user of the knowledge through research reports and professional or academic publications. This form of scientific knowledge is afforded considerable status and indeed researchers pay a great deal of attention to ensuring that the research is of a high quality according to the criteria that it has developed. Decontextualised scientific knowledge, and particularly that of quantitative methodologies, is held to be more absolute in its message than some authors would agree with. For example, Greenhalgh (1999) discusses how population-based findings do not hold true for individuals:"evidence based clinical decision making involves the somewhat counterintuitive practice of assessing the current problem in the light of the aggregated results of hundreds or thousands of comparable cases in a distant population sample, expressed in the language of probability and risk" (p 323). The 'misplaced concreteness' attributed to decontextualised scientific knowledge results in frustrations when trying to apply research-based evidence to individual clients and to services.

The other form of 'scientific' knowledge is in the form that is personalised and contextualised (Reed and Procter, 1995). This is not a remote form of knowledge but is developed by practitioners for their own client group in their own clinical areas. It may be published and communicated to other people but its primary purpose is to inform the development of local practice to meet local health need. Examples include knowledge developed through action research, a localised form of systematic intervention and evaluation, or ethnography, an exploration of the culture and relationships of practice. Because this type of knowledge is developed in ways that do not conform to traditional scientific methodologies, it faces a struggle to be accepted as scientific knowledge at all in some debates. This problem is largely due to the way in which such localised qualitative and naturalistic methodologies cannot be generalised to wider populations under the auspices of statistical analysis. This is not to say that it is not relevant to other settings or situations, just that the process of generalisation is more complex than simple statistical calculations.

Both forms of science may make use of a wide range of research methods and address a range of research questions – for example, analysing the needs of service users – or evaluating the effectiveness of a new intervention or service model. What underpins all forms of scientific knowledge, and where its strength lies, is in the process of its development. This seeks to maximise the quality of the information produced through systematic and transparent processes that can be clearly articulated to others so that others can made a judgement about the relevance of the knowledge for their own purposes.

Intuitive/experiential knowledge

The second form of knowledge is less transparent and public – it is the sort that builds up over time, and leads to 'hunches' about what needs to be done. It is therefore difficult to examine critically – you can't argue with a hunch. Blomfield and Hardy (2000) argue that the tacit, experiential sources of knowledge that practitioners use to inform their practice need to be promoted as important and valid contributors to effective clinical practice. Meerabeau (1995), however, cautions against overenthusiastic and uncritical promotion of intuitive knowledge, pointing out that its tacit nature means that it is difficult to explore, communicate or evaluate.

While intuitive and experiential knowledge might be very powerful, then, it is also difficult to challenge and examine critically. This can lead to it being dismissed as 'subjective' and idiosyncratic. Supporters of intuition and experiential knowledge, however, argue that its subjectivity makes it more relevant to the situations in which it is used – it is less general and more specific. Importantly, it may also be 'owned' more by the person using it – it has not been developed and transmitted by an unknown authority, but has resulted from personal experience that is understandable and of immediate relevance.

Moral/ethical knowledge

Moral or ethical knowledge stems from the values and principles that underpin debates about care and services. Doyal (1993), for example, suggests that there are two basic principles of ethics for practice. The first is the universal duty of good care – the use of expertise to protect the well-being of clients. The second is the universal duty to respect the autonomy of the client. These are two issues that at times conflict with each other – for example, when caring for someone who wishes to take a course of action that may cause them harm. This is what Raines (2000) describes as an ethical dilemma: "when two or more ethical principles apply in a situation, that support mutually inconsistent courses of action" (p 30). This is distinct from the moral distress experienced by many people who have firm ideas on what is right to do but feel unable to act on or implement that decision in a particular situation (Raines, 2000).

Ethical decision making and ethical dilemmas permeate even the most fundamental areas of practice. Seedhouse (1998), for example, asserts that: "morality is of such profound importance in healthcare that it is impossible to understand the nature of health work without also understanding the nature and purpose of ethical reflection" (p 36). Reed and Ground (1997) extend ethical consideration beyond the single clinical decision to locating that decision in the political dimensions of healthcare relationships:

> Many of the moral issues which nurses face are not particular events
> about which single decisions must be made, but permanent features
> of the relationships and structures within which nurses and patients
> find themselves. (Reed and Ground, 1997, p 94)

Unfortunately, one way to cope with moral distress is to develop an emotional distance with the recipients of care and as a result to not even recognise the ethical foundation of an issue. This distancing is fertile ground for the development of "the corruption of care" (Wardhaugh and Wilding, 1993) in which care provision betrays its very purpose of 'caring'. Any form of knowledge for practice has to be located in moral and ethical frameworks to safeguard practice and care provision. There are no aspects of care that are morally neutral despite the technical rationality of evidence-based practice that seduces one into assuming a false neutrality (Trinder, 2000).

Knowledge topics

In addition to distinctions that can be made about forms of knowledge (or where knowledge comes from), distinctions can be made about what the knowledge is about.

Service-context knowledge

Knowledge of the context of care and the care environment is critical to the ability of a practitioner to deliver effective care. Practice is highly dependent on the interactions between professionals, between agencies and between the patient and their environment. Liaschenko and Fisher (1999) refer to this as a form of 'social knowledge'. Practitioners need to match required care (or need) with an appropriate care provider/provision and so they need to know of the skills and working patterns of other providers. They argue that knowledge of the other people involved in care provision allows nurses to 'organise care for multiple individuals across time and space'. This knowledge extends beyond a social form of knowledge through to knowledge of the care and service infrastructure that may be deployed, and that historically shapes care provision.

Person/client knowledge

Liaschenko and Fisher (1999) identify a second form of social knowledge that emphasises the ability of the practitioner to know of the part that growing older plays in the person's life. This includes knowing about the social environment in which a person lives; the impact of growing older on the individual's ability to function; the stigma associated with ageing; and the extent to which the individual adopts the 'dominant cultural discourse' about ageing. 'Knowing the client' is something that practitioners hold as a unique identifier of their practice in a multidisciplinary field and claim as their vehicle for delivering holistic care (Allen, 2000). It is a claim that is being increasingly contested and challenged as requirements for evidence-based practice take a scientific turn.

A crucial dimension of this form of knowledge concerns who it is that holds the knowledge. Professional staff draw on the scientific and experiential knowledge base that they have accumulated over several years of professional education and practising with older people. The holders of person/patient knowledge, however, are older people themselves. It is a knowledge that is specific to their own lives and is rich in their personal biography rather than rich in scientific evidence.

Locus of expertise

A final aspect of knowledge for practitioners that must be considered is the locus, or point of location and control, of that knowledge. Traditionally, professionals have assumed the locus of expertise, and indeed this is reinforced by holding exclusive access to scientific and experiential knowledge. However, it is a position that is being challenged, in part through the increasingly open access of the public to knowledge, but also through the drives to recognise the level of expertise held by patients with long-term health needs and carers. Allen (2000) describes how 'expert carers' are challenging nurses' control over caring processes, nurses' claims to expertise and their authority to define standards of care. Drawing on patient/person knowledge undermines the nurses' claims to professional identity and challenges the ability of nurses to be the only people who can 'know' the patient. The increasing dilution of registered nurses – for example, through skill-mix reviews – further challenges nurses' claims to know clients since it is increasingly non-professionally qualified staff who work most closely with them (Allen, 2000).

Knowledge chains

Another way of thinking about the knowledge that practitioners use is to think about the processes of acquisition – knowledge chains. There are, in effect, three 'knowledge chains' in operation: that of practitioners derived from sources other than their immediate practice environment (for example, research); that of practitioners derived from their practice; and that of the service user.

1. The knowledge *for* practice results in the drivers for developments in practice being derived from outside any specific care environment – distal knowledge. Distal knowledge is relatively prescriptive and is not owned by practitioners themselves. In particular, service users have a role in the generation of this distal knowledge but only as subjects, or members of the sample, of a research study (and therefore at a collective level) or possibly as commissioners of the research. Much of this distal knowledge fits with scientific models of knowledge development, particularly science that seeks to demonstrate or uncover generalisable principles or laws.
2. Knowledge *from* practice is that which is derived from within a specific care environment. It is, therefore, dependent on the contextual issues within that environment such as staffing levels, the nature of the service and the process of engaging service users in care provision. As such, knowledge from practice, or proximal knowledge, does not meet many of the criteria used to judge the quality of knowledge such as its ability to be generalisable (Clarke and Procter, 1999) – or, at least, there are additional processes through which proximal knowledge must pass in order to be relevant to other care environments. It

must be decontextualised, core elements identified, transferred to another care environment, and recontextualised in the new care setting.

Proximal knowledge is derived by practitioners, who consequently have a very strong sense of ownership of that knowledge. Most importantly, proximal knowledge is able to be sensitive to service users at an individual and local level. However, one of the more major concerns about evidence-based practice is that the dominance of quantitative science may devalue, or even exclude, other sources of knowledge such as proximal knowledge (Trinder, 2000). This knowledge chain corresponds to the discussions above about qualitative science and experiential knowledge, and may also reflect the values of practitioners and clients – moral knowledge.

3. The knowledge of service users is that which is derived from their own experiences of self-management and the acquisition of information from family, friends and lay sources of information. Increasingly, however, the distal knowledge of practitioners is accessible to service users – for example, through the Internet. Service-user knowledge is experiential and moral, but it needs to be acknowledged and listened to. As the discussion that follows this points out, there are moves to make the knowledge of service users more transparent and influential in shaping services, but this demands some changes in our ideas of and responses to different forms of evidence.

Clarke and Wilcockson (2002) argue that while a great deal is expected of evidence-based practice, it is no panacea. Distal knowledge may be a tool (Trinder, 2000), but it is the proximal knowledge that allows practitioners in health and social care to know whether it is the right tool for the job, and whether it is the right knowledge for the needs of clients. As a result, there is relative stability of distal knowledge but instability in decision making based on the rapidly fluctuating proximal knowledge (situated decision making). Martin (1999), for example, highlights how "clinical judgments made by mental health nurses are time- and situation-dependent and consequently are unique".

It is in the area of bringing together proximal and distal knowledge that there is most concern expressed within the literature. Trinder (2000) writes that "comparatively little attention has been given to the question of how to combine evidence with clinical expertise or consumer perspectives" (p 214). Greenhalgh (1999) also calls for the integration of individual patient narratives with population-derived evidence in the context of evidence-based practice, and Rolfe (1998) argues that most desirable is a synthesis of scientific theoretical, experiential and personal knowledges.

Similarly, J.B. Clarke (1999) argues that different forms of evidence such as "clinical anecdote" and systematic reviews "should not be in competition but where possible be mutually supportive and informative.... A pluralistic outlook is vital for best practice and patient outcome" (p 92). This is a view shared by Greenhalgh (1999). In relation to reflective practice, Schon (1987) describes professional practice as a complex process that involves juggling situational demands, intuition, experience and knowledge.

Proximal knowledge is generated through the critical examination of care and service provision in relation to the needs of the service users. In a wider context, Brechin et al (2000) argue that "critical practice draws on an awareness of wider ethical dilemmas, strategic issues, policy frameworks and socio-political contexts" (p xi). On the whole, however, debates about advanced practice do not appear to concern themselves with 'seeing' patient need and subsequently reconceptualising care provision and the role of professionals (Clarke and Wilcockson, 2002).

Crucially, proximal knowledge involves understanding how one's practices and care interventions are reflective of little more than the philosophy to which we subscribe. For example, in dementia care, the biomedical model leads to care interventions such as pharmaceutical and behavioural management, while a socio-critical model leads to interventions such as family nursing and systemic practice (C.L. Clarke, 1999). Distal knowledge is unable to help us make choices between such philosophical underpinnings of our professional practice (Clarke and Wilcockson, 2002). Indeed, the more the shift towards the reductionist approach and technical rationality of evidence-based practice, the less practice becomes theoretically explicit (Im and Meleis, 1999). Philosophical guidance is more likely to be derived from policy developments and here it may not concur with the assumptions about practice held by individual practitioners or teams.

Where older people's knowledge fits in this book

The discussion above helps to set out some parameters that can help us locate the contributions of older people to this book. The discussions of scientific knowledge set out characteristics and criteria that clearly do not match the material from older people used in this book. This material is personal, ad hoc, subjective and creative, rather than a systematic reporting of facts. Yet the discussion above shows that there are other forms of knowledge that are useful in developing practice.

Experiential knowledge, for example, is important in informing practice in the way that it is personal and contextual. Using the experiential knowledge of others, however, is more complicated. Some of the things that make our own experiential knowledge significant to us, such as its immediacy and saliency, may well make other people's experiential knowledge significant to them, but invisible to others. An older person who has experience of the issues involved in growing older may well feel that this knowledge is important, but find that it is difficult to communicate, even if others are willing to listen. The development of campaigning groups attempts to overcome this barrier, by using a range of communication strategies, but they face problems in ensuring that their voices are heard when many other groups may be clamouring for attention, or ensuring that their messages are not misinterpreted as simple complaining or 'attention seeking'. For the individual older person, the difficulties are even greater. Without sophisticated communication tools, individuals are left facing the difficulties of giving a complex message to people who might not be skilled or motivated in listening.

Using the experiential knowledge of older people, then, requires as much from practitioners and researchers as it does from older people. This book has tried to show how this can be done, by using pieces of writing and discussion from older people, and framing these in ways that draw out messages for others and place these experiences in the context of what is known more formally, through research – scientific knowledge. This strategy does not seek to support or validate the experiential knowledge of older people that we present in the book, but simply to point to the connections that can be seen. In our practice and research, however, these connections are not so overt, and this book therefore has another aim, which is to help extend this connected way of thinking beyond this book into the world in which older people experience growing older.

Connected to this treatment of experiential knowledge is another type of knowledge discussed above – moral knowledge. This is not so much about knowing 'what is' but about knowing 'what should be'. This is based on values and ethics, and ideas that we have about ways to behave that are good and that have good outcomes – based, of course, on our ideas of what is good. These might be ideas about fairness, justice, human rights – which are the stuff of many political debates – or ideas about the values of personhood, client-centredness and the need to ensure that older people's wishes and preferences are respected and responded to.

These values underpin this book, as they do much practice and research. The aim of the book is to help make life better for older people, by widening a debate about what they need and want in a way that makes their voices central rather than peripheral to the voices of practitioners, academics and policy makers. As such, it is based on principles of justice and personhood.

The discussion above also touched on the connections between knowledge and power, in that those who have socially valued knowledge (such as scientific knowledge) have the power to make decisions, change opinions and define reality. This book, by introducing different forms of knowledge – that is, the experiential knowledge of older people – seeks to go some way towards equalising the differences in power between older people and those who provide services or research their lives.

These moral or ethical positions are not cries in the wilderness – they fit in with moves in policy and research to respond to calls for equal partnerships with older people. In turn these moves can be linked up to a more general growth in the impetus to greater equality with all people who use services. These drives can be described as 'consumerism', which has both positive and negative connotations. The positive connotations are that seeing people as 'consumers' rather than as people who are provided for, through some form of benevolent but authoritarian system, also involves seeing them as people with views and choices. The negative results of the consumerist model are that it misses out the complexities of need and preferences, and reduces using services to buying items from a shop. An overglib notion of consumerism glosses over the issues about how choice is supported and responded to, and how people are equipped to make choices, either by having good enough information or systems to support their buying power.

These caveats aside, there is some evidence of attempts to make consumerism – or its less materialistic formulation, partnership – a real force in shaping services and ideas. The National Service Framework (NSF) for Older People (DoH, 2001a), for example, has been established in the National Health Service (NHS), with one of its key principles being to promote person-centredness in services. Alongside this there has been a move to address issues of older people's participation in policy and planning – for example, through the Better Government for Older People programme. This developed schemes in target areas for improving consultation between older people and policy makers both at national and local level.

The process of developing partnership, however, is not a straightforward one, and Gilleard and Higgs (1998) rightly caution against being caught up in the rhetoric of consumerism without attending to the realities of older people's experiences. They point to the development of consumerism in health and social care over the past few decades, and to its application in services for older people in particular. They argue that the consumerist principle may work when people do have the purchasing power that true consumers have, but that in a mixed economy of provision, where older people have limited resources and limited opportunities for making their views known, such consumerism is not attainable. What can result, Gilleard and Higgs argue, is that the needs of older people, particularly those who are very frail, can be forgotten if it is assumed that older people are able and willing to articulate their views and act on them when choosing services. If the rules of engagement are set by those who do not understand the variety of experiences of older people, many will be marginalised. These observations can be brought to bear on many other developments that adopt the rhetoric of user involvement. One example from the UK is the Expert Patient initiative, which seeks to identify people who have experience with certain health problems, so that they can be used as a resource for other people with the same problems (DoH, 2001b). Closer examination of this, however, suggests that this expertise is defined by compliance with accepted medical models of the illness, rather than user-generated ideas and strategies. In this formulation of expertise, then, service users have to comply with accepted wisdom rather than challenge it, and so genuine partnership seems unlikely.

Similarly there have been moves to increase partnerships between older people and researchers. This can be traced through the increased use of qualitative methods that reflected the ideas of participants, rather than structured research approaches that derived their structure from academic or policy frameworks. From these developments there has been increasing involvement of older people in research, from sitting on funding committees, to being involved in designing and carrying out studies, to leading their own research programmes. Much of this development has occurred on an ad hoc basis, but this has become more formalised over the years, with bodies such as the Joseph Rowntree Foundation requiring applicants for funding to show user involvement. The practicalities of this development, however, may take some time to be worked out. Involving older people in research may require extensive support for them, in order to facilitate participation. This may involve some training in research methods, leading to a potential paradox – if older people are valued in research activity because they have a 'user view', then training may turn them into researchers, and this unique contribution may be lost. As more research teams explore these issues, then strategies will be developed to address them, as they have been in other areas of partnership research, but this will only happen if these issues are openly acknowledged and debated.

Conclusion

This introductory chapter has sought to give some flavour of the book, by giving an account of how and why it developed. We wanted to write a book that reflected the ideas and experiences of some of the older people we had been involved with in a range of activities, but were also staking a claim to be treated seriously on academic terms – this is not an anecdotal collection of material with no relevance outside the environment in which it was developed. As the discussion above has indicated, being taken seriously academically is a process that has to negotiate many of the traditions and definitions there are about what is legitimate knowledge. Contrasting the contributions of older people to this book with traditional scientific knowledge, particularly quantitative research that seeks to generalise its findings, leads to the conclusion that this is not the form of knowledge that we are offering here. The discussions of experiential and moral knowledge, however, are clearly relevant, and it is here that we would locate the material.

Using and evaluating the material from older people, however, still presents us with a number of challenges. As we discussed earlier, initial book proposals were met with some questions about the validity of the material, that the older people would either be inarticulate or, if they were able to express views, would therefore be 'unrepresentative' of older people. In response to this we would state that we make no claims that the material from older people is representative in the sense that it reflects the totality of the range of older people's experiences. What it does do, however, is reflect and articulate key issues in the lives of older people in a way that is useful to the central concerns of this book – developing practice and research in a way that is responsive to the needs and wishes of older people.

We have also discussed some of the political and organisational factors that influence ideas of legitimate knowledge, starting off with ideas about 'evidence-based practice', which are prevalent in current debates about the quality and effectiveness of services and professional practice. While this evidence can be thought of in quite narrow terms, we make the plea that this should be expanded to embrace the types of evidence that we are offering here – the knowledge of the particular and specific contexts of older people's lives, and their goals and experiences.

In making a case for the use of this experiential and moral knowledge, we are not discounting more traditional scientific knowledge, and indeed we feel that this is extremely important. We would not like to suggest that the only knowledge that we value is the immediate and the personal. We would argue that practitioners and researchers need all sorts of different forms of knowledge, but we also realise that making sense of these can be difficult and confusing. To this end, then, we have tried to combine different forms of knowledge. We begin each chapter with material from older people, as a way of grounding thinking and discussion in their experiences, before moving on to overviews and discussion of the research and policy debates around the chapter topic. At the heart of the book, therefore, is material that discusses feelings and experiences about growing old and ideas and definitions about health in older age. This material has been produced by older people through creative writing groups, songs and poems. This voice of older people illustrates and is supported by material that we as authors have been privileged to contribute to their narrative.

In the final sections of the chapters we return to material from older people, sometimes as we present exercises and activities that readers might engage in. This basic format is, of course, a flexible one, particularly where the research is about the views of older people.

We do not want to set up an artificial dichotomy between academic material and that from older people – gerontological research has a long tradition of seeking to explore older people's views, although it may have done so using frameworks and criteria that have been derived from debates about methodological validity that are more reflective of researchers' concerns than older people's. What we are trying to do, then, is to present all of this material in an integrated way, which will help readers to keep older people centre stage in their thinking.

References

Allen, D. (2000) 'Negotiating the role of expert carers on an adult hospital ward', *Sociology of Health and Illness*, vol 22, no 2, pp 149-71.

Blomfield, R. and Hardy, S. (2000) 'Evidence-based nursing practice', in L. Trinder and S. Reynolds (eds) *Evidence-based practice: A critical appraisal*, Oxford: Blackwell.

Brechin, A., Brown, H. and Eby, M.A. (2000) 'Introduction', in A. Brechin, H. Brown and M.A. Eby (eds) *Critical practice in health and social care*, London: Sage Publications.

Clarke, C.L. and Procter, S. (1999) 'Practice development: ambiguity in research and practice', *Journal of Advanced Nursing*, vol 30, pp 975-82.

Clarke, C.L. (1999) 'Dementia care partnerships: knowledge and ownership', in T. Adams and C.L. Clarke (eds) *Dementia care: Developing partnerships in practice*, London: Baillière Tindall, pp 5-35.

Clarke, C.L. and Wilcockson, J. (2002) 'Seeing need and developing care: exploring knowledge for and from practice', *International Journal of Nursing Studies*, vol 39, no 4, pp 397-406.

Clarke, J.B. (1999) 'Evidence-based practice: a retrograde step? The importance of pluralism in evidence generation for the practice of healthcare', *Journal of Clinical Nursing*, vol 8, no 1, pp 89-94.

DoH (Department of Health) (2001a) *National Service Framework for Older People*, London: DoH.

DoH (2001b) *The expert patient: A new approach to chronic disease management for the 21st century* (www.ohn.gov.uk/ohn/people/expert.htm).

Doyal, L. (1993) 'The role of the public in healthcare rationing', *Critical public health*, vol 4, no 1.

Gilleard, C. and Higgs, P. (1998) 'Forum. Old people as users and consumers of healthcare: a third age rhetoric for a fourth age reality?', *Ageing and Society*, vol 18, pp 233-48.

Greenhalgh, T. (1999) 'Narrative based medicine in an evidence based world', *British Medical Journal*, vol 318, pp 323-5.

Im, E. and Meleis, A.I. (1999) 'Situation-specific theories: philosophical roots, properties, and approach', *Advances in Nursing Science*, vol 22, no 2, pp 11-24.

Liaschenko, J. and Fisher, A. (1999) 'Theorizing the knowledge that nurses use in the conduct of their work', *Scholarly Inquiry for Nursing Practice: An International Journal*, vol 13, no 1, pp 29-41.

Martin, P.J. (1999) 'Influences on clinical judgement in mental health nursing', *Nursing Times Research*, vol 4, no 4, pp 273-80.

Meerabeau, L. (1995) 'The nature of practitioner knowledge', in J. Reed and S. Procter (eds) *Practitioner research in healthcare: The inside story*, London: Chapman and Hall, pp 32-45.

Raines, M.L. (2000) 'Ethical decision making in nurses: relationships among moral reasoning, coping style and ethics stress', *JONA's Healthcare Law, Ethics, and Regulation*, vol 2, no 1, pp 29-41.

Reed, J. and Ground, I. (1997) *Philosophy for nursing*, London: Arnold.

Reed, J. and Procter, S. (1995) 'Practitioner research in context', in J. Reed and S. Procter (eds) *Practitioner research in healthcare: The inside story*, London: Chapman and Hall, pp 3-31.

Rolfe, G. (1998) 'Advanced practice and the reflective nurse: developing knowledge out of practice', in G. Rolfe and P. Fulbrook (eds) *Advanced nursing practice*, Oxford: Butterworth-Heinemann.

Schon, D. (1987) *Educating the reflective practitioner*, San Fransisco, CA: Jossey-Bass.

Seedhouse, D. (1988) *Ethics: The heart of healthcare*, Chichester: John Wiley & Sons.

Trinder, L. (2000) 'A critical appraisal of evidence-based practice', in L. Trinder and S. Reynolds (eds) *Evidence-based practice: A critical appraisal*, Oxford: Blackwell Science.

Wardhaugh, J. and Wilding, P. (1993) 'Towards an explanation of the corruption of care', *Critical Social Policy*, vol 37, pp 4-31.

ONE

Ideas and models of growing older

Contents

Introduction	15
Theories of ageing	18
Policy implications	20
The social 'problem' of older people	22
Conclusion	26

Key points

- We need to review critically the usefulness of identifying older people as a distinct group in society.
- There are a number of ideas, models and theories about growing older, which affect the way we think about older people and the way they think about themselves.
- 'Deficit' models, which focus on loss of ability, present a negative view of growing older.
- 'Activity' models can present successful ageing as not ageing at all, and can impose impossible challenges and an unhelpful competitiveness on older people.
- The definition of growing older as a 'problem' can be formulated in different ways.

Introduction

"Getting old is not for cowards!"

This comment was made by a participant in a focus group of older people discussing their ideas about healthy ageing. The focus groups were made up of older people who attended a local authority-run day centre, and they had a variety of health and functional problems that limited their activities. In the focus group they talked about their experiences of growing older, and the way in which the process of ageing was accompanied by a sense of an increasing lack of fit between them and the rest of the world. The things that they had done, and in many cases still wanted to do, were becoming difficult and required greater determination and effort in an environment full of physical obstacles and social barriers. The quote given above came from a woman who had talked about the difficulties of everyday life and her resolve to overcome them where possible. It seems a good point to start this chapter, which is about ideas of ageing.

The message this woman is giving is that growing older is a particular experience that evokes a particular response in others. While we discuss ageism in more detail in Chapter Two and the physical aspects of growing older in more detail in Chapter Three, what we want to do here is set the scene for these discussions by examining some of the ideas in gerontological debates about what it is we define as older people, and what sort of challenges these definitions give rise to.

The discussions in this book's introduction concerned the types of knowledge we might use or develop when working with older people. The process of using this knowledge is, at a fundamental level, a process of making sense of our encounters with older people and theirs with us. This sense making also goes on at theoretical or conceptual levels, as we try to make general statements about ageing that fit with or explain our specific experiences. This search for theory is a feature of academic knowledge, and a coherent body of theory is seen as marking out an academic discipline or field in a way that specifies its concerns, its boundaries, its methods and its questions. The development of gerontology (the study of growing older) has been a process marked with periodic concerns about the need to develop coherent theories and frameworks that would mark out the territory and direction of gerontology.

The search for theory follows on from another debate in gerontology – that is, whether there is such a thing as 'older people'. This may seem a counterintuitive question to raise, as we all know, or think we know, older people when we see them. The point that some writers make, however, is that when we look critically at what are taken for granted as characteristics of older people, they begin to break down. With some groups in society we can see (or construct) some clear divisions between these groups and others, and between these groups and ourselves. When we talk about children, for example, we can use some legally determined or empirically researched chronological age as a cut-off point. Below this, humans are children, and above this they are not. When talking about people with mental health problems, we can try to use some diagnostic classification system or assessment schedule to say whether a person belongs to this group or not. There are, of course, problems with these lines of demarcation: individual variations in development make childhood a more elastic concept than we suppose, and mental health problems have to be placed in an ever-changing context of cultural definitions and norms. Nevertheless, these definitions are used, and part of their function is not only to specify the characteristics, problems and needs of particular client groups, but also to distinguish them from 'us', the 'normal' people.

In the case of older people, however, this will not do. While we can point to legal definitions of, say, 'pensionable age', empirical evidence does not support the idea that there are clear developmental changes once this age is reached. Individual variations and differences are too marked to make this credible. Not only is it difficult, therefore, to demarcate older people, separate them from other groups in society and specify their unique needs and problems, but it also becomes difficult to separate them from us. Older people are us, just a bit further on in development and experience. We will become old; we will become them. Being old is not like being young, something you grow out of – it is what we will all grow into. Being old is not a time-limited condition, like being pregnant, or something for which there might be a cure, like an illness – it is just being old. When we debate issues in the care of older people, therefore, we debate our own care.

Metaphorical distance, however, has been maintained by language, in the way that this has emphasised difference and has also become pejorative. It is easy to dismiss issues of language as trivial, but language is extremely important in the way that it not only reflects what we feel, but also shapes it. Referring to older people as 'geriatrics', for example, reduces them to examples of a medical specialty, and 'the elderly' emphasises their distinctness as a group. The use of the term 'older people', however – which is a fairly recent term – makes the point that there is a group who are simply people who are older than others. Critics point out that everyone is older than someone else, but in some ways this is a positive aspect of the term. It reminds me that I am older than some people and that you are older than some people, and that we all share this state of seniority. Most importantly, however, there is some evidence that older people themselves prefer this term (Walker, 1993).

Whatever term we use to describe older people, there is still a question about whether we should try to demarcate them in any way. Opinion is very much divided on this. At a pragmatic level, it seems obvious that meeting needs depends on being able to identify them, and that this is facilitated by being able to classify and summarise the groups of people who have these needs – targeting services can be more effective. On the other hand, this process raises a number of concerns. Many writers have made the point that the result of many policies based on differentiating older people from others is that older people are also separated from others in physical and social ways – by being placed in particular places to receive care (such as care homes or hospitals) or by being excluded from social activities and debates. Distinctions can also make excluding older people easier. Retirement policies and pensions for older people are an interesting example of this process. Pensions that are provided simply on the basis of a person reaching a particular age seem to be benevolent mechanisms for ensuring provision for older people. When they are interpreted as a rationale for compulsory retirement by employers, then their benevolence becomes questionable – they are used as an excuse to exclude older people from the job market. Because pensions are not equal to salaries, then older people inevitably experience reduced incomes, which affect their activities and participation in social events. They then become 'hidden' from others – they are not seen around, and their experiences are therefore not acknowledged in everyday discussions. Another way of hiding the structured inequalities experienced by older people is to portray them as affluent and

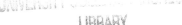

emphasise the power of the 'grey pound' – a process that, as Ginn (1993) points out, denies the problems that older people face.

The 'unpopularity' of older people very much depends on them being singled out as a group who are different from the rest of us. This demarcation simultaneously creates and reinforces stereotypes of older people and puts in place mechanisms for systematically classifying their needs as being the 'problems of old age' rather than problems that are shared across society. What seems a reasonable and sensible approach to identifying need can become a means of pigeonholing people and reducing them to stereotypes. Whether we adopt a position of 'compassionate ageism' (Binstock, 1984) where we feel pity for the frailty and problems of older people, or whether we portray them more positively as affluent and therefore less needy – thus approaching what Arber and Ginn (1991) have termed 'conflictual ageism' where older people are seen as taking resources away from other groups – both positions depend on stereotypes.

There are, therefore, some consequences of demarcating age that can be negative. Bill Bytheway wrote a thought-provoking book in 1995 in which he argued that a way to a non-ageist gerontology might be to abandon the presumption that old age exists (Bytheway, 1995). In response to this, Molly Andrews (1999) argued that to deny ageing was in itself ageist, and that we need to accept that people grow old – pretending that they don't denies this experience and the benefits it can bring. The debate continued with an article by Bytheway (2000) in which he argued that it was possible, indeed necessary, to problematise the assumptions we make about the existence of old age, without devaluing or ignoring the experiences of growing older. Such critical challenges, Bytheway argues, are necessary if we are to understand growing older, in any useful way. When it comes to policy making, practice and research, for example, assumptions about what it is to grow older can have far-reaching and potentially negative consequences.

Theories of ageing

Following on from these debates about definitions of older people are debates about concepts of growing older – theories of ageing. These theories seek to describe the changes that happen to people as they get older, at a physical, social and psychological level, identifying common, frequent or universal patterns. Physical theories of growing older are discussed in detail in Chapter Three, so the focus in this chapter is on what could be described as the socio-psychological theories that have been developed, always remembering that experiences of physical changes are inextricable from experiences of social and psychological change. At a simplistic level, if you age physically in a way that makes you look older and feel less active, then this will affect the activities you engage in and the way that you feel about yourself.

Socio-psychological theories can be divided into two types: those that describe growing older as a process of withdrawal and reduced engagement, and those that describe it as a period of activity. These latter theories are generally about what is called 'successful ageing' in that they are not necessarily descriptive theories about how people grow older, but are prescriptive theories about how people *can* grow older.

The first formulation of a theory that emphasised the withdrawal of older people from activity was the 'disengagement theory' of Cumming and Henry, developed in the 1950s. From a longitudinal study in the US, they concluded that those people reporting the greatest satisfaction with their life were those who had 'disengaged' from former roles and activities. Their contentment with their current lifestyle suggested that this process of disengagement was normal, natural and even desirable (Cumming and Henry, 1961).

Notions of disengagement as the usual or ideal form of ageing have been criticised on a number of grounds. The theory can be used as a rationale for not supporting or encouraging older people to remain active and engaged, and plays to the stereotypes of the 'Granny in the Rocking Chair' image. Within such a framework, expectations are set for low engagement and activity, with correspondingly low need for services and facilities. If we expect older people to do less and less as they grow older, then we need to do less and less to support them. Another criticism of disengagement theory is that it has a negative emphasis – it focuses on what people give up, and says little about what they gain. More recent theoretical discussions have given more emphasis to positive aspects of disengagement – most notably Tornstam's theory of 'gerotranscendence'. Tornstam (1996) has described this as a shift from the material and rational concerns of younger adulthood towards a perspective on life that transcends these elements, and that focuses more on the spiritual and meditative. Hence older age is a period of change and also of personal growth, with the implication that this process should be recognised, respected and supported.

Activity theories of ageing have a very different emphasis on the ideals and goals of maturity. Havighurst (1963) was one of the first to develop a theory, which drew from research, which indicated that those older people who were happiest with their lives were those who had remained active and engaged with social life. This could involve maintaining existing activities and relationships or it could mean developing new ones. Activity theory, under the rubrics of 'positive ageing' and 'successful ageing', has become a popular way of thinking about growing older, not least because it challenges stereotypes of loss and restriction. These ideas form the basis of much self-help literature and consumer material, perhaps because they stand in contrast to many professional and medical models of decline in later life. This material can include advice on diet and exercise, and also reflects a view of growing older that places few, if any, restrictions on older people. Discussions about sexual activity, for example, serve to reinforce the idea that older people today are not bound by any restrictions placed on them in past years, where older people were expected to become asexual. A more worrying element is that which seems to be negative towards any suggestion of change with age. Advertisements for plastic surgery, face creams and hair dyes may reflect the idea that ageing is to be avoided at all costs, and 'giving in' to it is a sign of weakness or laziness.

The emphasis found in the successful ageing literature is on physical functioning (see, for example, Klein and Bloom's 1997 handbook) – something that can exclude those who are restricted in their activities as they grow older. This idea of optimal physical functioning, however, has been connected to psychological functioning, in that there is also an emphasis on having a 'positive attitude' to growing older. This positive attitude consists of a refusal to accept the physical consequences of growing older as being inevitably life limiting, or to see growing older as a process of decline that cannot be halted. While some of this literature encourages people to challenge their assumptions and stereotypes, there is also a potential negative consequence – that people feel guilty or inadequate if they are unable to overcome difficulties. The development of the idea of successful ageing, in the US in particular, has been described by Strawbridge as "implying a kind of contest. But people should never be told that they failed ageing because they had arthritis" (Strawbridge, 2000, p 14).

The debate about theories of ageing is largely about the extent to which they can adequately describe or explain the experiences of people as they grow older. With these criteria to meet, theories have to be inclusive in that they address the experiences of as many older people as possible, without being so broad that they become vacuous. As a guide to research, theories need to indicate what the key phenomena to be investigated are, and how they might be related to each other, as well as developing ideas about methodologies and methods. For theories to inform practice, they need to have clear connections with debates about the types of support older people might want, how this can be determined and how services can be tailored to match their needs. For theories to have policy relevance, they need to be able to direct thinking about how need can be defined and met, and how services can be shaped. In these ways, debates about theories are not just self-indulgent navel-gazing on the part of gerontologists, but have potential to affect, in direct and indirect ways, the lives of older people.

Policy implications

These issues can often be most easily seen at a political and policy level, where processes of distinguishing between people on the basis of age materialise into legislation, funding decisions and service provision. The decisions that are made at a political level therefore impact on practice and care. This may be in the way that the resources and funding for care are determined, priorities for spending are set, and goals and aims for services are formulated (Boyajian, 1988). Where state resources are limited (always remembering that the state has already made decisions about what level of resources it should have, through its taxation policies), then the competing claims of various different groups have to be weighed against each other. In this process of weighing, a number of considerations may be made. First, it may be thought that the state does not have a responsibility to meet these needs – that the provision of state support is either demeaning to people because it reduces their independence, or it is unjust to those who have been prudent enough to make their own provision. Second, if some state responsibility is acknowledged, then a number of other considerations come into play about the strengths of the claims of different groups.

In deciding between the claims of different groups, a number of cultural and social values come into play. Societies can, for example, attach merit to certain groups because their dependency arises from an activity that is approved of. War heroes, for example, may be regarded more highly than, say, those who abuse drugs. This is because the former group acquired their disability through activities that are perceived to be of benefit to others in society, while the latter group may be reviled because their problems are seen as self-inflicted and of no benefit to others, possibly making society more uncomfortable, unpleasant or dangerous to live in.

Reciprocity

Here there are some notions of reciprocity being evoked – the idea that the contributions that a group of people make (or have made in the past) should be rewarded and met with equivalent contributions. If this form of reciprocity prevails, then older people are likely to benefit: their past contributions – for example, in a Europe that has seen much military, political and cultural conflict in the last century – will be held up as justification for providing them with support now. If, however, the idea of reciprocity is time limited – that only current contributions are acknowledged – then the position of older people becomes more vulnerable. If older people are not working or do not have active social or familial roles, then they may be seen as 'parasites' on the active, working, money-making younger population.

Another temporal dimension of reciprocity, however, is the commitment that we might feel to future generations. As Becker (1986) has argued, this is a somewhat puzzling idea, and seems to be based on some sort of allegiance to the notion that perpetuating the human race (or at least our own ethnic version of it) is of great importance. Another element of this commitment to future generations is, perhaps, based on self-interest – we look after the young in order that they will look after us if we need help when we are old. It may be the case, then, that when choosing between meeting the needs of older people or those of children and younger people, one formulation of reciprocity would lead us to favour future generations. The irony is, of course, that if this is done for reasons of self-interest then we abandon older people in the hope that younger people will not do the same to us in the future.

There are, of course, other cultural values, which impinge upon the decisions made about the distribution of resources to different groups. Western society, for example, is often described as being youth-orientated, in the way that people see youth as desirable and old age as distasteful. This set of values can make older people an unpopular choice for resource allocation. These negative attitudes to others have, of course, been explored by many writers, who point to literature and current cultural images as reflecting these aesthetics (for example, Till, 1993; Blaikie, 1994). As Norman (1987) has put it, "Both as individuals, and as members of society, we find it extremely difficult to be honest about our attitudes to old age and old people. There is an ambivalence at the root of our being". Norman details this ambivalence further when she talks about feelings that "cannot with decency be openly expressed" such as "contempt of the young and strong for the old and weak; fear of the mortality which old age represents; guilt which is translated into anger; and resentment over the need to use scarce resources and precious time on people 'who have had their life'" (Norman, 1987, p 3).

In current UK policy debates about services and support for older people we are bombarded by headlines about the 'problems' of an ageing society. The Age Concern Millennium Debate of the Age, for example, began with statements about the increasing burden on health and social services (Age Concern England, 2001). Figures about the increasing numbers of older people and reduced numbers of younger people surround discussions about the way that society is developing. The impact of these changes on welfare and economic systems is endlessly rehearsed, usually with the observation that perhaps our welfare system has been too successful. People are living too long because of the great advances in healthcare and living standards and, ironically, this success threatens to drag our welfare services down. The spectre is presented of vast numbers of old and dependent people needing support from a dwindling number of young people. Older people have become a problem.

The social 'problem' of older people

Sally Macintyre (1977) analysed this notion of older people as a social problem and identified two different formulations that it can take – her analysis is still useful today. She begins by quoting Fuller and Myers, who in 1941 commented that: "Social problems are what people think they are, and if conditions are not defined as social problems by the people involved in them, they are not problems to those people, although they may be problems to outsiders or to scientists" (Fuller and Myers, 1941, p 321). Macintyre's argument is that not only have older people not always been seen as a problem, but that the types of problem that they are thought to present have changed over time.

The era when older people were not seen to be a problem was, in Macintyre's reading, a period in which older people were not seen as different from other people – when they were not singled out as a separate group. As the Majority Report of the Royal Commission on the Poor Law of 1909 commented: "the practice of considering the aged as a class by themselves for purposes of relief is one of modern growth" (part 4, para 304, cited in Gray, 1979).

Throughout early policy developments – such as the Elizabethan Poor Laws, which dealt with the needy – older people were not distinguished in any way from other groups of people needing support or 'relief'. Macintyre (1977) argues that older people only became 'officially' recognised in policy formation towards the end of the 19th century.

It is worth pointing out, however, that other commentators have suggested that older people were seen as a problem before the 19th century, and were distinguished as a specific group. Minois (1989), for example, has traced discussions about older people back to antiquity, and points out a number of examples of the 'age problem' being debated.

Interestingly, however, the problems seem to be very different from the ones we think we have today. In the Roman Empire, for example, the problem of old age was that old men had too much power and influence. Minois (1989) describes Roman law as giving the paterfamilias 'exorbitant' rights over his family, including rights to:

- give away his children to another paterfamilias;
- sell his children as slaves;
- condemn any member of his family to death.

Understandably, old men were resented by younger people, who were only free of this tyranny when the paterfamilias died.

Nevertheless, Macintyre's (1977) analysis of more recent welfare policy in this country seems to hold true – the recognition of older people as a discrete group who required specific services is only clearly apparent relatively recently.

When older people were distinguished as a 'special' group of the poor and needy, Macintyre (1977) argues that this was tied up with ideas about 'deserving' and 'undeserving' poor. Some of the strategies for dealing with need, such as 'indoor' or workhouse relief, were partly designed and administered as ways of discouraging people from applying for help, and to motivate them to provide for themselves, a strategy based on the assumption that many of the poor were able to fend for themselves but were too lazy or dissolute to do so. Older people, however, could not be accused of such moral degeneracy – even the most vigorous detective of abuses of the public purse could see that older people were simply not able to provide for themselves, particularly in a world where the Industrial Revolution had put a premium on heavy manual labour in factories, and where older people were therefore not able to support themselves.

Macintyre, however, further discusses how, after the identification of older people as a social problem, the problem itself is open to different formulations. The first formulation is that the problem is a *humanitarian* one – in other words "a perception of old age as bringing problems of various kinds to individuals, problems which the community should attempt to ameliorate through increased provision" (Macintyre, 1977, p 49). The humanitarian view was the one that, Macintyre argues, predominated in the UK at the beginning of the 19th century – it stimulated the separation of older people from other needy groups, and set policy goals as being the appropriate and adequate provision of support.

Macintyre (1977) goes on to describe how the problem of old age was reformulated as time went on. This was particularly evident as the debates in the UK about the new welfare state took place, and plans for this were developed. For example, William Beveridge, the architect of the welfare state, more than once cautioned against too-liberal provision for older people – the welfare state that he envisaged would be funded through the contributions of young working people, and therefore their welfare was paramount.

> On the one hand, the provision made for age must be satisfactory otherwise great numbers may suffer. On the other hand, every shilling added to pension rates is extremely costly in total.… It is dangerous to be in any way lavish to old age, until adequate provision has been assured for all other needs, such as the prevention of disease and the adequate nutrition of the young. (Beveridge, 1942, para 236)

The problem of old age then became one of how to reduce the demands of older people on others, or to meet their needs at a containable (and reduced) cost. Macintyre describes this as the *organisational* formulation – "consideration of how best to reduce the social costs imposed on the community by the elderly population" (1977, p 44).

If we use Macintyre's framework as a way of exploring the impact of policy on practice, then we can look at the implications for the provision of care and support. If the policy formulation is a humanitarian one, then the goals of care are to meet need and address problems in as effective a way as possible. The concern is primarily that older people are not receiving enough care, or good enough care. We could expect, therefore, that resources would be made available, or at least efforts would be made to provide them, and that there would be concerns about the quality of the care that was delivered, and that it was provided in the right way and at the right time. Because this would, hopefully, entail some concern with the views of older people themselves, then we could also expect that the autonomy of older people would be promoted.

If, however, the policy formulation is an organisational one, and the central concern is to minimise cost, then the implications for practice and provision are very different. Not only are the resources for care limited, but the whole goal of the service is to provide minimum standards of care with these minimum resources. Practice becomes a matter of scrimping and saving, with few staff and little equipment. The goals of care are about 'warehousing', to use Evers' term (Evers, 1981). Good practice, which might include the promotion of autonomy and development of advocacy roles, becomes extremely difficult to establish. Anyone who adopts these values may therefore find them difficult to put into practice.

Current policy developments in the UK and elsewhere demonstrate the tensions between the humanitarian and organisational formulations of the 'problem' of old age. These tensions are not demonstrated only by governments, but also by campaigning groups and advocates for older people. In 2000, for example, Age

Concern (a British campaigning charity) launched 'The Debate of the Age', which aimed to focus minds on the needs of a growing proportion of older people in society. While their goal was to develop a humanitarian debate about how services and policies could be designed to best meet these needs, the campaign to start the debate used organisational formulations to stimulate interest. Figures about the numbers and proportions of older people in the population over the next decades were presented alongside figures about the decline in the numbers of younger people working and paying taxes to support them. The message was mixed – older people deserve and need help and respect, but on the other hand they are a drain on resources.

Not surprisingly this mix is seen in many other debates about policies for older people, in many different countries. The 'demographic time bomb' is evoked as a way of pointing to the urgency of the problem, and as the public purse has more demands made on it, organisational drivers push policy towards trying to develop ways of providing less support for less money. At the same time, the rise in consumerism and increasing protests and campaigns by older people are humanitarian drivers to develop services that meet the needs of older people in ways that respect their dignity and autonomy, and promote a good quality of life.

The two formulations are not necessarily incompatible – good services are not necessarily produced by large budgets – but marrying the two may require some creative thinking. In one approach, an emphasis on older people as consumers has been adopted as a way of potentially rethinking provision. Reframing service users as consumers, rather than simply patients or clients, alters their relationship with providers. Instead of passive acceptance of whatever the authorities think best, there is a more active and critical demand for whatever older people think is best. As some commentators have pointed out, however, this approach can only change things to a limited extent (Blaikie, 1994). While commercial companies have to listen to consumers in order to remain viable, and consumers of products have options on what they buy, providing services for older people does not necessarily fit this pattern. Where services are provided by the state, the threats of provider insolvency are reduced, and where they are provided by the private sector, consumer knowledge and vulnerability does not make for critical challenging of what is offered. Where consumers have limited spending power because of reduced income, services are often purchased on their behalf, through insurance schemes that are either private or state organised. Such proxy purchasing is not based on the preferences of older people but on the wishes of those paying for the service. These factors may make 'true' consumerism impossible to achieve, and so some commentators have argued that the most that can be achieved is to have some regulation of the purchasers to promote consultation with and responsiveness to older people (Gilleard and Higgs, 1998; Thornton, 2000). Notions of 'structured dependency' – the view that older people are disempowered by their exclusion from work and resultant reduced spending power – are evoked to support this argument (Barnes and Walker, 1996).

Some of these regulatory methods involve inspection processes where either services themselves or the process of accessing them are subject to scrutiny. Again, however, inspectors are acting as proxies for older people, and realisation of this leads to ever more complex policies, where inspectors are scrutinised by different parties, who themselves must demonstrate responsiveness to older people. The National Care Standards Agency, for example, has been established in the UK to regulate a number of different types of provision, but is itself monitored by government, who in turn seek to reassure voters that older people are being well cared for.

Notions of consumerism – or, in less fiscal terms, partnership – depend on ensuring that the voice of older people is heard and responded to. This, however, brings us back to the questions that this chapter started off with – who are older people? If we concentrate on the views of the articulate, we may miss the views of those who are not, and attempts to be inclusive may founder because of problems of access to and availability of a wide range of older people.

Conclusion

Ideas about ageing and ways of defining older people, then, are fundamental to the way that we respond to them in policy and therefore in practice. The context of practice – in other words, what services exist, their goals and objectives, and their resources – depends on policies, which in turn depend on the way we think about older people. The process is, however, more a circular one than a linear one, in that the way practice happens can feed into policy debates. Vivid examples of this are provided by disasters and scandals that stimulate concern and change, but it is also possible for effective practice to provide a foundation for policy developments. 'Effectiveness', however, is in turn defined according to humanitarian or organisational formulations, and can therefore never be taken for granted.

What this chapter suggests, therefore, is that ideas about growing older are important in the way that they shape the experiences of older people. Returning to the discussion at the beginning of this chapter, however, we would like to go further and say that they shape our experiences too. If we reject definitions of older people that see them as different and separate from us, then we are left with the realisation that they are much the same as us. Their experiences of growing older, therefore, are ours, and we need to ask ourselves whether we would want to come to the conclusion of the woman in the focus group, whose comment began this chapter. Do we want growing old to be a process of fortitude, stoicism and suffering. Do we have to be brave, or is it possible that we could grow old as cowards?

Exercise

Öberg and Tornstam (2001) carried out a study in which they asked Swedish people ranging from 20 to 85 years old to respond to a questionnaire about their subjective ages. Respondents were asked to indicate their:

- 'feel age' – how old they feel themselves to be;
- 'look age' – how old they think that they look to others;
- 'ideal age' – the age they want to be.

The researchers asked the respondents to complete the following statements:

1. In my inner self I feel as if I am ... years old [insert age in space].
2. I would most like to be ... years old [insert age in space].
3. I think other people see me as ... years old [insert age in space].
4. I am ... years old [insert age in space].

Try this for yourself. Are all your ages the same? What might they be 20 years from now? If there are differences, what might this say about your experience of growing older? You could try this on someone older than you and someone younger than you. What are their responses, and what might they say about their experiences of growing older?

Öberg and Tornstam (2001) asked other questions, about body image and activities, and concluded that the majority of respondents had lower subjective ages than their chronological age. In other words, most felt younger, wanted to be younger and thought that other people saw them as younger than they were. Importantly, however, discrepancies increased with age – younger people showed little differences between their subjective age and real age, whereas they summarised the responses of people in their eighties as being "they think they look like 70, they feel like 60 and wish to be 50" (p 20). Following on from the discussion in this chapter, how might these findings shape the way we think about older people?

References

Age Concern England (2001) *The debate of the age*, London: Age Concern.

Andrews, M. (1999) 'The seductiveness of agelessness', *Ageing and Society*, vol 19, no 3, pp 301-18.

Arber, S. and Ginn, J. (1991) *Gender and later life: A sociological analysis of resources and constraints*, London: Sage Publications.

Baltes, M.M. and Baltes. M.M. (eds) (1990) *Successful ageing: Perspectives from the behavioural sciences*, New York, NY: Cambridge University Press.

Barnes, M. and Walker, A. (1996) 'Consumerism versus empowerment: a principled approach to the involvement of older service users', *Policy & Politics*, vol 24, no 4, pp 375-93.

Becker, L.C. (1986) *Reciprocity*, London: Routledge.

Beveridge, W. (1942) *Social insurance and allied services*, Cmd 6404, London: HMSO.

Binstock, R. (1984) 'Reframing the agenda of policies on aging', in M. Minkler and C. Estes (eds) *Readings in the political economy of aging*, Farmingdale, NY: Baywood, pp 199-212.

Blaikie, A. (1994) 'Ageing and consumer culture: will we reap the whirlwind?', *Generations Review*, vol 4, no 4, pp 5-7.

Boyajian, J.A. (1988) 'On reaching a new agenda: self-determination and aging', in J.E. Thornton and E.R. Winkler (eds) *Ethics and aging*, Vancouver: The University of British Columbia Press, pp 16-30.

Bytheway, B. (1995) *Ageism*, Buckingham: Open University Press.

Bytheway, B. (2000) 'Youthfulness and agelessness: a comment', *Ageing and Society*, vol 20, pp 781-9.

Cumming, E. and Henry, W. (1961) *Growing old: The process of disengagement*, New York, NY: Basic Books.

Evers, H.K. (1981) 'The creation of patient careers in geriatric wards; aspects of policy and practice', *Social Science and Medicine*, vol 15, no 1, pp 581-8.

Fuller, R.C. and Myers, R.R. (1941) 'Natural history of a social problem', *American Sociological Review*, vol 6, pp 321-8.

Gilleard, C. and Higgs, P. (1998) 'Forum. Old people as users and consumers of healthcare: a third age rhetoric for a fourth age reality?', *Ageing and Society*, vol 18, pp 233-48.

Ginn, J. (1993) 'Grey power: age-based organisations' response to structured inequalities', *Critical Social Policy*, vol 38, pp 23-47.

Gray, M. (1979) 'Forcing older people to leave their homes', *Community Care*, 8 March, pp 19-20.

Havighurst, R.J. (1963) 'Successful aging', in R.H. Williams, C. Tibbitts and W. Donahue (eds) *Processes of aging*, vol 1, New York, NY: Atherton, pp 299-320.

Klein, W.C. and Bloom, M. (1997) *Successful aging: Strategies for healthy living*, New York, NY and London: Plenum Press.

Macintyre, S. (1977) 'Old age as a social problem: historical notes on an English experience', in R. Dingwall, C. Heath, M. Reid and M. Stacey (eds) *Healthcare and health knowledge*, London: Croom Helm.

Minois, G. (1989) *History of old age: From antiquity to the Renaissance*, Cambridge: Polity Press.

Norman, A. (1987) *Aspects of ageism: A discussion paper*, London: Centre for Policy on Ageing.

Öberg, P. and Tornstam, L. (2001) 'Youthfulness and fitness – identity ideals for all ages?', *Journal of Aging and Identity*, vol 6, no 1, pp 15-29.

Strawbridge, W. (2000) 'Chronic illness: coping successfully for successful aging', *Aging Today*, vol 21, no 5, p 14.

Thornton, P. (2000) *Older people speaking out: Developing opportunities for influence*, York: Joseph Rowntree Foundation.

Till, R. (1993) 'Ageing in literature', in P. Kaim-Caudle, J. Keithley and A. Mullender (eds) *Aspects of ageing: A celebration of the European Year of Older People and solidarity between generations*, London: Whiting and Birch, pp 140-7.

Tornstam, L. (1996) 'Gerotranscendence – a theory about maturing in old age', *Journal of Ageing and Identity*, vol 1, pp 37-50.

Walker, A. (1993) 'Older people in Europe: perceptions and realities', in P. Kaim-Caudle, J. Keithley and A. Mullender (eds) *Aspects of ageing: A celebration of the European Year of Older People and solidarity between generations*, London: Whiting and Birch, pp 8-24.

TWO

Attitudes and images

Contents

Introduction	31
Ageism and stereotypes of older people	33
Cultural and societal factors that shape views and expectations of older people	35
Older age stereotypes acting alongside other stereotypes of gender, ethnicity, class and sexuality	36
Older people's experiences of ageism	37
Exploring ageism and attitudes	39
Empowerment	42
Implications for change	42

Key points

- Many of society's views of older people are ageist – that is, they assume that people have negative characteristics simply because they are older.
- Images of older people range from the 'sweet old grandparent' to the incapable invalid.
- Ageist attitudes permeate many aspects of policy and practice.

Introduction

> "You could tell by the way she looked at me – she just thought that here was another oldie who would be a pain in the neck. You could tell she was sick of me before I'd even opened my mouth." (Quote from an older person discussing the attitude of a shop assistant)

This chapter deals with one of the most important issues for older people and those working and living with them. Ageism can be seen as underpinning all of our responses to older people, and to our own ageing. As such, then, it shapes the experience of older people in a fundamental way, in the way that they interact with younger people, and in the choices that are open to them. We feel that it is important, therefore, to explore this issue in some depth – recognising, however, that the literature on ageism is vast and that what we do here is concentrate on points that we feel are crucial to developing practice with older people.

Underpinning any aspect of 'ism' is a differential value being placed on something, be it skin colour, social class, gender or age. Ageism is not something that belongs to (or is caused by) the individual who is older, but it belongs to the social world in which they live. It is this social world that determines where its values lie. In developed and, perhaps even more so, in developing countries, ideas about what contributes to society (and so is more valued) are linked to financial or material contributions to society and independence from the need for support from the rest of society. Value is increasingly placed on what people do (their employment, for example) rather than what they are (a mother, for example) or what they believe in (their moral code of conduct, for example). As societies become orientated towards function–ability, and in particular financial function–ability, so those who do not live up to society's expectations find themselves falling by the wayside. As a result we can see older people, and other non-financially productive people as being identified as socially excluded.

The social exclusion of older people runs very deep into the fabric of how developed countries are constructed. There are, for example, points of retirement from paid employment, expectations of withdrawal from political decision making, and assumptions about the gap between the values of older people and those of younger generations. This cascades into a process of social diminishing of the value accorded to older people such that older people find it increasingly hard to find a role that is valued outside their own family, or even within it at times.

The so-called 'grey power' of older people, however, may herald a renaissance of their social inclusion, at least within the commercial sector of society. The financial resource of some older people is not unrecognised and with it comes the power of any consumer group to influence a marketplace. However, it serves merely to reinforce society's shift towards valuing financial function–ability rather than any indication of wider tolerance and inclusion.

The concerns of older people and social exclusion are similar to those of any group who find themselves socially excluded. First, the characteristic that marks them as 'different' is located with them as an individual. It is the individual's fault that they are older and the responsibility for and of its consequence lies with the individual alone. Typically, there are two possible responses of the individual: to 'hide' the characteristic that leads to the social exclusion such that looking young, or being young at heart, are goals to be pursued; or to accept the exclusionist characteristic but reject its secondary social consequences. The first response has cosmetic and hair-dye firms rubbing their hands with delight at our need to look younger than we are. The second response draws potential admiration for audacity or bravery for acts 'at such an age too!' or criticism for not 'acting their age', and everyday acts such as riding a bicycle risk ridicule. Second, society does not see itself as having a responsibility systemically to accommodate age-related issues and as a result there are no systems to respond to older people: instead they must be accommodated on a one-to-one basis, again emphasising the troublesome nature of older people to the rest of society. In addition, the age factor that leads to social exclusion results in older people being seen to be a burden, on their relatives as well as on the state. As discussed in the preceding chapter, age itself becomes framed as problematic and these problems assume a primacy over any advantages of age or any reciprocity of the older person with their relatives or with the rest of society.

It becomes hard for people to see beyond the 'age issue', just as it is hard for people to see beyond the wheelchair that someone is sitting in or the white cane with which they walk. The functionalism of society combines with the biomedicalisation and reductionism of healthcare to create dangerously powerful assumptions and expectations about, of and from older people and other sectors of society. These entrench ageist approaches through their focus on physical ability, mind–body dualism, and behavioural and financial independence. Such an approach fails to respect the qualities that are strengths of older people.

In this way, we can see that the debate about ageism is not so much about chronological age as about congruence with that which is valued in society. We can understand the interplay of age and society, and framing age as a social disability allows us to recognise that the 'problems' and disadvantages of older age result not from older people themselves but from society itself and its values system.

Ageism and stereotypes of older people

There are many images of old age, all of which are informed by underlying social values and which express very clearly a widely varying range of social attitudes towards old age. Perhaps the two most fundamentally opposed are, put crudely, those of sickness versus normality as the enduring conditions. This is a theme that can be traced back to antiquity, and was identified more than 2,000 years ago by the Roman Cicero (106-43 BC). Cicero's view was rather more subtle than merely identifying the extremes of a continuum. He argued that old age afforded an opportunity to bring one's life to fulfilment but emphasised that there were differential experiences between 'normal' and 'sick' old age – that is, that we should *not* confuse old age with illness. This is a theme picked up by Bytheway (1995) in his important text on ageism.

While there is a danger in overinflating the historical perspective (in the final analysis the 21st century is not exactly analogous to the 20th or 19th any more than to the 1st millennium BC), it can equally be misleading to take too short term a view. Phillipson (1998, p 109) has argued that the idea of older people as a separate group in the population only stems from the end of the 19th century, citing a 1930s' study by Slater which referred to the fact that it was only then that Poor Law policies differentiated older people from sick people. A similar claim, as we saw in the previous chapter, has been made by Macintyre (1977), citing the Poor Law Act of 1905. Other authors, however, have argued that while older people might not be mentioned specifically in policy documents, they are certainly talked about as a distinct group in other arenas. Minois (1989), for example, has traced discussions about older people back to antiquity, and points out a number of examples of the 'age problem' being debated, including the concern in Roman times about older people being too powerful. The idea that older people were suddenly 'discovered', then, is a rather simplistic and inadequate speculation. Quite apart from substantial cultural differences that exist in terms of the different roles undertaken by older people in different societies, the same could be said of children – Pinchbeck and Hewitt (1973) have written a seminal two-part work on the historical role of childhood in English society. Childhood, like old age, has been constructed and defined differently across history and cultures, but has always existed.

Bytheway (1995, p 15) draws attention to the fact that historical perspectives of the old are poorly researched. Much time could be spent on conjecturing about the past and although historical views, often rose-tinted (especially those harking back to the 'good old days'), are important in their contribution to shaping current views, it is perhaps more productive to identify present-day influences. Phillipson (1998, p 14) attributes to the developing discipline of critical gerontology the view that ageing is a socially constructed event. This is an essentially sociological perspective, and is certainly a plausible argument.

However, it cannot be the whole story for, quite apart from the fact that academic disciplines tend to reflect and interpret the realities of their subject matter, it becomes clear from a cursory review of the world about us that old age is constructed and defined by a range of factors: economic, political, medical, physical and environmental – as well as social. The role of the 'grey' vote is beginning to assume significant proportions in the UK as it has for some time in the US (demonstrated, for example, by the pensions protests of 1999-2000): the key factors in this issue are politics and economics. At another level, the matter of ageism in the workplace has become a significant issue, with different employers taking different stances, and is inextricably linked with economics and demographics. A third example is medicalisation of old age through developments in drug therapy of conditions that are associated, although not exclusively analogous, with old age. Each of these examples serves to demonstrate the complexities of definition and the attendant difficulties in unravelling the issues. In sociology, the phenomenon of social stereotyping by observing collective behaviours and characteristics and attributing these to social groupings as generalised attributes has been well explored by many writers. The danger of this approach to making sense of the world lies in the consequential discrimination that arose – that the process of stereotyping lends itself to developing negative ideas of groups of people, without encouraging critical reflection.

Older people are no less bedevilled by the problems of stereotyping through the perpetuation of ageist attitudes than any other social group. However, they are uniquely vulnerable to its pernicious effects because of their unique circumstances that, in many sectors of society within and across cultures, ensure their systematic disempowerment and oppression.

Cultural and societal factors that shape views and expectations of older people

Bradley (1997, pp 151-77) explores age in a number of interesting ways. Starting from the premise that the 'classless' society is a myth and that there are widening social inequalities, she examines the growing complexities of patterns of stratification, significantly titling the introductory chapter, 'Age: the neglected dimension of stratification'. In particular she explores the sociological themes of age stratification theory and generations and generation units. Indeed, no contemporary definition of old age can be separated from the changing definitions of family structure and the changing roles of family. Bradley also identifies intergenerational studies as an emergent field of study within gerontology and addresses the need for "aging education"; that is, that the school curriculum should address a range of perspectives from understanding "that aging is a natural, normal, lifelong process" to "identifying the sources of ageism that can plague society" (1997, p 107). Perhaps it would be more emphatic to affirm that ageism *does* plague society.

Another theoretical perspective within 'life course' studies endeavours to explain the experience of old age: this echoes issues that we have touched on above, including old-age aspects of functionalism and modernisation, dependency theory and the political economy, and postmodernist approaches.

Psychological theories also have much to say about old age. Some of this literature is based on long-standing, and by implication questionable, assumptions, which do not always address issues of empowerment or stereotyping and may have culturally narrow origins. Other contemporary issues, such as life review in a shifting context of employment and retirement; the nature of familial relationships as members of postmodern models of the family grow into old age; ideas of old age leading to successive disengagement; and the concept of 'successful ageing' (which we touched on in the previous chapter) are issues that have become more important since some of these theories were developed.

Cumming and Henry (1961) developed their notion of 'disengagement theory' as a means of explaining the life task at the end of the life cycle, almost a way of suggesting that withdrawal from the known world into a much more narrowly proscribed environment was a positive form of psychological adjustment to the ageing process. This is at one level, perhaps, no more than descriptive of the experiences of some, but that is not to say it is always desirable or even inevitable. Such a view contrasts strongly with notions of, for example, care in the community and denies the realities experienced by many of a differently full and enriching old age. Havighurst (1963) based his notion of 'activity theory' on the idea that older people were forced to withdraw from society as it increasingly excluded them. It was argued that the most positive response to this disabling process was to retain into older age as much as possible of the activities that were enjoyed during middle age and, if necessary, to develop new activity. Thus this approach was in complete contrast, and acted as an antidote to, the principles of disengagement theory. Yet another model in the panoply of theories of old age is 'successful ageing' (Baltes and Baltes, 1990) where ideas of selection, optimisation and compensation interact to deliver a satisfying and sustainable lifestyle.

Many of these models are accompanied or complemented by the idea of tasks or phases. For example, Havighurst (1963) identifies a range of developmental tasks in old age:

- adjusting to physical changes;
- adjusting to retirement and changes in income;
- establishing satisfactory living arrangements;
- learning to live with partner in retirement;
- adjusting to death of partner;
- forming affiliations with ageing peers;
- adopting flexible social roles.

However, Atchley (1994) suggests that the following stages are characteristic of retirement:

- pre-retirement
- 'honeymoon period'
- rest and relaxation
- disenchantment
- re-orientation
- routine
- termination.

However, all of these approaches have some limitations largely because of the time in which they were developed in terms of failing now to match the changed shape of later life in contemporary society or being prescriptive in a context that does not recognise the changing arena of ageing experience. It is important therefore to acknowledge that *any* model of old age can only be as relevant as its capacity constantly to reflect and respond to the changing cultural and societal factors that shape the views, experiences and expectations of older people.

Older age stereotypes acting alongside other stereotypes of gender, ethnicity, class and sexuality

The reality is that there is no adequate, single model of ageing and that there are interacting dynamics of age, ethnicity, gender and class (Bradley, 1997) that combine to produce a powerfully containing mechanism for old age. This issue of multiple jeopardy arising from exposure to multiple oppressions is a theme that runs through much of the literature on oppression and is no less applicable to old age than it is to any other topic. Tinker (1997, pp 188-92) raises the question, in relation to ethnicity, of the type of provision – mainstream, specific or separate – in relation to community and individual needs. There are also linked aspects of generational perspectives. Brabazon and Disch (1997, p 199) refer to the question of why ethnic community intergenerational programmes have not historically occurred in the US, concluding that this is because of strong existing intergenerational patterns which are, however, under threat as social, economic and cultural changes put pressure on family ties. This is true for the UK as well: for example, the tensions raised as a result of younger generations of Asian families challenging the institution of arranged marriages can have as profound an impact on the older generation as on the younger. The increase in numbers of fractured families and the move away from the generational support provided within extended family networks is yet another example.

Finally, although referred to tangentially above, the phenomenon of institutional ageism is a matter that permeates all experiences of ageing. From finding employment to keeping it, from age-related cut-off points in health treatment eligibility criteria to user-driven choices in community care services, and from pensions entitlement to the means-tested or begrudging distribution of free television licences and winter heating allowances, older people in society are prey to disempowering and oppressive practices which speak volumes about the way in which society values its older citizens.

Older people's experiences of ageism

For older people, the impact of ageism can be significant in a number of ways. It affects the way that they are regarded by other people, not only those directing policy and resources, but also at an interpersonal level, with the people that they meet everyday. Some of these ageist attitudes may be difficult to spot – even the people who hold them may not be fully aware of them. This also, of course, makes ageist attitudes difficult to challenge or change, and this is especially the case if they are hiding under a mask of benevolence and caring. This might manifest as 'caring' that is patronising – making comments about how we 'love' older people, perhaps because they are 'sweet' or 'grateful' or 'old-fashioned'. While these attributes may sound like positive comments, they are based on stereotypes of older people; moreover they are stereotypes that portray older people as passive and inept.

These 'caring' attitudes are one part of the ageist spectrum – the other end is the openly derogatory, and there is a range of positions in between. While these attitudes are unpalatable in the general public, they represent even greater cause for concern when they are evident in the actions and discussions of service providers who have a responsibility for delivering care and support to older people. There is an extensive body of research that indicates that ageist attitudes are common in health and social care professionals. Koch and Webb (1996), for example, found that the narratives of the older people in hospital indicated that they felt that they were subject to segregation from younger people, and enjoyed less supportive care. The reasons for these attitudes are variously explained by different authors, but in the main rest on two observations. The first is that professionals are part of a society that constantly demonstrates ageist attitudes, and that professionals would therefore be subject to ageist messages and discourses, as would any other member of that society. The second observation is that, for some professionals, older people represent obstacles to successful practice. This is particularly the case if successful practice is defined as rapid response and treatment, which cures or solves problems within a short timescale and restricted budget. Older people who take a long time to recover from illness (if they ever do), or who have complex and multiple problems that require complex and long-term responses, do not fit into the performance indicators of many institutions and organisations. The term 'bed-blockers' when applied to older people in hospital illustrates this well – they are defined by the way that they block the system and frustrate the organisation's needs, rather than in terms of their own needs.

For older people living in a society where ageist attitudes abound, the difficulties are huge. Every encounter with a younger person (and sometimes with people of their own generation) takes place in the shadow of ageism. We know something about the way that older people respond to ageism, through research that has explored this issue and through listening to what older people's groups and organisations have to say about it. Age Concern England (2001), for example, has pointed out some of the inequalities in services and treatment offered to older people as opposed to younger people – for example, being denied surgery or treatment.

The impact of ageism on older people seems, therefore, to be easily identifiable at a societal or an institutional level, but in addition the impact of ageism has an interpersonal dimension. Minichiellio et al (2000), for example, have carried out a study with 18 older people, who were asked questions about their response to and experiences of ageism in in-depth interviews. Interestingly, some responses indicated that, for some older people, ageism was not a term that meant much to them and they had never heard of the word. Some participants, however, were familiar with the term, and were able to give a sophisticated definition. Minichiello et al (2000) point out, however, that: "Although the *word* 'ageism' may have no immediate meaning to some older people, the *concept* of ageism and its characteristics has considerable relevance and meaning" (p 259, emphasis in original). The older people in this study reported the exclusion of older people in society, and commented about older people being made to feel a burden. Interestingly, however, some of the older people in the study talked about ageism as something that happened to other older people, but not necessarily themselves. Indeed, much of the conversation was about maintaining a distance between themselves and old age, and older people themselves also demonstrated ageist attitudes.

The complexities of the findings from Minichiello et al's (2000) study suggest that the debates about ageism and the strategies to overcome it will need to address a whole range of issues, including raising awareness of ageism among older people themselves. Ageism cannot simply be regarded as an attitude held by the advantaged young over the disadvantaged old, but is much more endemic than that.

Exploring ageism and attitudes

Exploring the ramifications and complexities of ageism, then, requires a range of strategies involving both young and old people. One strategy, which has been developed by a group of older people in Newcastle in the UK, uses drama to get the message across. The group 'Old Spice' was formed in 1996 by a collective of older people involved in a number of local initiatives, such as Action for Health (Senior Citizens in Newcastle), and whole systems events supported by the local authority, which brought together older people and people from a range of different organisations and agencies. Old Spice have performed sketches and songs to a range of audiences, including older people and professionals. In 1999 a theatre group, Frank Theatre, which used drama techniques to explore mental health issues, joined with Old Spice in a workshop to explore the use of drama to examine and change attitudes.

One of the workshop activities involved Old Spice performing a sketch about a woman and her daughter being visited by a care worker to assess her needs. Andy Griffin wrote the sketch, in collaboration with Old Spice. An extract follows.

CARE WORKER *(to daughter)*	And is this your mother, is it?
SUSAN *(daughter)*	Yes, this is Mrs Stanley.
CARE WORKER *(to mother)*	Ah, Mrs Stanley, I presume?
MOTHER	That's right … how do y- … *(cut off)*
CARE WORKER *(interrupting mother … to daughter)*	She's now in her eighties?
SUSAN	That's right.
MOTHER	85!
CARE WORKER *(to daughter)*	Well, there's no need to worry. *(Starting to fill in a form)*
MOTHER	What about?
CARE WORKER *(to daughter)*	She's quite frail, isn't she?
MOTHER	Who?
SUSAN	She does *look* frail.
CARE WORKER *(to daughter)*	We can put her down for meals on wheels. *(To mother loudly)* I said we can put you down for meals on wheels. *(To daughter)* Three times a week.
MOTHER	What for?
CARE WORKER *(to daughter)*	We can see about a home help.
SUSAN	Mother's very independent.

CARE WORKER *(to daughter)*	But she's 85, my dear. *(To mother)* Not a youngster, are we?
MOTHER	NO!
CARE WORKER *(to daughter)*	We can have someone come in to clean in the morning … and we have a 24-hour call system. *(Pause)* Is she clean?

The sketch continues, until Mrs Stanley, sick of being ignored by the care worker, announces that she's going to the shops, and asks her daughter if she should get her anything while she's there. The care worker is taken aback by this independence and leaves, thoroughly flustered by someone who insists on rejecting her well-meant professional advice and help.

Throughout the sketch Old Spice make a number of points about ageism and the way that it affects how older people are treated. For example, the frequent instances of the care worker talking over Mrs Stanley's head to her daughter, to ask a range of personal questions, demonstrate the way that older people can be regarded as incapable of giving valid information, even about themselves. The testimony of a younger person is assumed to be more accurate, more valid or more reliable. The invasion of privacy and dignity entailed in the question "Is she clean?", illustrates another way in which ageism can be evident in thinking about older people – that dignity and privacy are not important to them, in the way that they are to other people. The barrage of services that the care worker tries to put in place, without any real thought about the particular needs and preferences of Mrs Stanley, is based on a set of assumptions about older people in general – the trigger is Mrs Stanley's chronological age rather than any need she has.

In the drama workshop with Frank Theatre, in which Old Spice performed this sketch and explored the ways of developing the material further, to get audiences to think about their own attitude, a number of strategies were explored. One of these was 'hot seating' where members of the cast would sit in a chair (the 'hot seat') and answer questions that the audience might ask their character. Mrs Stanley, for example, might be asked how she felt about the care worker, and would reply that she felt angry or humiliated. Susan might be asked how she felt, and the person playing this role might talk about the ambiguities of her position. The care worker might be asked about her feelings, and might reply by outlining some of the conflicting pressures of the job. 'Hot seating' allows the audience and the cast to explore issues in a way that illuminates the complexities of different stances – it is not simply that the care worker is a bad person or an ageist person.

Another exercise used in the workshop was 'role on the wall' where the audience is divided up into groups and each given one of the characters as a focus for discussion. The groups then generate a range of words or phrases that express ideas that the group have about the character, their motivations, needs and options. These are brought back to the larger group, who share their ideas and explore different possible courses of action. A third exercise explored in the workshop was 'building bridges', where the audience were asked to think about how they would take the workshop ideas back into their everyday lives. They are asked to think of words and phrases that sum up their feelings, and to pick an image that captures this, depicted in a 'freeze frame', which they can either draw or act out.

Old Spice has used these exercises with a range of different audiences since the drama workshop with Frank Theatre. These have included older people's groups and educational sessions for professionals. The full programme lasts 35 minutes and consists of sketches, songs and poems. These are presented in different ways for different audiences – for example, using overhead projectors to display the words of the sketches for people with hearing difficulties, and using interpreters for audiences where English is not understood. Copies of scripts have been given to other agencies for their use, and an Old Spice member presented the work at a World Health Organisation (WHO) conference workshop in Athens.

What the Old Spice performances do, and this is illustrated particularly well by the sketch 'And is this your mother is it?', is to take everyday exchanges, or at least exchanges that we could all imagine happening, and draw to our attention the underlying ageism. The fact that the care worker could begin a conversation with "And is this your mother is it?", rather than by introducing herself to Mrs Stanley, suggests that older people are not paid the courtesies that we pay other groups. That a raft of services is put in place for someone, without any discussion with them, suggests that the organisation of these services does not acknowledge the individuality of older people, or support their autonomy.

Discussions with Old Spice members have identified some interesting responses from the audiences. One member has described how, when the sketch starts off, with the social worker's first line, the older people in the audience smile in recognition. As one Old Spice member says, "You can see it in their eyes, they know that voice. It might not have happened to them, but it's happened to somebody they know, and it might happen to them soon, if they have to have any dealings with professionals".

When the audience contains professionals, however, Old Spice members report that the reactions are different, and more varied. Some professionals blush with embarrassment, as they recognise themselves in the social worker; some become indignant and angry at the social worker; but some seem to take the sketch for granted, as a straightforward account of practice, and are either uncritically amused by the jokes or bored by what they see as an unremarkable exchange.

The questions asked in the 'hot-seating' exercises also range from audience to audience. While older people in the audience might challenge the social worker or the daughter about the ethics of what they are doing, professionals may ask slightly different questions, sometimes technical, about Mrs Stanley's needs or the resources available. They may ask about feelings as well, of course, but some of the sessions can begin to sound like a case conference, with professionals suggesting other strategies or services. Again, this seems to miss the point – it is not the thoroughness of the assessment that is the key issue, nor the adequacy of the care plan. It is the experience of being assessed, and being seen as a problem to be solved simply because of age, which is at the heart of the sketch. Those professionals in the audience who focus on the mechanics of assessment and care planning not only fail to hear the central message, but also demonstrate and reinforce it: by switching into 'problem-solving' mode so automatically, they demonstrate the barriers that this approach has for making a more personal and human connection – seeing Mrs Stanley and her daughter as problems and not people.

Empowerment

The discussion so far has outlined some of the issues around ageism and illustrated its impact on older people. This discussion raises some questions about what can be done to combat ageism and to prevent the negative experiences of older people. One line of thought is that what we should be doing is trying to empower older people to make their own choices, set their own agendas and present the images of their choice. The uncomfortable truth so far as empowerment is concerned, however, is that it can only be won at a price. That price will be as discomforting for those who must have power removed from them, in order for it to be redistributed, as it is for those who wish to obtain it. While Greengross (in Thursz et al, 1995) might comment that, "Older adults, as full citizens and participating members of their society, should have the same rights and their voice the same power and influence as other groups living in their community" (p 205), it will take positive action for that goal to be achieved.

If older people in society are to claim power, then it is important that there are mechanisms for their collective activity as well as for the individual. There are existing examples of respect/veneration of older people in society – for example, as founts of knowledge, figures of religious reverence, holders of political power. Avarez (in Thursz et al, 1995, pp 105-9) refers to "Elder empowerment and cultural revolution" and Phillipson (1998, pp 13-14) explores issues of empowerment in political economy, humanities, biographical and narrative perspectives in gerontology. It is clear that for citizens to develop emancipation, it must start before the onset of old age, however defined, and it is equally clear that dimensions of 'sickness' and 'normality' remain far from being the sole parameters in defining social attitudes towards old age.

Implications for change

This chapter has, in many ways, painted a depressing picture of an ageist society, where older people are systematically undervalued. It is a picture that has prompted a number of responses from those who are concerned about it, from groups representing older people, to professional bodies, to policy makers. These responses range from calls to promote positive images of older people in the media, to calls to improve the financial circumstances of older people through pensions and employment policies. However, it has also offered examples of positive action: older people insisting on presenting their experiences to others.

What is needed is a fundamental change in the way that we think, not just about older people but about how we judge the value of everybody, and what is important to us as human beings. This is a huge agenda, and one in which it is difficult to know where to start. As professionals it makes sense to start by thinking about our practice, the way that we behave when practising, the attitudes that shape our practice and the impact that our practice can have on older people. It would be instructive, for example, to imagine our response to the Old Spice sketch described above, 'And is this your mother is it?'. Would we be blushing in shame, indignant or unconcerned? Have we ever talked over the head of an older person, assumed that they would not be able to understand us, underestimated their abilities or asked intrusive and intimate questions in ways that are insensitive?

Many of us would have to say that we had done some of these things, and we might come up with a number of reasons – too little time, too many people to care for, experiences of dependent older people that have coloured the way we meet others, and many other reasons. We might even feel that doing these things was not so bad – after all, the older people did not seem too upset or affronted. The message of the sketch, however, is that having too little time does not justify acting only on assumptions and stereotypes – it is not effective practice and can be deeply offensive. The response of the older people in the audience, the gleam of recognition when they hear the opening lines, tells us that ageism or the threat of ageism is an everyday experience for older people, and one that can be created by the professionals who are supposed to be providing support to them, but instead are undermining them.

Exercise for groups or individuals

You could re-enact the sketch, giving group members scripts to read from (you may want to edit them to introduce a male social worker, a father and a son and so on, to suit the group). This can be done in small groups of three, or with one group of three playing the roles, and other members of the group as an audience. If you decide to have one group presenting, it might be useful to give them the script in advance and have time for discussion before the performance, in order to give them support.

If you have small groups acting the scene, you can ask them to change roles, and repeat the sketch as a different person (for example, the social worker could become the mother, and the daughter could become the social worker and so on). The small-group discussion can then be about any differences members felt between the two roles. If you decide to have one group present to the others, you can then use the exercises that Old Spice has developed. The 'hot seating' exercise is suitable for groups that are very confident about this type of work: they need to be able to ask questions and role-play the replies with imagination, but also need to be able to role-play without taking on the roles too much – if some of the questions are hostile, for example, the role-players should not interpret this as a personal attack, but a criticism of the character that they played. If a group is not experienced, then the other exercises might be better – the 'role on the wall' exercise, or the 'building bridges' exercise for a group from a practice background.

Discussion groups and individual study

An alternative would be to simply use the scripts as reading materials and as a basis for discussion in a group or reflection in individual study. Suggestions for how to structure this discussion and reflection are given in the following bullet points. You could also use this structure if you have performed the sketch.

- Review the Old Spice sketch and identify the key themes that it illustrates. Make a list of these themes.
- How does your practice reflect or address these themes? For example, the sketch shows a social worker who ignores the older person and talks directly to her daughter. Are there any areas of your practice where assumptions are made that older people will be unable to speak for themselves (this may be, for example, through a policy that relatives are always consulted before the older person is)? There may be a difference between 'official' policies, where the organisation has developed rules or guidelines for practice, and 'unofficial' policies, where practitioners have developed ways of working that are based on their experiences or the advice that they have had from colleagues.
- The sketch also gives examples of an assessment that is driven by the availability of services, rather than client need. In your practice, do you feel that this is sometimes the case? Of the services or care that you can offer, what are the features that make them acceptable or unacceptable to service users?
- Next, list the range of audience reactions reported. Do these match up with your reactions? Can you understand reactions that are different to yours?
- The sketch is meant to stimulate thought and discussion about ageist attitudes but also to lead to change in practice. What areas of change are suggested by the sketch? What would need to happen for change in practice to take place, for example, should there be training, different ways of managing services, and what are the implications for resources? Think about an ideal world where resources are unlimited – what would you like to see happen?
- If things did change, how would you know? What sort of evaluation process would identify the change?

References

Age Concern England (2001) *The debate of the age*, London: Age Concern.

Atchley, R.C. (1994) *Social forces and ageing*, Belmont, CA: Wadsworth.

Baltes, M.M. and Baltes. M.M. (eds) (1990) *Successful ageing: Perspectives from the behavioural sciences*, New York, NY: Cambridge University Press.

Brabazon, K. and Disch, R. (1997) *Intergenerational approaches to aging: Implications for education, policy and practice*, Binghamton, NY: The Haworth Press.

Bradley, H. (1997) *Fractured identities*, Cambridge: Polity Press.

Bytheway, B. (1995) *Rethinking ageing*, Buckingham: Open University Press.

Cumming, E. and Henry, W. (1961) *Growing old: The process of disengagement*, New York, NY: Basic Books.

Havighurst, R.J. (1963) 'Successful aging', in R.H. Williams, C. Tibbitts and W. Donahue (eds) *Processes of aging*, vol 1, New York, NY: Atherton, pp 299-320.

Koch T. and Webb, C. (1996) 'The biomedical construction of ageing: implications for nursing care of older people', *Journal of Advanced Nursing*, vol 23, pp 954-9.

Macintyre, S. (1977) 'Old age as a social problem: historical notes on an English experience', in R. Dingwall, C. Heath, M. Reid and M. Stacey (eds) *Healthcare and health knowledge*, London: Croom Helm.

Minichiello, V., Browne, J. and Kendig, H. (2000) 'Perceptions and consequences of ageism: views of older people', *Ageing and Society*, vol 20, no 3, pp 253-78.

Minois, G. (1989) *History of old age: From antiquity to the Renaissance*, Cambridge: Polity Press.

Phillipson, C. (1998) *Reconstructing old age*, London: Sage Publications.

Pinchbeck, I. and Hewitt, M. (1973) *Children in English society*, vols 1 and 2, London: Routledge and Kegan Paul Ltd.

Thursz, D., Nusberg, C. and Prather, J. (1995) *Empowering older people: An international approach*, London: Cassell.

Tinker, A. (1997) *Older people in modern society* (4th edn), Harlow: Addison Wesley Longman.

THREE

The body growing older

Contents

Introduction	47
Biomedical models of physical ageing processes	49
Intrinsic ageing theories	51
Extrinsic ageing theories	52
Disposable soma theory	53
Longevity and health in older age	53
Self-assessed health	55
Managing and responding to ill-health	56
Older people's views of health	57
Implications for quality of life and successful ageing	59
Conclusion	61

Key points

- There are a number of theories of ageing which seek to explain why bodies grow older.
- Some of these suggest that physical ageing is not inevitable.
- The social aspects of growing older impinge on people's self-image and functioning.
- For older people, health may not be thought of purely as a physical state, but as fulfilling social activity.

Introduction

> "Well, I don't get about as much as I used to.... I don't miss it, though ... it's time to settle down."

This quote, from an interview with a nursing home resident, can be interpreted in different ways. Her comments could be seen as resignation and pessimism, anathema to some who promote the idea of active ageing as a defiant stance against expectations of physical frailty. They could also be seen as a realistic and proper response to increasing age by those who assume that older people will be less active and should, indeed, 'settle down'. Both of these interpretations, however, may be too simplistic, and further information about this woman indicates some of the complexities behind her comments.

She had grown up on a farm, where her father had worked, and had married a farm hand. Her stories of life on the farm were somewhat removed from idyllic images of rural bliss that are popular in fiction and drama – her stories were closer to the bleak stories of Hardy than the sentimental tales of other novelists. Her stories of getting up on dark winter mornings to feed the cattle, and descriptions of having to deliver calves without the assistance of an unaffordable vet, reflect a life of rural poverty, hardship and difficult physical work. Throughout her life she worked in jobs that required manual labour, as a cleaner, a factory worker and as a school cook. She enjoyed these different jobs for different reasons – the hours were good, her fellow workers were friendly and fun, the environment was warm – but her real love was farm work, because she loved the animals and the fresh air.

For such an active woman, who enjoyed physical work, her increasing health problems, arthritis and heart failure, which restricted her activity, could be assumed to be a source of regret and sadness. She did not, however, seem to feel this. Her descriptions of cold frosty mornings on the farm were vivid and poetic, but so were her descriptions of sitting in the warm lounge of the nursing home, watching passers-by outside scurrying to work.

> "I love it in the winter, when we're all snuggled up and you can see the poor folk outside racing to work. They look so miserable, their faces could trip them up – I'm pleased I'm finished with all that."

These interview extracts point to a way of experiencing the physical effects of growing older in a way that is somewhere between the frenetic active ageing lobby and the view that older people should disengage from activity. This woman had enjoyed physical activity in the past, but showed no regrets that she was not very active any more, but instead was taking pleasure in her new-found opportunities to relax and be comfortable.

This response to a body growing older stands in contrast to many of the prevalent anxieties that we have in western societies about growing older. Images of youthful people on TV and in magazines are used to sell products, and even those products designed for older people are advertised using images of very young-looking older people, often engaged in some energetic activity. There is some evidence that older people themselves endorse the value of youthfulness. Öberg and Tornstam (2001) found that the people of all ages that they interviewed agreed on the importance of looking youthful, and that the proportion of people agreeing rose with age. Öberg and Tornstam cite Featherstone (1994) who has identified the cultural message about age as 'Youth = Beauty = Health', where the three elements are connected and equally valued and desired. Öberg and Tornstam's work supports this perspective, also finding that being slender was important to participants.

Some critiques of this focus on fitness, beauty and youthfulness have centred on the way that it is impossible to achieve without a great deal of effort, and often money, and this excludes large numbers of people from meeting these standards. Feminist critiques have pointed out the way that the concern with the appearance of the ageing body reflects the way in which the body is inscribed with social codes – the body is both a private, lived experience and a social, public construction (Harper, 1997). A youthful-looking body is not just valued in abstract aesthetic terms, but for the power, sexuality and ability it represents.

The focus on fitness has been critiqued by writers who see this as a medicalisation of the body (see, for example, Estes and Binney, 1991). The emphasis on keeping healthy, supported by a range of health promotion initiatives for older people, on the one hand can be seen as a way of opening up possibilities for older people, and countering the expectations of decline that are prevalent in many portrayals of growing older. On the other hand, it can be seen as an attempt to objectify the body and discount subjective experiences of living with a body growing older: ageing processes become something to be controlled and fought against – as Bytheway says, "we are encouraged to 'age well', but never to 'fall ill well'" (1997, p 12).

These issues form a background to the discussion in this chapter, which moves from biomedical models of ageing, to a consideration of health problems to older people's perspectives on well-being, ending up with a critique of some of the notions we have about 'successful ageing'. Perhaps the key theme of this chapter, however, relates to Featherstone and Hepworth's (1991) description of the ageing body as 'a mask'. This mask represents the external body, judged by its appearance and function, subject to prevailing cultural values, and used as a classifier of the person as old, with all the implications this has. Behind the mask, however, is the lived body, the body that the person knows and experiences according to their own individual context and biography. In discussions about the body growing older, then, we must be careful to distinguish between the mask and the lived experience of older people.

Biomedical models of physical ageing processes

The ageing body is, by orthodox biomedical models, a body that is functioning at less than optimum levels. The development of the body from birth to adult maturity is described as a process of increasing capabilities and powers. From maturity, however, the picture is one of decline and decay, a process of loss and restriction. Anyone who has attended any conferences or workshops on ageing will have come across the quote from Shakespeare, which is trotted out so frequently, describing old age as:

> "Sans teeth, sans eyes, sans taste, sans everything." (*As you like it*, Act II, Scene VII)

This is often delivered as a solemn warning of what old age can be, but perhaps it says as much about the person who chooses to illustrate their presentation with this quote than it does about older people. Portraying ageing as a process of loss, without any gains, would seem a very limited view of what the experience of growing older might be, and one that lacks imagination, empathy or critical reflection. Longino (2000) has characterised the biomedical view as being based on five doctrines:

- the separation of the body from the mind;
- the view of the body as a machine that can be repaired;
- the search for explanations at progressively more basic physiological levels (reductionism);
- the body as the focus of medical control; and
- a view of aetiology that holds that each disease has only one cause.

These characteristics can be seen in many of the debates about ageing processes, and about the health problems associated with growing older. As Longino (2000) argues, biomedical models have had "profound and wonderful effects on human health" (p 45). The processes of growing older, however, give rise to a reconsideration of the appropriateness of the biomedical model for understanding ageing. As we will see, the ageing body is a complex and multifaceted phenomenon, which is not well served by physical reductionism or mechanical models.

There are several theories and debates in biomedicine about the definition and causes of ageing. Debates about definitions of ageing seek to distinguish between what is a normal and probably universal process of physical change, and what is an abnormal disease process. Joint changes, for example, could be due to everyday wear and tear, the result of activity over a lifespan, but also to a disease process, such as arthritis, which has had a range of hypothetical aetiologies suggested, from auto-immune disorders to environmental toxins. The arguments have continued over many years and are important not just in their representation of two different scientific views, but also in their implications for healthcare and longevity. If we just 'wear out', then ageing is natural but inevitable, and so must be accepted with as good a grace as we can bring to it. If ageing is not inevitable, but a result of damage or disease, then this opens the door to the development of 'cures' or 'treatments' for what we call ageing. This confers the prospect of much longer, healthier and more active lives, although immortality for individuals is likely to be out of reach.

Bennet and Ebrahim (1992), in their medical textbook, illustrate this by presenting an example of an older person who has problems getting in and out of the bath, but whose doctor may have told them that this is simply due to their age. Bennet and Ebrahim, however, point out that this may be due to a number of disease processes, such as diabetes, osteomalacia or osteoarthritis, to name but a few of the potential causes. These are treatable, if not necessarily completely curable, but only if they are detected. Attributing difficulties to 'normal ageing' therefore may mean people whose conditions could be improved miss out. This perspective, of the need for assiduous detection of disease, is credited to one of the originators of geriatric medicine, in the histories presented in many geriatric textbooks. The story told is of a Dr Marjorie Warren, who in the 1930s took up a post at the West Middlesex Hospital on a 'workhouse ward' where older people were housed in a climate of therapeutic pessimism and neglect. The effects of the regime – no active treatment or exercise – were to increase disabilities and dependency. Dr Warren and her colleague, Dr Howell, instituted a regime of active medical diagnosis and treatment with dramatic effects for some patients, and in the words of Bennet and Ebrahim (1992) "this marked the start of clinical gerontology, the scientific study of ageing and disease" (p 59).

Nonetheless, as people grow older, they seem to experience reductions in function that are not due to disease. While this process may vary from person to person, it remains a common experience. The physiological changes can include thinning of bones, and decreases in eyesight and hearing, as well as more superficial changes such as loss of hair and hair colour and loss of skin elasticity.

These are changes that seem to be caused by a general 'wearing out' process, rather than disease. Strehler (1964) has suggested that for a process to be attributed to ageing rather than disease, it must be universal (it must happen to every member of the species), progressive (there is no possibility of reversal), intrinsic (not dependent on chance but on the make-up of the organism) and deleterious (leading to decrease in function rather than increase). The problem with this framework, however, is that it can be difficult to ascertain these characteristics. While for simple and short-lived organisms some of these characteristics may be established, for human beings who live long and complex lives in a variety of environments and with a range of life experiences, it is not so simple. Using this framework, however, has given rise to some conclusions about ageing processes and some theories of how they may happen. These theories are complex and numerous, coming from different research efforts, and as such are difficult to describe simply. Moreover, there are many 'crossover' theories, which have combined different research findings from different fields. The description that follows, then, is necessarily simplistic and cannot hope to explore the details of the theories mentioned.

Intrinsic ageing theories

These theories suggest that there are internal programmes or mechanisms that determine the ageing process in species and individuals, and which are intrinsic to their make-up. Some derive from research done at the cellular or molecular level, on how cells divide and die. There is, for example, a well-observed limit to the number of times human fibroblasts will divide when grown in a cell culture, which seems constant at around 50 and does not vary with any changes to laboratory conditions (Kirkwood, 1977). Extrapolating this to the human body as a whole would suggest that the same is true at a macro level – after a point, our cells simply stop renewing. Ageing in this model, then, is the cessation of cell division, according to predetermined limits.

Related to cellular theories are the genetic theories of ageing, which suggest that the processes of cell division are genetically programmed for each species, and possibly for each individual. This genetic programming is independent of environmental factors, although may be affected by them – a rabbit kept as a household pet, for example, has a more comfortable life than its counterparts in the wild, and is protected from predators and accidents, and will probably survive longer. It will not survive that much longer, however, and if its offspring were returned to the wild, they would have the same lifespan as any other rabbit.

The mechanism for genetic programming may be a combination of factors – we may simply be programmed to have a higher cell division limit, or we may be programmed to have better protection against diseases and damage. While there may be some strategies we could adopt or develop in the future to delay ageing, intrinsic theories suggest that we are, as a species, allotted a lifespan that we can do little, at the moment, to affect. This is borne out by epidemiological research that shows that while the numbers of people living longer can increase – with better food, sanitation and healthcare – the absolute length of life, the maximum number of years anyone can live for does not seem to be changing. There may be some potential for genetic interventions in the future, and there is a research effort to identify possibilities (including the 'gene for ageing' beloved of the press) but for now intrinsic theories seek to understand what is, for the moment, an inevitable process.

Extrinsic ageing theories

Ageing has also been described as a process of error accumulation in genetic material due to external factors. As cells divide, they become increasingly prone to errors, which reduce their ability to function effectively and lead to senescence and death. This means that there is damage to the DNA (deoxyribonucleic acid), the genetic material that is carried from one generation of cells to another. DNA may become damaged simply through the process of replication, or through environmental agents, or through the processes that the body uses to survive and defend itself against attacks and disease.

Extrinsic factors include things such as ultraviolet (UV) light (which has a particular ageing effect on skin), toxic agents (such as chemicals in water and air), viral or bacterial infections and excesses or deficits in diet. All of these factors have been implicated in the changes associated with age at a cellular or organ level, and similarly 'recipes' for a longer life have involved doing things that either protect against these factors or help the body to cope with them. Searches for the 'fountain of youth' have a long history, with Öberg and Tornstam (2001) giving examples from the Middle Ages and the journeys of the Spanish explorers some 500 years ago. More recent examples that they cite include

Victorian recommendations to take arsenic to prevent wrinkles, and extracts of sperm to prevent other ageing signs. More recently, interest in vitamin supplements and complementary medicine as ways of preventing ageing has increased (Andrews, 2002). Theories of ageing based on extrinsic factors, then, can lead to recommendations about either the avoidance of toxins or the increase of beneficial elements. Articles and advertisements for vitamin supplements are an example of this way of thinking, that ageing is something that we can affect if we organise our lives in particular ways. The implication of this, of course, can be that suggestions that we can control our ageing, by living a healthy life, can also be used to blame people who do show ageing changes – they can be seen as failing to act responsibly or prudently.

Disposable soma theory

In addition to the categories mentioned above, there is another theory that goes some way to unifying different views and findings, the 'disposable soma' theory (Kirkwood, 1977). This is perhaps as much conceptual as empirical, in that it suggests a different way of thinking about what we know. It suggests that the 'germ-line' – that is, the genetic elements that are transferred to human beings by their parents through the process of reproduction – is immortal, in the sense that while the cells that carry the germ-line may die, the information they carry is constantly passed on through the generations. In this sense we do not grow old but, as Kirkwood has suggested, we sacrifice some cells to preserve the germ-line, and it is this process of sacrifice that gives rise to the changes that we label as ageing. The disposable soma theory suggests ways in which ageing of individuals is irrelevant to the survival of a species, and that physical decline is one price that must be paid for this.

Longevity and health in older age

Distinguishing ageing processes from disease processes is a fundamental concern of biomedical–ageing research, but this does not mean that the two can be completely separated from each other. The ageing process may make people more vulnerable to illness, or it may be that living longer allows time for health problems to develop. This does not mean that age-related health problems are inevitable and universal, and there is a great variation between individuals.

There are, however, some general patterns that have been described by research studies and national surveys. Longevity seems to be increasing – for example, in the UK life expectancy for women is now estimated at 80.2 years, and for men 75.4 years. This, however, varies across the UK, with the gap between the 'best' area (Kensington and Chelsea) and the 'worst' area (Manchester) being 7.7 years for men and 6.6 years for women (DoH, 2002). This contrasts with life expectancy in previous years. In the UK in 1900, for example, life expectancy at birth was 44 (men) and 48 (women) (DoH, 2002). These figures for longevity therefore suggest that this is something that can be affected by social contexts. That life expectancy has increased over the last century, for example, has been attributed to a number of factors, such as better sanitation and living conditions, as well as developments in the treatment of common, previously fatal diseases (Sidell, 1995). These developments have a profound effect on life expectancy figures, importantly because they reduce infant mortality rates. If more babies and children survive, then the average age at death increases for the population. The effect of change, then, is not so much on the health of adults and older people, but on children, who are vulnerable to the hazards of disease and poor living conditions. The disparity in current life expectancy according to area suggests that there are still complex social factors at play, involving the environment, social disadvantage and deprivation and culture. While death in western societies can be described as something that mainly happens to older people, the figures also point to inequalities in health.

This general increase in lifespan, furthermore, does not necessarily mean that people have fewer health problems, but simply that they are living longer. Studies of morbidity – that is, the extent to which people live with health problems that do not kill them – suggest that older people may be looking forward to more years of life, but that these years may be affected by poor health. Figures from the Office of Population Censuses and Surveys (OPCS, 1993) suggest that both acute and chronic health problems increase with age. Older people suffer acute problems such as accidents and injuries, with older women suffering more than men. Older people also suffer more chronic illness, with the OPCS finding that approximately 70% of people over 75 have a long-standing illness. Sidell (1991) has analysed the 1987 Health and Lifestyles Survey data and found that arthritis was the most commonly reported condition for women, with heart disease being the most common for men. Overall, Sidell argues, women's levels of illness tend to increase with age, but men's tend to decrease, although this can depend on the type of illness and there are exceptions to this pattern.

A disease process, however, does not necessarily have a deleterious effect on lifestyle. Sidell's (1995) analysis of the 1990 General Household Survey (GHS) data, for example, showed that when asked about whether illnesses are limiting, in the sense that they restrict daily living, people did not always agree, although the overall pattern of increase with age still holds true. These numbers, however, are greater in the OPCS disability study of 1988, which included older people living in institutions such as nursing homes (Martin et al, 1988). The GHS data also allows some other variables – such as occupation, marital status and housing – to be linked to chronic illness and disability, and analysis suggests that disability is greatest among widows, people from non-manual occupations, those with few educational qualifications and people living in council housing.

More recently, the Health Survey for England (2000) found that 40% of men and 42% of women living in private households reported having a disability, but this rose to 83% and 88% for men and women living in care homes. Disability increased over the age of 80 and the most commonly reported type of disability was locomotor disability followed by difficulties in personal care. The survey also collected data on co-morbidity, or the occurrence of multiple problems, finding that about 25% of men and women in private households reported one disability, 13% two disabilities and 6% reported three or more disabilities. In care homes, multiple disability was much more common, with 40% of men and 45% of women having three or more disabilities. In both private households and care homes, for both sexes, the disabilities most often occurring together were locomotor and personal care disabilities.

The Health Survey used the World Health Organisation (WHO) classification system for impairment and disability, which represents a move away from thinking about health as simply being the absence or presence of disease, and towards thinking of health as the ability to do the things that people feel that they should do or that they want to do. This comes closer to what we know about the way that older people themselves think about their health but, as the next section shows, does not fully address issues of subjective well-being in older people.

Self-assessed health

While many of the surveys reported above have relied on older people self-reporting illness or disability (rather than an independent third party such as their GP), this reporting acknowledges only the existence of a recognised illness or disability. Older people may, however, experience a range of symptoms and problems that do not fit with any medical diagnosis, but which can be distressing and restricting. These symptoms can include, for example, painful joints, headaches and stomach problems, which have not been attributed to a diagnosed disease. Mental or psychological problems such as sleeplessness, worry or lethargy can also occur without a specific illness being diagnosed (Sidell, 1995). Some insight into whether this is important to perceptions of health can be gained by comparing illness and disability levels to self-assessed health status – in other words whether people rate their health as good or bad. Comparisons between health rating and the incidence of health problems show some interesting patterns. While it would be expected that the incidence of problems of ill-health would correlate with self-rated health status, this is not always the case. Some older people seem to rate themselves as being in good health despite having illnesses, while some rate themselves as being in poor health despite reporting few or no illnesses. Overall, however, older people seem to rate themselves as being in good health in comparison to their peers (Cockerham, 1983). This observation is backed up by qualitative studies (for example, Wenger, 1988; Sidell, 1995; Bryant et al, 2001), which suggest some explanations of these anomalies – for example, that their health matches their own expectations of growing older, that they see ill-health and old age as synonymous and do not feel old, and that they are embarrassed to admit to poor health. Alternatively they may themselves attribute physical changes to age and assume no therapeutic options.

Embarrassment about poor health may fit with the findings of Blaxter and

Paterson (1982) that illness was seen as a 'moral category' – that is, that it was associated with moral failings such as indulgence, hypochondria, grumbling or a lack of self-care. This link with morality in western societies has been attributed by some to the dominance of the protestant work ethic, which equates personal worth with the ability and willingness to be active in directing one's own life, through work or through self-reliance. For older people who share this cultural belief, a chronic illness can prevent them from meeting these criteria and being considered a fully functioning person, with equal status to others. The cultural value placed on characteristics such as self-reliance and independence, however, is not universal, and varies from culture to culture. While independence may be valued in the West, and particularly the US, other markers for successful ageing are used elsewhere: for example, being assisted by a supportive family is very much valued in Japan and individual identity is only experienced and expressed through the family identity. In the West, however, it seems that independence is highly valued, and illness is a threat to this. Those who become ill or disabled may experience an assault to their sense of self, if this is based on independence, and may find themselves 'discredited' by others. This process of discrediting is where other, perhaps younger or perhaps more healthy people relate to the ill older person as less than fully adult. Discredited people can be treated as different from others, patronised and with fewer rights to make decisions – being an invalid can also make one *in-valid*. Charmaz (1983) also suggests that people can participate in discrediting themselves, by internalising these values.

These theories go some way to explaining why older people may describe themselves as healthy, when their medical diagnosis suggests that they are suffering from an illness. It may also go some way to explaining the findings of some studies that have explored older people's definitions of ill-health. They have found, on the whole, that older people equate ill-health to a condition that prevents them from functioning adequately and carrying out the activities expected of them or valued by them.

Managing and responding to ill-health

Various strategies used by older people to manage ill-health have been reported by researchers. Managing the symptoms of illness becomes a major task, particularly if these are unpredictable. Strategies may involve the use of medication, prescribed or over the counter. Medication regimes can be complicated and difficult – for example, someone who has diabetes may have to monitor their blood sugar levels and adjust their insulin dose or diet accordingly. Some medications have unwelcome side-effects, which in turn require management. Other treatments may be very visible, such as oxygen masks, and mark out the person as different from others. Bury (1988) found that these factors were weighed up when people decided whether to comply, adapt or abandon medication regimes.

Management strategies may also involve the use of complementary therapies

(Andrews, 2002) but in the UK these are not usually available through state-funded healthcare, and are usually paid for by the individual. While they may be seen as effective and promoting a sense of well-being, their cost may put them out of the reach of many older people. There is also the strategy of regulating activities. Weiner (1975), for example, found that people with arthritis 'paced' their activities to avoid problems, which involved regulating the amount, type and frequency of activity. This may be to avoid exacerbation of problems, but also to avoid disclosing difficulties to others.

Other strategies may be more subtle. People may, for example, only buy clothes that are easy to get on and off, or avoid certain foods, or eat at certain times. All strategies, however, are linked to normalisation – that is, the attempt to live a 'normal' life, according to the expectations that someone has about themselves, or that they feel others have about them. This may involve efforts to disguise or minimise their difficulties, or to overcome them, and can take up much energy, effort and resources. Responses to ill-health that involve such disguise processes may lead to the findings that older people rate their health better than would be expected given the problems that they have, as noted earlier, but also to views of health that are based on the ability to function 'normally' rather than any identification of pathology.

Older people's views of health

As a converse to this view of ill-health as something that prevents functioning, health has been described by older people in functional terms – that is, the ability to do things. Bryant et al (2001) carried out a qualitative study asking older people about their perceptions of health. The sample of 22 older people was drawn from a larger study that had looked at self-reported health and objectively measured health in a sample of older Americans. From the findings of the parent study, older people were identified who had under-rated or over-rated their health compared to the predictions based on their measured health status. The researchers found that there were a number of elements to interviewees' discussions and definition of health and well-being, including physical condition, a sense of security, a 'good' mental attitude, and the ability to go and do things. This last element was further explored, and analysis produced four components: having something worthwhile to do, having the ability to do it, having the resources to do it, and having the will to do it. Bryant et al (2001) point out that this view of health as 'doing things' contrasts with the medical view that doing things results from, rather than contributes to, health (the medical view of health typically being the absence of disease or disability).

Similar findings had been reported by other studies, but many other explorations of the links between activity and health display a circular logic, which suggests that activity promotes health – that is, that higher levels of activity are associated with higher health scores (see, for example, Everard et al, 2000). Bryant et al's (2001) study argues that activity is health, in the eyes of older people, and that physical health status is not an end in itself, but a means to an end: that of going and doing things.

Some studies have looked at the concepts of self-efficacy and sense of coherence, and these ideas offer ways of connecting subjective and objective experiences of health. Self-efficacy is an individual's perception that they have the ability to do things, rather than any physical measure of ability. The suggestion is that people with weaker self-efficacy beliefs will be reluctant to engage in activities (Bandura, 1977). Curtailing activity may have progressive negative effects, as people do not experience successful performance of activities, and their self-efficacy beliefs decrease. There is evidence that this model of self-efficacy also pertains to older people. Tinetti et al (1994) found that in older people higher self-efficacy beliefs about the ability to perform activities of daily living are associated with higher self-reported levels of physical and social functioning. Self-efficacy beliefs have been measured for a number of different domains, including health, finances, and interpersonal relationships, and the patterns do seem to be similar – self-efficacy beliefs in each domain are linked to willingness to engage in this activity. A study by Seeman et al (1999) extended these ideas and explored the relationship between self-efficacy ratings and future onset of self-reported disabilities in a longitudinal study of older people, taking those who had high baseline self-efficacy scores in interpersonal and instrumental domains, and following them through time. They concluded that self-efficacy beliefs had an impact on perceived physical abilities, but were not related to actual physical abilities. Seeman et al (1999) suggested that self-efficacy beliefs might be important factors in lifestyle changes for older people, and their perceived quality of life.

The concept of 'sense of coherence' has also been brought to bear on understanding older people's perspectives on health. Antonovsky (1979) has defined sense of coherence as:

> a global orientation that expresses the extent to which one has a pervasive, enduring, though dynamic feeling that one's internal and external environments are predicable and that there is a high probability that these things will work out as well as can reasonably be expected. (Antonovsky, 1979, p 123)

In later work, this was refined to three main components – comprehensibility, manageability and meaningfulness – and all of these components have relevance to understanding older people's views of health and well-being. Sidell (1995) has used the sense of coherence framework as a basis for discussing older people's views of their health, and in particular the threat posed by chronic illness, which can pose huge challenges to making sense of health problems. Blaxter (1993), for example, found in a study of older people with chronic illness that much effort was expended in uncovering 'chains of causes', that is, why they had the problems that they had – a process that Williams (1984) has described as 'narrative reconstruction'. Explaining the rise of health problems in a way that makes sense of the past and the present allows the future to be presented as more manageable. Sidell (1995) gives the example of one person, Sarah, who has arthritis, but who sees herself as a very active person. She explains her arthritis as due to wear and tear, which preserves and supports her view of herself as active and, while using medication, refuses to allow it to restrict her activities. Another example, that of Jim who had prostate problems, shows a more complex pattern by his denying publicly the incontinence problems that he experiences, and coping with them by withdrawing from activities. Jim's coping strategies involved avoidance of what was an embarrassment, and construction of a narrative that minimised the impact on his life by presenting other explanations for his withdrawal from social gatherings, such as a lack of interest or time.

Implications for quality of life and successful ageing

As was discussed at the beginning of the chapter, biomedical theories of ageing are many and varied, and because of their diversity can only address selected aspects of ageing. They offer various possibilities for delaying ageing, with extrinsic factor theories perhaps having the most to offer at the moment. There are, however, other questions that can be asked of this advancement of science – questions about whether we want to delay ageing and extend life. Some of these questions have been raised by suggestions that what we should be striving for is not to increase the quantity of life, but its quality. Related to this is the 'compression of morbidity' (Fries, 1980) model of ideal ageing, which states that the best way to grow older is to function independently with little illness or disability, until a brief acute illness causes death. This ideal assumes that what reduces quality of life is the experience of illness and loss of function, and so cutting this to as short as possible a period would be what everyone wants.

This idea, however, makes many assumptions about growing older, and about what might be the aims and aspirations of older people. It assumes that physical decline and disability is something to be feared and avoided, and that it reduces quality of life to such an extent that it becomes no longer worth living. As such it seems like an idea developed by people who have not yet experienced growing older to any meaningful extent, and who are applying their own anticipated responses to predict the views of others. This seems a shaky foundation for developing policy and practice for older people and, as the next section discusses, can be challenged by a number of accounts from older people that suggest that the physical effects of growing older can be accepted and accommodated and enjoyment of life maintained. This material, developed from a social/psychological perspective on physical ageing, offers a different view to biomedical models.

Most striking is the idea that, as discussed above, physical and psychological functioning is not valued by older people as an end in itself, but as the basis for enjoyment of activities. There is, however, a complex relationship between what a person wants to do, what they physically can do, what they think they can do (sense of self-efficacy), and the support that they get to do it. This broadens the relationship between physical and mental health and quality of life to include particular personal contexts and expectations.

Some of these points are reflected in the current debates about the notions of 'successful ageing'. Bowling (1993) has traced this idea back to 44 BC when Cicero wrote an essay on it, and Torres (1999) has identified more modern roots to 1944 and the establishing of a Committee on Social Adjustment to Old Age. Torres further goes on to identify four main definitions of successful ageing found in the literature, namely reaching one's potential, the ability to adapt to changes, remaining youthful in outlook, and remaining productive. Some of these definitions can be linked to the discussions above, about what older people feel, but some of them would seem to reflect a particular western view of successful living in adulthood in general, applied automatically to older people. This is particularly the case of definitions that emphasise 'youthfulness' (see, for example, Rowe and Kahn, 1987, whose article in *Science* comes close to suggesting that successful ageing means not ageing at all).

Some models – for example, that of Baltes and Carstensen (1996) – have developed notions of coping and optimisation as strategies for successful ageing, which do resonate with the accounts of older people and which have the virtue of being adaptable to specific individual and cultural contexts. The Baltes model identifies 'selective optimisation and compensation', suggesting that older people can adapt to circumstances by making strategic choices, and that this can lead to growth and development. Others, as Torres (1999) argues, are implicitly based on western cultural assumptions about independence and autonomy as being desirable. Torres highlights the danger of making such assumptions when she cites the example of the Project AGE study, which was a cross-cultural study (Keith et al, 1990). Americans were found to associate successful ageing with self-reliance, while older people in Hong Kong were mystified by the idea of self-reliance in older age, and saw their family's willingness to provide support as a mark of ageing successfully. American older people tended to value optimism, courage and motivation, while older people in Hong Kong valued tolerance and being easy-going. These stark cultural differences indicate the problems in assuming a universal model of successful ageing, but also open up the possibility of differences within cultures as well. While models may be shaped by lifelong cultural experiences, we also know that these are not monolithic, and there is variation among members of the same cultures in many ways. Cross-cultural comparisons point to the possibility of within-culture differences in life goals and life satisfaction (Gubrium and Lynott, 1986).

As mentioned in Chapter One, Strawbridge (2000) has identified some of the problems of models of successful ageing that are based on the idea that to be successful in ageing is to maintain physical levels of fitness and engage in physical activities. He has criticised media stories about, for example, older athletes who can achieve as much if not more than younger competitors, and suggested that they marginalise those who cannot match these achievements. His study showed that older people who have health problems tended to feel that they were not ageing successfully, and he comments that the phrase 'successful ageing' is a very American term, "implying a kind of contest. But people should never be told that they failed ageing because they had arthritis" (p 14).

Conclusion

This chapter began with some comments from a woman who, in an interview, seemed to have accepted her reduced capability for activity as she grew older, but got pleasure from things that she did do in the care home where she lived. She is worth keeping in mind as an example of a response to a body growing older that contrasts with some of the debates in research and policy (usually conducted by younger people), which have attempted to tackle the 'problem' of the ageing body. First, we turned to a discussion of biomedical models of the ageing body, which suggest explanations for the changes in physical functioning that are observed as people grow older. These explanations, in part, seek to distinguish between ageing and disease, and suggest strategies for preventing ageing. These strategies depend on whether ageing factors are intrinsic or extrinsic: intrinsic factors indicate genetic modification strategies that are not, as yet, developed, but extrinsic factors indicate possibilities for modifying lifestyle and environment.

Probably of more interest to older people, however, is the incidence of health problems in older age, and our discussion then turned to life expectancy, the incidence of disease and disability in old age. This showed that there were differences within the UK in life expectancy, and that health problems in general increase as you grow older. This does not mean, however, that older people 'feel' ill, and self-reported illness is lower than observed illness for some groups. What is suggested by the literature is that there are a number of moral drivers that lead older people to see illness as a weakness, so they are keen to underplay it, and furthermore illness per se is not necessarily the most important factor for older people thinking about health – it is the reduction of ability to do things that leads to subjective feelings of health. Both of these observations may go some way to explaining discrepancies between objective and subjective health reports, and moreover they point to the complexity and range of possible models of health for older people.

Explorations of what these models might be suggest again that the absence of disease or disability is not the key issue for older people, as much as the ability to 'go and do' things. The impetus for this may come from pressures to act as though younger or deny age, and avoid moral judgements that can be made about giving up, or hypochondria or attention seeking. The impetus may also be about having fun – the ability to go and do things that are worthwhile, enjoyable and meaningful. The following quotes, which come from a focus group exploring notions of 'comfortable healthy ageing' (Reed et al, 2003), suggest that it can be a mix of the two.

One woman, for example, talked about the strategy she had developed to maintain activity:

> "I think when you get older you have to pace yourself, you know, you ... you must realise that you can't physically do what you could do when you were younger, and you pace yourself."

Another focus group member talked about the way in which the group accepted each other's difficulties:

> "I think that's why we enjoy coming in here [to the day centre]. We're all elderly. We're all disabled in one way or the other and we enjoy each other's company because you don't have to keep explaining oh I've got this, I'm going blind and ... you don't have to go through that."

The chapter ends on a cautionary note, therefore, about the problems that could follow from adopting an idealistic goal of successful ageing, particularly if this is based on the avoidance of any limitations accrued with ageing. This has echoes of biomedical models, which see ageing as the accumulation of deficits and the decline in ability attendant on growing older. As Strawbridge (2000) has pointed out, this is a western competitive model, and runs the risk of excluding the many older people who do experience health problems and disabilities and those who do not subscribe to these goals.

Exercise

- Make a note of the physical activities that you have been engaged in today. This includes washing, dressing, eating, walking and sitting, hearing, seeing and talking.
- Which of these activities were the most important to you and why?
- If you could only engage in these activities to a limited extent, and needed special support or equipment, what things would become difficult for you to do?
- Think about the plans that you have for the rest of today, or tomorrow. What would be impossible, difficult or would be just as straightforward if you had limited abilities?

References

Andrews, G.J. (2002) 'Private complementary medicine and older people: service use and user empowerment', *Ageing and Society*, vol 22, no 3, pp 343-68.

Antonovsky, A. (1979) *Health, stress and coping: New perspectives on mental and physical well-being*, San Francisco, CA: Jossey-Bass.

Baltes, M.M. and Carstensen, L.L. (1996) 'The process of successful ageing', *Ageing and Society*, vol 16, no 3, pp 397-422.

Bandura, A. (1977) 'Self-efficacy: towards a unifying theory of behavioural change', *Psychological Review*, vol 84, pp 191-215.

Bennet, G. and Ebrahim, S. (1992) *Healthcare in old age* (2nd edn), London: Edward Arnold.

Blaxter, M. (1993) 'Why do the victims blame themselves?', in A. Radley (ed) *Worlds of illness*, London: Routledge, pp 124-42.

Blaxter, M. and Paterson, L. (1982) *Mothers and daughters: A three generational study of health, attitudes and behaviour*, Oxford: Heinemann Educational.

Bowling, A. (1993) 'The concept of successful and positive aging', *Family Practice*, vol 10, pp 449-53.

Bryant, L., Corbett, K. and Kutner, J. (2001) 'In their own words: a model of healthy aging', *Social Science and Medicine*, vol 53, no 7, pp 927-41.

Bury, M. (1988) 'Meanings at risk: the experience of arthritis', in R. Anderson and M. Bury (eds) *Living with chronic illness: The experience of patients and their families*, London: Unwin Hyman, pp 90-116.

Bytheway, B. (1997) 'Talking about age: the theoretical basis of social gerontology', in A. Jamieson, S. Harper and C. Victor (eds) *Critical approaches to later life*, Buckingam: Open University Press, pp 7-15.

Charmaz, K. (1983) 'Loss of self: a fundamental form of suffering in the chronically ill', *Sociology of Health and Illness*, vol 5, no 2, pp 168-95.

Cockerham, W.C. (1983) 'Ageing and perceived health status', *Journal of Gerontology*, vol 38, pp 349-55.

DoH (Department of Health) (2002) *Reducing inequalities in health: An action report*, London: DoH.

Estes, C.L. and Binncy, E.A. (1991) 'The biomedicalisation of aging: dangers and dilemmas', in M. Minkler and C.L. Estes (eds) *Critical perspectives on aging*, Amityville, NY: Baywood, pp 117-34.

Everard, K.M., Lach, H.W., Fisher, E.B. and Baum, M.C. (2000) 'Relationship of activity and social support to the functional health of older adults', *Journal of Gerontology*, vol 55B, no 4, pp s208-12.

Featherstone, M. (1994) 'Kultur, knapp, konsumtion. Stockholm symposium', cited in P. Öberg and L. Tornstam (2001) 'Youthfulness and fitness – identity ideals for all ages?', *Journal of Aging and Identity*, vol 6, no 1, pp 15-29.

Featherstone, M. and Hepworth, M. (1991) 'The mask of ageing and the postmodern life course', in M. Featherstone, M. Hepworth and B. Turner (eds) *The body: Social process and cultural theory*, London: Sage Publications, pp 371-89.

Fries, J.F. (1980) 'Ageing, natural death and the compression of morbidity', *New England Journal of Medicine*, vol 303, no 3, pp 130-5.

Gubrium, J.F. and Lynott, R.J. (1986) 'Re-thinking life-satisfaction', in B.B. Hess (ed) *Growing old in America*, New York, NY: Transaction Books.

Harper, S. (1997) 'Constructing later life/constructing the body: some thoughts from feminist theory', in A. Jamieson, S. Harper and C. Victor (eds) *Critical approaches to later life*, Buckingam: Open University Press, pp 160-74.

Health Survey for England (2000) *Disability among older people*, London: The Stationery Office.

Keith, J., Fry, C.L. and Ikels, C. (1990) 'Community as context for successful aging', in J. Sokolovsky (ed) *The cultural context of aging*, New York, NY: Bergin and Garvey.

Kirkwood, T.B.L. (1977) 'Evolution of ageing', *Nature*, vol 270, pp 301-4.

Longino, C. (2000) 'Beyond the body: an emerging medical paradigm', in A. Warnes, L. Warren and M. Nolan (eds) *Care services for later life: Transformations and critiques*, London: Jessica Kingsley, pp 39-53.

Martin, J., Melzer, H. and Elliot, D. (1988) *The prevalence of disability among adults*, OPCS Surveys of Disability in Great Britain Report No 1, London: HMSO.

Öberg, P. and Tornstam, L. (2001) 'Youthfulness and fitness – identity ideals for all ages?', *Journal of Aging and Identity*, vol 6, no 1, pp 15-29.

OPCS (Office of Population Censuses and Surveys) (1993) *General household survey 1991*, London: OPCS.

Reed, J., Cook, G., Childs, S. and Hall, A. (2003) *Getting old is not for cowards: Comfortable healthy ageing*, York: Joseph Rowntree Foundation.

Rowe, J.W. and Kahn, R.I. (1987) 'Human aging: usual and successful', *Science*, vol 237, no 2, pp 143-9.

Seeman, T.E., Unger, J.B., McAvay, G. and Mendes de Leon, C.F. (1999) 'Self-efficacy beliefs and perceived declines in functional ability: MacArthur studies of successful aging', *Journal of Gerontology*, vol 54B, no 4, pp P214-22.

Sidell, M. (1991) *Gender differences in the health of older people*, Research Report, Department of Health and Social Welfare, Milton Keynes: The Open University.

Sidell, M. (1995) *Health in old age: Myth, mystery and management*, Buckinghamshire: Open University Press.

Strawbridge, W. (2000) 'Chronic illness: coping successfully for successful aging', *Aging Today*, vol 21, no 5, p 14.

Strehler, B.L. (ed) (1964) *Advances in gerontological research*, vol 1, New York, NY: Academic Press.

Tinetti, M.E., Medes de Leon, C.H., Coucette, J.T. and Baker, D.I. (1994) 'Fear of falling and fall-related efficacy in relationship to functioning among community-living elders', *Journal of Gerontology: Medical Sciences*, vol 49, pp 140-7.

Torres, S. (1999) 'A culturally-relevant theoretical framework for the study of successful ageing', *Ageing and Society*, vol 19, no 1, pp 33-51.

Weiner, C. (1975) 'The burden of rheumatoid arthritis: tolerating the uncertainty', OPCS, in A. Strauss (ed) *Chronic illness and the quality of life*, St Louis, MO: Mosby.

Wenger, G.C. (1988) *Old people's health and experience of the caring services: Accounts from rural communities in North Wales*, Liverpool: Liverpool University Press.

Williams, G. (1984) 'The genesis of chronic illness: narrative reconstruction', *Sociology of Health and Illness*, vol 6, no 2, pp 174-200.

FOUR

The lived environment

Contents

Introduction	67
Housing	67
The community environment, pedestrians and transport	74
Conclusion	77

Key points

- The environment in which older people live is an important determinant of their quality of life.
- Domestic spaces need to be designed to cope with different and changing needs, providing a 'home for life'.
- Public spaces and facilities need to be planned with accessibility and participation in mind.
- Improving the lived environment for older people will improve it for everyone.

Introduction

This chapter is concerned with quality of life and the lived environment, by which we mean the contribution that surroundings and circumstances make to the maintenance of a healthy lifestyle for older people. In particular it is concerned with exploiting the possibilities of being able to continue to occupy general housing stock and make use of community services and facilities that are open to all. With a specific focus centred on housing, transport, risk and security we shall take a selected number of key ideas and look at examples that might both challenge and extend our ideas on healthy ageing.

Housing

"I had to give up a home and every time I pass it I look at it and I think 'you shouldn't have done that'. But I did." (*House for Life*, 2001, p 15)

The quote above, by an older person, is from a report that presents the findings of a housing group of older people and housing professionals that was established (following a whole systems event in Newcastle in 1995) to look at housing issues for older people in Newcastle upon Tyne. Having first developed a guide to accommodation for older people, the group then set out to find ways of ensuring that "more older people are given the information, support and services which [would] enable them to live independently in their own homes" (*House for Life*, 2001, p 6).

There is a pervasive popular perspective on ageing that contributes to the view that, as people become older, they inevitably need progressively less space. It is quite a powerful view, which is often reinforced – for instance, by those approaching retirement – by such ideas as 'downsizing' homes on the basis that their children have grown up and left home or perhaps that their capacity to manage the garden has become reduced owing to failing strength or mobility. These are very real considerations, which we certainly must not dismiss, and apply equally to any sector of the housing market – from social housing through to owner-occupier, rental and residential and nursing care homes. (Chapter Eight has a discussion of strategies for equity release where older people may realise the assets tied up in their property.) However, this view can be argued to mirror unhelpfully the deficit model of ageing by implying some sort of inevitable law that the external physical world will shrink proportionately to the atrophying ageing person, and it colludes with the idea that life closes in, that there is less to do and therefore less need for personal space in which to do it. The changed and changing demographics of ageing suggest that, while these ideas hold validity in the very later stages of life and in the context of inadequate health and fitness, there is an extension to the period before then which holds greater scope for independent living.

Quite apart from the sense of loss that can be experienced as a result of giving up a familiar and valued home because it is time to face planning for the future, it is important not to allow such ideas to remain unexplored. There are two major considerations that can either challenge the inevitability of such an outlook or invite further thinking about the timescale of such a move.

Excess capacity or new uses?

The first consideration is that, rather than prove to be ultimately unnecessary, so-called 'excess' living space might be adapted for use in changing circumstances. The child's empty bedroom becomes the guest bedroom for grown-up children who have left home, for grandchildren, for hobbies, a home 'study' to house the computer or for many other varied uses. This is an area of interest across a wide range of disciplines, from social geography through to architecture and social gerontology. An interesting study by Helen Nelson (2001) cites many examples of older people reconsidering the uses to which their domestic space can be put and equally, reinforcing the opening quotation, poignant examples of where space has been voluntarily surrendered in the mistaken belief that it was superfluous. Percival (2002) explores the differing ways in which domestic space is important – for example, for entertaining, with sufficient space to invite the family and act as host, with one interviewee saying of her limited dining facilities, "I feel I've robbed my children and grandchildren of something in a way" (p 734). Other examples include overnight guest space and the personalisation of space to enable spouses to conduct their different leisure activities in different rooms.

Above all, the flexibility to manage sufficient space acts as a powerful expression of the "importance of self-determination in the home environment" (Percival, 2002, p 735). Percival goes on to caution about the inevitable consequential paradox: that while access to sufficient space is important, there can develop difficulties in its cleaning and maintenance, to the extent that there may be advice to downsize to a more 'manageable' apartment of sheltered accommodation. This is a conundrum that strikes at the very centre of health and welfare service provision for older people. Too often the emphasis is on the provision of personal services, with provider agencies – for example, in domiciliary care – able to offer support for personal tasks such as dressing and bathing, but not for, say, housework. If ever there was a demonstration of the interrelatedness between health and social well-being, then this is an issue that epitomises it.

A 'house for life'...

The second consideration is that apparently unmanageable homes can be made more manageable through forward planning using adaptations and 'smart' technology (where items that are traditionally stand-alone can be used in conjunction with other functions – for example, multiple function light switches – or where manual tasks such as opening a door can be automated) so that older people can continue to occupy them for longer than might have been thought possible. It should be noted that some aspects of smart technology are not without their criticisms, especially ethical considerations (Thomas Pocklington Trust, 2003). The quote at the beginning of this chapter continues: "It's irrevocable [having to give up a home], but I just pass it on for knowledge to people that, now we know what can be done in your home, think about it and stay where you are" (*House for Life*, 2001, p 15). Just what *can* be done is the whole purpose of the House for Life report. The housing group embarked on an "ambitious and challenging" programme: first, to adapt a real house in which it would be suitable for older people to live; and, second, to mount an exhibition of the range of aids, adaptations and services that could assist older people in living independently. Throughout their work there was an emphasis on involving older people from the outset, on the principle that outcomes were thereby more likely to be meaningful and acceptable to other older people.

The housing group set Newcastle City Council's Community and Housing Directorate a challenge by inviting them to make available an older property with staff and finances to adapt it in line with recommendations made by the housing group, and to allow it to be available as a demonstration house open to the public for a limited period, followed by allocating it to older tenants who would make best use of the adaptations in the long term. The role of the housing group would be to coordinate the project overall, support and fund the involvement of older people, and organise and manage the show house. The remit of the project was to make the outcomes applicable to council tenants, private tenants and owner-occupiers. Within four months of being submitted to the city council, the proposal had been approved, a suitable property identified and staffing resources allocated to the project. The report sets out in some detail the processes of consultation and learning that were undertaken by the housing group members with inputs from a range of professional, voluntary and statutory service providers as well as older people themselves. It is worthwhile listing in entirety the range of adaptations that were made to the property:

- rewire with whole-plate switches, with sockets at a height of 300 mm and 1,000 mm;
- hard-wired smoke and carbon monoxide alarms;
- level access throughout the ground floor, including front door, kitchen door and patio doors;
- wide doorways for wheelchair access throughout the house;
- patio doors in the sitting room allowing easier access to the garden and more daylight;
- provision of a downstairs toilet;
- kitchen adaptations including lever taps, separate hob and oven and folding ironing board suitable for a wheelchair user;
- central heating with combination boiler and low surface temperature radiators with temperature control valve on each radiator;
- conversion of the bathroom and toilet into a single bathroom to make it wheelchair accessible, including a bath with overhead shower;
- vertical lift (chosen in preference to a stairlift because of the narrow and sharply curving staircase in the property);
- ceiling rack hoist in the bedroom;
- security system including intercom and burglar alarm;
- low maintenance front garden and raised beds around patio.

While in use as a show house there was also a range of additional information available to visitors concerning equipment, energy advice, lifts, hoists, alarms, social services, grants and benefits and other available finance. Among other positive comments, visitors reported it to feel like an ordinary house and satisfaction that the alterations had been carried out to the specifications of older people rather than led by architects and officers. While the report makes it clear that this was not achieved without some tensions, especially in taking as much time as was necessary for the older people representatives to make their choices, it also is careful to value the advisory and technical inputs of professional, statutory and voluntary service providers – indeed, a hallmark of the housing group's approach to the project was its meticulous planning and consultation. The priority responses to the question 'what would most help you stay in your home?' were identified as:

- kitchen and bathroom adaptations;
- downstairs toilet;
- community care alarm;
- the confidence to know that some of the things shown would be made available to when needed.

In many respects, and without in any way underemphasising the significance of this project, the individual components of the house existed already. But what was different was the way in which the process was both devised and conducted. The report makes clear that this project was indeed a genuine partnership between the stakeholders, with the views and needs of older people being paramount. Thus the process was equally as important as the outcomes, one of which was that the "standards from the House for Life (especially for kitchen and bathroom improvement) are now being incorporated into the City Council's investment programme for its own housing stock" (*House for Life*, 2001, p 2). Unsurprisingly, kitchen and bathroom adaptations were identified as key improvements by the older people whom Percival (2002) interviewed for his study.

These examples amply demonstrate ways in which older people can plan, and be empowered to plan, for their future and to maintain control over their lives (Chapter Five has a specific discussion of technology for people with dementia and memory problems). It would be naive to ignore the resource implications, but there are significant messages here for both policy makers and practitioners in health and social care services. The enfranchisement that can be achieved by doing so is best expressed by one of the participants in the House for Life project:

> "Having my own front door has always been important to me, but I will have difficulty managing in my house if I become disabled.... I now know what I can do to go on living independently and having my own place. It's no good having your own front door if you can't get in and out of it. And you don't want to be a prisoner in one room ... now I can see how you can make every room accessible ... get in and out easily with level access ... even open the door from your armchair ... be linked to an alarm system and get help when you need it. So I am going to be able to go on having my own front door." (*House for Life*, 2001, p 31)

...and 'Lifetime Homes'

There is a growing recognition that, as people grow older, they wish to live where they choose and how they choose, and to be supported in so doing. It is also acknowledged that this is a fundamentally complex and changing cohort, which is far from homogeneous. A Joseph Rowntree Foundation-funded study by Appleton (2002a) provides a concise overview of the literature and identifies the context in which general housing must be available in order to be successful. Collectively, identification of the characteristics of the cohort and the community context in which they live occupies more of the report than is devoted to the built environment. In a similar vein, 'Lifetime Homes' is a concept generated from a Joseph Rowntree Foundation project aimed at developing design features that will ensure that new homes are adequate for the needs of most households, incorporating features that are adaptable as people's circumstances and needs change. Appleton (2002b) has developed this concept for the Joseph Rowntree Foundation's vision of a new community at New Osbaldwick, on the outskirts of York, which aims to create a mixed tenure community, including provision for older people, taking into account an extensive inventory of 16 complex and particular areas of need (see Appleton, 2002b, pp 41-2).

These are innovative ideas when it comes to housing provision for older people, for much of the literature is devoted to the provision of special housing (such as sheltered housing, residential care and nursing homes and high dependency units) and it is easy to lose sight of the need to respond to demands for normative rather than differentiated provision. However, there are caveats. It is important to recognise that, by definition, these are not facilities that most older people will be able to access. Currently they are essentially demonstration projects, but demonstrations that are increasingly being adopted through, for example, accessibility legislation on building standards. It is equally important to be reminded that not all older people live in settled accommodation: a joint report by the Salvation Army and Help the Aged (undated), *Old before our time*, explores, through an action research project in Bristol in 2001, special issues surrounding the resettlement of homeless older people.

Highlighting continuing difficulties

Quite apart from addressing requirements for fitting out the home, there are also fundamental issues concerning managing within it. Winter time can often trigger instances of such matters:

> For most of us, winter's just an inconvenience. It means we can't eat outdoors, wear light clothing and enjoy long warm days. But for Britain's 12 million over 60s, the changing seasons can be seen as a life or death concern. Most confess to dreading winter coming and with it the cold and the dark. Small wonder. Given that so many

over 60s have experienced ill-health, money worries and crime as part of previous winters.

So wrote Miriam Stoppard in her introduction to the report of an independent survey commissioned by British Gas in association with Help the Aged, *Winter matters* (British Gas/Help the Aged, 2002), aimed at exploring the feelings of older people about the onset of winter and its implications for them in terms of illness, income, security, the cold and loneliness. It is significant that this survey, of a sample of over 1,000 older people drawn from regions across mainland Britain, focuses on their worries, and so there is little of the optimism that is to be found in the House for Life project. Nevertheless it serves as a sharp reminder of worries that may well be heightened in the winter time but which, no doubt, do not necessarily vanish with the coming of spring. The study shows respondents saying that 40% are concerned about money matters, 50% about falling ill, 33% about having adequate heating in their homes, 60% about high bills and 50% about being burgled. The evidence from the survey is that one in three of the respondents suffered a severe winter infection during the previous year and that approaching one in ten was hospitalised as a result. The extent to which homes were not as well insulated as they might have been was significant, even where grant aid was available to assist with installation. The study paints a distressing picture of the worries of the respondents and, while the results differentiate between different income groups, it is nonetheless the case that older people inhabit some of the poorest of housing stock.

Thus it can be seen that provision of adequately equipped housing stock alone is, at one level, merely the starting point. Making provision for, among others, financial pressure and health and social needs is a vital part of the equation.

Risk and safety

Living is a risky business and houses can present particular safety problems for older people. A good example is the danger posed by stairs, which can become dangerous when care is not exercised or when particular sorts of behaviour can exacerbate the likelihood of falls. A study by Haslam et al (2001) suggested that older people could be both aware of the hazards presented by stairways – for instance, in the dark or when they were taking medication or alcohol – and yet also engage in behaviour such as leaving obstructions on the staircase. Focus groups conducted with older people for this study also indicated that participants had not thought very much about the potential dangers that stairs presented, or how they might alter their behaviour to become safer when using them. The discussion in Chapter Nine about risk and safety also illustrates points about safety for older people, through the use of scripts for sketches used in an educational programme for older people.

Haslam et al's findings (2001) identified a number of key issues surrounding safety and stairs: environmental factors (stair design, stair covering, handrails, environmental aspects of lighting); behavioural factors (patterns of usage, carrying items, leaving objects on stairs, hurrying, use of lighting, footwear and clothing, cleaning, pets, stair avoidance); and personal factors such as balance, general strength, vision and the use of spectacles. These factors could occur singly or combine to create potentially greater or lesser degrees of hazard, and overall it appeared that there was considerable scope for safety education in reducing the likelihood of falls associated with stairs.

In a different though associated context, a report by the Thomas Pocklington Trust (2003) explored the housing and support needs of older people with visual impairment. The report maintains that policy, especially on housing support, has kept up neither with demographic trends nor with the incidence of visual impairment in older people. Support needs identified included: support with activities of daily living; modification, layout and space changes in the home environment; difficulties in group living environments shared by residents who did not have an understanding of the special needs of visually impaired older people; and concern about the undue quietness or 'hushedness' of some shared spaces, which unsettled and distressed respondents. Discussion on the provision of shared, specialist accommodation was mixed, particularly expressing concerns about institutionalisation, and most respondents expressed a wish to retain independent living for as long as they could. High on the lists of preferred provision were issues to do with social contact and inclusion, and the development of sensory impairment teams with rehabilitation strategies that acknowledged and could respond to the wide variety of preferred activities and lifestyles.

While these are two quite different studies, they both equally serve to demonstrate the wide range of issues that can affect older people in their living environments. Being safe is as much about being aware and being able to respond appropriately in an adequately resourced setting. It is not about rendering sterile either the living space or the living experience.

The community environment, pedestrians and transport

While this chapter is mostly concerned with the built environment, the overall lived environment of older people is, of course, more extensive. As was hinted earlier, there is little value in having an independent home – a front door of your own – only to become a prisoner behind it, whether through immobility, fear for personal safety or unavailable access to appropriate means of transport or travel. Chapter Seven illustrates how important community engagement can be for older people. Appleton (2002a) presents a convincing range of studies that demonstrate that location is just as important as the building. For older people, the safeness of their community is as important as anything else and is a significant contributory factor to psychological health as well as to physical health. The safety, or lack of safety, of public space can be manifested in the management of a number of diverse issues: noise, children's play areas, litter, graffiti, substance abuse, condition of surrounding buildings, pedestrian access, fear of crime, street lighting, drunkenness, and so on.

Now, these are issues that affect the lives of all citizens but there are particular implications for older people. Where areas are felt to be less safe there is likely to be a retreat into private realms, perhaps even 'fortified' by perimeter fencing, special lighting, uniformed security guards, gates, CCTV cameras, and so on. And while these security aids may promote security within the enclave – whether it be an individual home, a residential care or nursing home, or a retirement village – the evidence is persuasive that outside of the 'fortification' the world can seem to be even more unsafe. Thus, unless the issue of community safety in its broadest sense is carefully addressed, there is a greater likelihood that the wider community might become a 'no-go' area, which, in turn, is likely to inhibit travel and access to leisure and other facilities, thus directly affecting quality of life.

Age Concern England (the National Council on Ageing), in their (2001) submission to the House of Commons Environment, Transport and Regional Affairs Committee's inquiry into 'Walking in towns and cities', pointed out that not only did older people have less access to cars than most of the public (although access levels are generally increasing), they further argued that walking served an important function in promoting the health of older people and in contributing to their general sense of well-being. Indeed, it is a well-accepted position that older people who maintain their mobility are less likely to have falls or develop osteoporosis. They also pointed out that government policy generally led to increased road building while at the same time noting that public support for improved walking facilities, which are relatively cheap to introduce, was not reflected in government policy or provision. The Age Concern submission contains persuasive arguments of the needs of older people in respect of:

* improved condition of pavements;
* improved road safety;
* action on car parking (especially on pavements);
* the provision of more, strategically placed seating in public places;
* improved lighting in streets and at bus stops.

In doing so, the submission noted that, although people aged 65 and over are the least likely to be victims of violence, older women are more afraid of walking alone at night than women of younger age groups.

One developing initiative that will contribute to some of these concerns is that of 'home zones'. Essentially a home zone is a residential street where the needs of both residents and pedestrians are prioritised over those of vehicles. Biddulph (2001) explored the lessons to be learned from a number of these schemes in northern Europe and the UK. One central tenet of their development is to consult with groups of people, including older people, who are not usually consulted in matters of planning. Originally applied to existing sites, developers are now beginning to apply the principles to new-build sites. In particular, some of the benefits are to achieve greater social activity, better understanding between drivers and pedestrians and a more attractive and safer environment.

Another broader perspective for travel safety for older people derives from work on effective women's safety and crime prevention strategies. Known as 'the whole journey' and arising from pioneering work undertaken by such initiatives as Safer Travel Groups on Transport for London, the Suzy Lamplugh Trust (see *Making the connections*, Social Exclusion Unit, 2003, for a consideration of the broad issues), it refers to the need to recognise that travelling on any particular journey is comprised of a number of stages, all of which need to be undertaken safely: from stepping out of the front door, to walking to the bus stop or station, to waiting at the bus stop or station, to travelling on the mode of transport, alighting at the other end and then reaching one's final destination. Taken in these stages it can be seen that there are many points in the journey where the environment may change and which may be subject to a range of different regulatory bodies and controls. The underlying thrust behind this approach is to encourage cooperative multi-agency planning between the various bodies who have responsibility for the various stages of travel – local authorities, police, transport operators, highways authorities, and so on – with a view to integrating the travel experience.

The Economic and Social Research Council (ESRC) has funded the Growing Older Programme, based at Sheffield University (http://www.shef.ac.uk/uni/projects/gop/) but running projects around the UK, aimed at developing our knowledge of extending quality of life for older people. One of the projects, on transport and ageing, has reported interim findings (Gilhooly et al, 2003). Key among these were: older people were found to be reluctant to ask for lifts from friends or relatives, even for hospital or other health-related appointments; the relationship between quality of life and car access, suggesting that access to a car was an independent predictor of quality of life; similarly, greater access to public transport was associated with improved quality of life, even though satisfaction with public transport was low. A number of the findings resonate very closely with the 'whole journey' material. Respondents identified 28 potential barriers to using public transport: highest were concerns about personal security at evening or night time (65.1%) and difficulties in carrying heavy loads (59%); lowest were risk of being in a crash (7.6%) and concerns about personal security during the day time (9.3%). The study confirmed concerns about the whole journey, including walking to and from bus stops and stations. There was also anecdotal evidence that aspects of ageism displayed by transport operators were related to perceptions of profit reduction associated with the compulsory provision of concessionary fares for older people. Train operators, however, were seen as being more concerned about addressing the needs of older people than bus or underground service providers.

Conclusion

As well as the specific learning points from the House for Life project, its very title can also act as a metaphor for those conditions that are both desirable and necessary to enable people to remain in their own homes and to continue to be in control of their lives as they grow older. This chapter has raised issues of representation, design, collaboration, awareness, need and hope. It is based as much on what *could* be done as what is currently *being* done, and there are substantive issues to do with availability and resources that are beyond the scope of this present text. Nevertheless, there is much which can be built upon, especially in the modelling of good practice in partnership working and in applying the lessons from research to practice: these are matters for which every reader can take some responsibility.

Exercises

Using the material in this chapter as a starting point:

- Develop a checklist for an 'older person-friendly house', then take a tour of inspection of *your* home and see how it measures up to the criteria. Make a note of its assets/positives and problems/negatives.
- Negotiate agreement with an older person to be interviewed by you about their experiences of public transport. Compile a list of questions to ask, including inviting them to talk you through a particular journey they might take or wish to take: ask them to identify any barriers to, and any positive aspects of, making the journey.

References

Age Concern England (2001) The submission of Age Concern England to the House of Commons Environment, Transport and Regional Affairs Committee's inquiry into 'Walking in towns and cities', August.

Appleton, N.J.W. (2002a) *Planning for the majority: The needs and aspirations of older people in general housing*, York: Joseph Rowntree Foundation/York Publishing Services.

Appleton, N.J.W. (2002b) *Planning for older people in New Osbaldwick*, York: Joseph Rowntree Foundation/York Publishing Services.

Biddulph, M. (2001) *Home zones: A planning and design handbook*, Bristol: The Policy Press.

British Gas/Help the Aged (2002) *Winter matters*, London: British Gas/Help the Aged.

Gilhooly, M., Hamilton, K., O'Neill, M., Gow, J., Webster, G. and Pike, F. (2003) *Transport and ageing: Extending the quality of life via public and private transport*, Research Findings 16, March, Sheffield: University of Sheffield.

Haslam, R.A., Sloane, J., Hill, L.D., Brooke-Wavell, K. and Howarth, P. (2001) 'What do older people know about safety on stairs?', *Ageing and Society*, vol 21, no 6, pp 759-76.

House for Life report, 1999-2000 (2001), compiled by B. Douglas, June, Newcastle: A Better Life in Later Life/Newcastle Healthy City Project.

Nelson, H. (2001) 'Residential mobility in later life: a study of the moving decisions of older people in Newcastle upon Tyne', unpublished PhD thesis, Newcastle upon Tyne: Northumbria University.

Percival, J. (2002) 'Domestic spaces: uses and meanings in the daily lives of older people', *Ageing and Society*, vol 22, no 6, pp 729-49.

Social Exclusion Unit (2003) *Making the connections: Final report on transport and social exclusion* (www.socialexclusionunit.gov.uk/publications/reports/html/transportfinal/office_d_pm.html) February, London: Social Exclusion Unit, ODPM.

Salvation Army Older Homeless Research in association with Help the Aged (undated but action research project carried out in 2001) *Old before our time*, Bristol: The Salvation Army Social Services Centre.

Thomas Pocklington Trust (2003) *The housing and support needs of older people with visual impairment – experiences and challenges*, occasional paper, London: Thomas Pocklington Trust.

FIVE

Memory: self, relationship and society

Contents

Introduction	79
Cognition, dementia and functional ability	80
Cognitive disability	81
The importance of cognition and relationships	82
Care beyond cognition	87
The evolution of memory loss	88

Key points

- People with memory problems work actively to manage their memory loss and to remain engaged in society.
- Complex societies such as developed countries place a high value on cognitive ability, and so magnify the disability associated with memory loss.
- Environments and interpersonal relationships can be adapted to reduce any disability and to promote the self-determination of someone with memory loss.
- A point of debate concerns how important memory is to the essence of being oneself. Increasingly relationships are being viewed as central to the experience of memory loss.
- The arts offer a non-cognitively-based approach to working with people with memory loss.
- We need to find a new paradigm of dementia care that moves beyond the technical-rationality of cognition.

Introduction

In an editorial of an international journal, two people with dementia wrote of their aspiration that:

> ... through transformative action ... we can learn that our current social constructions in regards to dementia are not immutable reality but only moments in a dialectic. (Friedell and Bryden, 2002, p 131)

They use the language of their professions as academics! What they advocate is self-advocacy; what they urge is that media such as an academic journal be vehicles of challenge to orthodox views of memory loss, cognition and mental health. They are not passive in their adjustments to having dementia but then nobody is who has memory loss. We forget this at our peril – the result would be a grave disservice to the countless individuals who anticipate or experience memory loss, who are working very hard to accommodate it and continue with their everyday lives, and who we may approach with a paucity of understanding.

'Memory problems' is either a neat semantic device to help us avoid using words like 'dementia' or is a term loaded with every socially exclusionary perspective that can be thought of. Unfortunately, it is also associated in the same breath with people who are older – something to anticipate with dread as a consequence of the passage of time. Not true, of course. McKeith and Fairbairn (2001) describe the prevalence of dementia at the age of 75 years as approximately 10%, so nine out of every ten 75-year-olds do not have a dementia, although they do describe this doubling with every five years of increasing age. This chapter will explore these tensions and their underpinning social attitudes and cognitive changes. Throughout is woven the words of people who find themselves cognitively challenged in our societies.

Cognition, dementia and functional ability

'Developed' countries in the western world place a high value on cognitive skills. Our societies are layered and fragmented in a way that results in unprecedented dependency on others. As a result, individual members of our society must find their place and fulfil it in a timely and efficient way. It is rare for people to be self-sufficient and they must know how to manage the machinery of social and cultural life if their needs for nutrition, recreation, shelter, transport, and so on are to be met. For example, meeting nutritional needs requires the ability to go to a shop, select items and make a purchase, then to operate machinery to cook the food and the psychomotor skills to transport prepared food to the mouth, chew and swallow it. The dependence on cognitive skills to undertake such a complex social and technical activity for something as fundamental as meeting nutritional needs exemplifies how complex developed societies are and how they then magnify deficits in cognitive skill. For example, you would not be able to undertake such an activity if you were unable to drive/catch a bus/ walk in the correct direction to bring you to the shop, or if you found that the coins in your hand held no meaning for you, or if you were unable to associate the turning of a knob on the cooker with the generation of heat to cook your food. Imagine too your distress when on arriving home you found it occupied by people whom you did not recognise but who appeared over familiar with you!

In contrast, Oakley (2003 and personal correspondence), in an anthropological study of healthcare in Namaqualand in Africa, found that there was no stigma associated with memory loss and that individuals and the community always found a way of coping. Perhaps the capacity to accommodate cognitive change is greater in developing countries. In more 'developed' countries such as the UK, we have a society in which memory loss and cognitive difficulty results very quickly in a loss of functioning. And it is this interplay between the cognitive changes of the individual and their ability to function in society that creates distress for the individual. They are easily outpaced and outplaced in the functional machinery of society.

The energy devoted by people with memory problems to keeping up and keeping on top of society's machinery leaves them frustrated and exhausted. The poem below featured in a newsletter of a local branch of the Alzheimer's Society. In referring to care provision by the society, it illustrates so much of the misplacement felt by people with dementia from the wider places in society.

If this is not a place (Anon, 2002)
If this is not a place, where tears are understood,
    Then where shall I go to cry?
And if this is not a place, where my spirit can take wings,
    Then where shall I go to fly?
I don't need another place, for trying to impress you, with just how good
    and virtuous I am,
No, no, no, I don't need another place, for always being on top of things.
Everybody knows that it's a sham,
    It's a sham.
I don't need another place for always wearing smiles, even when it's not
    the way I feel.
I don't need another place to mouth the same old platitudes;
    Everybody knows that it's not real.
So if this is not a place, where my questions can be asked,
    Then where shall I go to seek?
And if this is not a place, where my heart cry can be heard, where, tell me
    where, shall I go to speak?
So if this is not a place, where tears are understood,
    Where shall I go,
    Where shall I go to fly?

Cognitive disability

Once we recognise, however, that it is the complexity of society that contributes to reducing the functional ability of people with memory problems, we open up a range of ways of amending the environment and the context in which people function to assist people. Some of these are technology-orientated, others emphasise interior design.

Assistive technologies such as found in smart houses are increasingly available (Pollock et al, 2000; Chapman, 2001). (Chapter Four contains a description of the way this was used in a house designed by older people.) Hagen et al (2002) describe the ENABLE project that is being run through eight European centres to develop and evaluate a range of assistive technologies. These include devices that are operated by the person with memory loss and those that are installed by others and used by the individual. Examples include: a locator for lost objects, the object bleeping when its picture is pressed; automatic lights that turn on when the person gets out of bed, so reducing the chance of falling; and a bath water level monitor and controller that turns off the taps if the water reaches a certain level. Other assistive technologies include monitoring and surveillance systems and devices, such as electronic tagging, safety alarms activated by the person, and incident–triggered alarms such as fire alarms.

Some environments are adapted to reduce disability more simply, provided through thoughtful design and the use of environmental cuing. Calkins (2002) describes how a bathroom in a residential care setting may be designed to create a welcoming and reassuring environment that considers the visual, auditory, tactile and olfactory environments. The basic message is to keep it simple and keep it like home – so do not use the bathroom to store spare equipment and trolleys that others might need to enter the room to retrieve during someone's bath; include warm, soft surfaces and generous towelling; use scented soaps and soft lighting. Calkins and Brush (2002) similarly consider designs for dining rooms. Innes (1999) describes the impact that a paint design has had, which includes murals on the bathroom walls of seaside scenes to promote reminiscence.

Marshall (2000) describes the need for 'homely' environments for people with memory loss to live in, the purpose of which is to: compensate for 'disability' (although perhaps this should read as impairment); maximise independence; enhance self–esteem and confidence; demonstrate care for staff; be orientating and understandable; reinforce personal identity; welcome relatives and the local community; and allow control of stimuli. Further suggestions for environmental design when working with people with memory problems are explored by Phair and Good (1995) and furniture itself is also under scrutiny, with Dick (1999) describing, among other items, the Delta Chair, which includes knobs on the armrests to encourage hand muscle movement and balancing aids for rising from the chair.

The importance of cognition and relationships

But the poem above, *If this is not a place*, also indicates another area that we need to engage with. The cognitive dependency of more developed societies results in our placing a high value on cognitive ability, and at times this is at the expense of other abilities. In the poem, the writer also talks about their spirit. From the words, we understand this spirit to be as capable of 'flying' as ever. Perhaps the spirit of the individual survives cognitive decline. Our challenge then is indeed to find places for it to fly – for people with memory loss to feel fulfilled. Perhaps our challenge is to come out of our cognitively bound way of thinking and realise that the enduring abilities of someone with memory loss are more likely to be found in the creative and spiritual domains of life. Our challenge is to find ways in which people can function in our society through the resource of their creativity and spirituality rather than through their (declining) resource of cognitive ability. Coleman and Mills (2001) take up this baton, stating that "contemporary societies need to develop new cultures of dementia care drawing on insights from the world's faiths and traditions" (p 62).

A word of caution though! Professor Morris Friedell writes that after diagnosis with Alzheimer's disease "he found himself transmogrified into a woman. He was supposed to be weak at sustained attention ('flighty'), poor at logic and long-range planning, but great at living in the moment, at smelling the flowers and at appreciating the warmth of touch" (Friedell and Bryden, 2002, p 131). Similarly, Christine Bryden, a senior public servant who has spent her life analysing, organising, planning and exercising strong executive skills, found upon diagnosis that she was "supposedly stripped of these abilities" (Friedell and Bryden, 2002, p 132). Her response was to write a book (Boden, 1998). For those without memory loss to take away cognitive ability from others is cruel and demeaning of us all.

Challenges such as these permeate the ways in which we can seek to work with people with memory loss, reducing a dependence on cognitive ability (without taking it away) and maximising access to other ways of presenting information and preserving a sense of self. For example, a booklet produced by the Scottish Down's Syndrome Association titled *What is Dementia?* (Kerr and Innes, 2000) depends a great deal on drawings to communicate through a printed document. Obviously, the Association is very experienced in working with people with complex cognitive problems, and a group of people with a learning disability, Surging Ahead, also worked on the booklet's production. A paper by Wilkinson et al (2003) provides a very useful insight into the perceptions of this often marginalised group of people with dementia. The following extract (overleaf) from *What is DEMENTIA?* illustrates how the environment might be managed to allow someone with dementia to feel (dis)abled by their environment.

Critical to appreciating the disability that is associated with memory loss is an exploration of the contribution that cognition makes to our sense of 'self' and what we mean by 'being normal'. Peter Ashley (2002), a trustee of the Alzheimer's Society UK and a person with dementia, described his personal experience as a three-year period of assessment that culminated in the diagnosis of a dementia and how there was a "subsequent realisation that there was still an opportunity for the patient to continue to engage in some of life's 'normal' pursuits" (p 67). This is a theme reflected in an Australian group that call themselves 'The M and Ms': not wanting to meet as a conventional support group and not wanting "to be left out of life's experiences", this group of people with dementia and their care partners have created occasions together that are "supportive, shared and

Extract from *What is DEMENTIA?*

Reproduced with kind permission by the Scottish Down's Syndrome Association

with the sole intent of making memories" – the Making Memories Group (Webb, 2002).

All of these issues connect with what we understand our 'selves' to be. The more cognition and memory are seen to be essential parts of ourselves, the more our self is compromised by memory problems. One perspective is that of Morris Friedell, a retired professor of the University of California who has dementia and for whom life without the capacity to think and to remember is a life with a lesser quality: "living in the here and now is not sufficient; one must be capable of cherishing memories and envisioning the future" (Friedell, 2002, p 360). He goes on: "I need to search my past for my deepest memories and motivations. I need the strongest roots I can find" (Friedell, 2002, p 361). Here we can see a search in the inner self, from within, for the most defining characteristics and features of the individual and their origins – what he finds is that, for him, his strong roots originate in his people's experiences in the Holocaust and his own children's suffering.

Others argue that life of some quality goes on despite memory loss and dementia – Jane Crisp in Australia describes how many aspects of her mother's self, not least her love of words, persisted throughout the course of dementia (Crisp, 1999). The 'M and Ms' group described earlier is seeking out ways of ensuring that there is an enjoyable future.

The distinction that seems to be being made here is between, on one hand, the inherent dependence of a sense of self on the individual's cognitive ability to locate themselves in their life course (as described above by Friedell, 2002) and, on the other hand, the ability of others to remain in a relationship with the individual and through the relationship maintain a sense of self. The latter, more interactional, perspective is starting to be flagged up by others. For example, Nolan et al (2002) argue that a shift from person-centred care to relationship-centred care is necessary for there to be a new generation of care interventions and services developed that are inclusive of people with dementia.

The foundations for this relationship-orientated perspective have been around for a decade or more, with the seminal work of Sabat and Harre (1992) indicating the role of others in maintaining the self in dementia through their interactions. The approach similarly underpinned the model of dementia care proposed by Tom Kitwood (1992) throughout the 1990s and that has had a very significant influence on dementia care provision across the globe, and relationship-centred care is also echoed in the work of others (for example, Coleman and Mills, 2001). Indeed, Coleman and Mills (2001), exploring spirituality in dementia care, argue that being relationship-centred is central to the Christian concept of the person. We are left to ponder on whether it is central to other faiths in the world too.

It is pertinent to explore what this distinction between 'self as a cognitive entity' and 'self as a product of interrelationships' actually means in day-to-day practice when working with people with dementia. From the interactionist standpoint (that people exist in their relationship with others and their surroundings), Kitwood and Bredin (1992) argue that as cognitive ability changes, interrelationships become increasingly essential if a sense of self is to be maintained (Clarke, 1999a) – a view also advanced by Orona (1990) and Sabat and Harre (1992). This perspective urges us to nurture those relationships, offering family-centred care interventions, for example, and maintaining continuity of people and environment around the individual, something that very often does not happen since as we move people through the care system we expose them to changing staff and facilities.

There are plenty of critics of the medicalised route through care provision and that pervades research. Hall (1996) argues that the processes of care within a psychiatric medical model – for example, the diagnostic process – result in "a contrived and sanctioned dehumanisation of the person" (p 18). Similarly, Richards (1994) argues that professional assessment may be disempowering for the client. The diagnostic label is central to subsequent social constructions of the illness experience (Brown, 1995) and influences expectations, which in turn creates a self-fulfilling prophecy for the individual and their family (Hall, 1996). Diagnosis with any enduring mental health illness can have a devastating impact on the individual's identity as they become exposed to the disempowering and dehumanising attitudes of society (Handyside and Heyman, 1995; Hall, 1996). For example, Harding and Palfrey (1997) argue that the label of dementia "appears to be required of all save the sufferers themselves" (p 125).

Exposure of memory loss through diagnosis may serve merely to expose that which people with dementia are working to keep hidden and private (Robinson et al, 1997). Keady and Nolan (1994), for example, found 'covering up' to be a key stage in the early experience of dementia.

On the other hand, the social consequences of diagnosis of memory loss may be welcome. Broom and Woodward (1996) identify diagnosis as the key to obtaining medical insurance for services in the US. Further, symptoms are validated and can be negotiated as 'the illness not the person' within family relationships, thus serving to protect the position of the person with dementia within their family context (Clarke and Heyman, 1998). Patterson and Whitehouse (1990) argue that in this way assessment ceases to be disabling but, rather, increases awareness within a family of their own strengths and abilities.

The 'self as a product of interrelationships' perspective is also echoed by McKee (1999) in relation to research with people with dementia. With reference to a study of the quality of care for people with dementia, he describes very movingly how:

> The concept of quality of life ... allows for the possibility of someone with dementia being a 'person'. Such a person lives in a community which, even if limited by four walls and a locked door, still contains social networks and interpersonal relations. The quality of care, however, reduces the person with dementia to no more than a patient or resident within a ward or a home. (McKee, 1999, p 153)

McKee goes on to describe how, as a psychologist undertaking research, his role in another study was to assess people with dementia using their morbidity and their destiny as outcome measures for a study of family caring.

> When assessing the cognitive status of the person with dementia, I felt as if I was a heartless magician, demonstrating to the people the growing instability of their memory, providing them with an explicit display of the shrinking limits of their minds. I found the work distasteful in the extreme.... These social relations [described by Kitwood (1990) as a malignant social psychology] allowed me to enter a person's world, ask a series of demeaning questions, and reduce that person to a series of depersonalised scores. (McKee, 1999, p 155)

The 'self as cognitive entity' perspective results in dementia being seen as so pervasive that the person is substantially and irreversibly changed. Such a position permits people to be treated as 'socially dead' before their physical death (Sweeting and Gilhooly, 1997). It allows a distancing between those with and those without dementia and reinforces the definition of themselves as normal and sane (Hall, 1996). For example, Reed (1999) describes a study of transition to nursing home for older people and notes the readiness of some residents to differentiate between themselves and others whose 'minds are going' or who are 'daft' in order to emphasise their own mental health. This led to behaviours from residents without memory loss that ranged from resentment and annoyance to paternalism. It was not unnoticed by residents with memory loss either, one commenting in interview: "They want their own friends. They don't want someone like me. –

How do you mean? – Well, they don't want someone mixed up" (Reed, 1999, p 181).

This is the 'them' and 'us' situation criticised by Kitwood (1993) and Hill (1999), yet Reed (1999) emphasises that non-confused residents themselves may feel their sense of self threatened by care management patterns that fail to differentiate those with memory loss from those without. These destructive patterns of social interactions undermine any sense of 'self', Sabat and Harre (1992) noting the lack of cooperation of other people in maintaining and developing the public self (rather than the impact of memory loss itself). Kelly and Field (1996) argue that while a core sense of self and identity persists, the consequences of chronic illness have to be "incorporated permanently into conceptions of self and are likely to become a basis for the imputation of identity by others" (p 255).

Care beyond cognition

In emphasising the importance of cognitive functioning there is a failure to acknowledge any other form of reality. Shomaker (1989), Frank (1995) and Crisp (1999), however, illustrate the reality and rationality of someone with dementia, which exists without constraints of, for example, notions of the present time (temporality). Increasingly, a focus of intervention is being explored which draws on music and drama and other non-cognitive ways of expression and communication. For example, John Killick has for some years used the visual and verbal arts as a medium to communicate the ideas of people with dementia and to engage with them (for example, Killick and Allan, 1999), and has more recently worked with a drama group called Elderflowers (Killick, 2003). Others use singing (Brown et al, 2001; Gibson, 2002) and dance to communicate through touch and rhythm (Jerrome, 1999), as a therapy intervention (Donald and Hall, 1999) and as reminiscence opportunities (Coaten, 2001). Brooker (2001) describes the enhancement to well-being derived by a group of people with dementia who went on an activity holiday and spent their days canoeing, abseiling, swimming and ballooning.

The more we move away from the cognitive domain of understanding memory loss, the more we move away from attempting to 'correct' memory loss and explore therapeutic ways in working alongside the memory loss. Equally, the level of our intervention shifts too from being focused on the individual to including a focus on the physical environment, the social surrounds, the family and community. Memory loss is a very complex neurological and social process that has a massive implication for the functional ability of individuals within more developed countries. Our interventions, and ways of reaching to be with people with dementia, are necessarily complex as well.

It is, of course, very important not to romanticise memory loss and there are many who see the fright and anxiety of those with dementia as testimony to the very destructive effects that the disease can have. The following extract is drawn from a paper written by Morris Friedell (2002) as he searches to understand and explain the impact of his dementia on his quality of life.

> For me the horror of AD [Alzheimer's disease] is summed up in a statement by Dempsey and Baago (1998, p 84): "While the physical being of an individual with a dementing illness remains intact, the very essence of a person – the psycho-social self – slowly disintegrates". It can be questioned how true this is. Nevertheless, their statement well expresses the horror, with its uncanniness of the slow disintegration of a self whose essence, presumably, is to integrate. Just how could one even conceive of a self slowly disintegrating? (Friedell, 2002, p 361)

The evolution of memory loss

The industry of healthcare intervention has been perhaps slow to turn its attention to older people with memory problems, but the 1990s, stimulated by pharmaceutical developments, have seen a massive growth in assessment and diagnosis facilities. Memory loss is not necessarily associated with a form of dementia and the more able we are to offer treatments, the more important it becomes to differentiate one cause of memory loss from another. In the UK, memory clinics have developed as centres for diagnosis and assessment. Some of the causes of memory problems, which can be misdiagnosed as dementia, are acute and can be resolved within days – for example, infections. Other causes masquerade as dementia but are different major mental illnesses such as depression. There is of course a complex relationship between acute confusional states (delirium), depression and dementia that results in them sometimes coexisting and always presenting a challenge to assessors who are seeking to isolate a diagnosis. In addition to the '3Ds' of delirium, dementia and depression, Eastley and Wilcock (2000) identify the following causes of more chronic confusional states (p 42):

- neurodegenerative (for example, Alzheimer's disease);
- vascular (for example, infarction);
- endocrine disorders (for example, thyroid disease);
- vitamin deficiencies (for example, B12);
- systemic diseases (for example, anaemia);
- neurological disorders or trauma (for example, normal pressure hydrocephalus);
- infection (for example, HIV – human immunodeficiency virus).

There are two portraits that we can draw of the early stages of memory loss. One is the technical-rational picture of a journey to a GP, referral to a specialist assessment centre, exposure to a battery of tests and then diagnosis. The other is a more publicly veiled process. In a phenomenological study with 20 men diagnosed with early-stage dementia, Pearce et al (2002) describe an ongoing, circular process in which people attempted to "manage their sense of self by balancing their wish to maintain a prior sense of self against their need to reappraise and construct a new sense of self" (p 173).

It is important to bear in mind too the maxim described by Brodaty and Green (2000) that "when a person is diagnosed with dementia, there is (almost) always a second patient. Dementia is not just one person's illness. The stone cast sends ripples through families, friends and society" (p 193). Care interventions then cannot be focused solely on the person with memory loss but must include also the social milieu in which that person lives. Crucially, however, we must cease displacing the person with memory loss from the centre of intervention in order to care for their family carer. The carer-focused research agenda of the 1980s has been criticised as subjugating the person with Alzheimer's disease to "... an entity to be studied rather than someone who can directly contribute to an understanding of the illness and its course" (Cotterell and Schulz, 1993, p 205). The therapeutic pessimism of dementia care in particular is no longer tenable (Clarke, 1999b).

We must also move to a position in which we acknowledge and support the mechanisms that people with memory loss deploy themselves to support their functional ability. People are active managers of care interventions, balancing the intrusion of memory loss, health and social care interventions with their own lifestyle. Much work in this area has focused on chronic illness – for example, Coates and Boore (1995) in relation to diabetes care – and Keady and Gilleard (1999) illuminate this area of active management in relation to the early experiences of dementia. People do not necessarily simply react to their memory loss, passively complying with the demands of care interventions.

In relation to dementia specifically, Berrios (2000) describes dementia as a concept that has evolved over the centuries but which has been associated invariably with psychosocial incompetence and with being a terminal state – it was not until 1900 that dementia was established as an intellectual (cognitive) impairment. However, Berrios (2000) concludes by saying that "during the last few years, the cognitive paradigm has become an obstacle, and a gradual re-expansion of the symptomatology of dementia is fortunately taking place" (p 10). We are yet to witness this new formulation of dementia and memory loss.

Exercise

We all forget things some of the time. Think about:

- the last time you forgot your keys;
- the last time you forgot a telephone number you use frequently;
- the last time you forgot the name of someone you know quite well;
- the last time you forgot what you were looking for;
- the last time you forgot what you were going to do.

How important were these memory lapses? Were you embarrassed or did it cause you a lot of difficulty? Did you feel that it was normal absent-mindedness, or did it challenge your sense of yourself as a competent person? Have you developed a strategy for making sure that it never happens again?

Thinking about your experiences, what do you understand about the importance of memory in everyday life and in maintaining a sense of self? How would this help you in working with older people with memory problems?

References

Anonymous (2002) 'If this is not a place', *Alzheimer's Morpeth and District Branch Newsletter*, Autumn.

Ashley, P.J.S. (2002) 'A personal experience of dementia', *Conference abstract book*, Barcelona: 18th International Conference of Alzheimer's Disease International, p 67.

Berrios, G. (2000) 'Dementia: historical overview', in J. O'Brien, D. Ames and A. Burns (eds) *Dementia* (2nd edn), London: Arnold.

Boden, C. (1998) *Who will I be when I die?*, Melbourne: HarperCollins.

Brodaty, H. and Green, A. (2000) 'Family carers for people with dementia', in J. O'Brien, D. Ames and A. Burns (eds) *Dementia* (2nd edn), London: Arnold.

Brooker, D. (2001) 'Enriching lives: evaluation of the ExtraCare activity challenge', *Journal of Dementia Care*, vol 9, no 3, pp 33-7.

Broom, D.H. and Woodward, R.V. (1996) 'Medicalisation reconsidered: towards a collaborative approach to care', *Sociology of Health and Illness*, vol 18, pp 357-78.

Brown, P. (1995) 'Naming and framing: the social construction of diagnosis and illness', *Journal of Health and Social Behaviour* (extra issue), pp 34-52.

Brown, S., Gotell, E. and Ekman, S.-L. (2001) 'Singing as a therapeutic intervention in dementia care', *Journal of Dementia Care*, vol 9, no 4, pp 33-7.

Calkins, M. (2002) 'Design a better bathroom: relaxing and comfortable', *Journal of Dementia Care*, vol 10, no 3, pp 26-7.

Calkins, M. and Brush, J. (2002) 'Designing for dining: the secret of happier mealtimes', *Journal of Dementia Care*, vol 10, no 2, pp 24-6.

Chapman, A. (2001) 'There's no place like a smart home', *Journal of Dementia Care*, vol 9, no 1, pp 28-31.

Clarke, C.L. (1999a) 'Dementia care partnerships: knowledge, ownership and exchange', in T. Adams and C.L. Clarke (eds) *Dementia care: Developing partnerships in practice*, London: Baillière Tindall.

Clarke, C.L. (1999b) 'Partnership in dementia care: taking it forward', in T. Adams and C.L. Clarke (eds) *Dementia care: Developing partnerships in practice*, London: Baillière Tindall.

Clarke, C.L. and Heyman, B. (1998) 'Risk management for people with dementia', in B. Heyman (ed) *Risk, health and healthcare: A qualitative approach*, London: Chapman and Hall.

Coaten, R. (2001) 'Exploring reminiscence through dance and movement', *Journal of Dementia Care*, vol 9, no 5, pp 19-22.

Coates, V.E. and Boore, J.R.P. (1995) 'Self-management of chronic illness: implications for nursing', *International Journal of Nursing Studies*, vol 32, pp 628-40.

Coleman, P.G. and Mills, M.A. (2001) 'Philosophical and spiritual perspectives', in C. Cantley (ed) *A handbook of dementia care*, Buckingham: Open University Press.

Cotterell, V. and Schulz, R. (1993) 'The perspective of the patient with Alzheimer's disease: a neglected dimension of dementia research', *Gerontologist*, vol 33, pp 205-11.

Crisp, J. (1999) 'Towards a partnership in maintaining personhood', in T. Adams and C.L. Clarke (eds) *Dementia care: Developing partnerships in practice*, London: Baillière Tindall.

Dempsey, M. and Baago, S. (1998) 'Latent grief: the unique and hidden grief of carers of loved ones with dementia', *American Journal of Alzheimer's Disease*, vol 13, no 2, pp 84-91, March/April.

Dick, R. (1999) 'Just another disability: designs on dementia', *Journal of Dementia Care*, vol 7, no 6, pp 21-3.

Donald, J. and Hall, S. (1999) 'Dance: the Getting There group', *Journal of Dementia Care*, vol 7, no 3, pp 24-7.

Eastley, R. and Wilcock, G. (2000) 'Assessment and differential diagnosis of dementia', in J. O'Brien, D. Ames and A. Burns (eds) *Dementia* (2nd edn), London: Arnold.

Frank, B.A. (1995) 'People with dementia can communicate – if we are able to hear', in T. Kitwood and S. Benson (eds) *The new culture of dementia care*, London: Hawker.

Friedell, M. (2002) 'Awareness: a personal memoir on the declining quality of life in Alzheimer's', *Dementia*, vol 1, no 3, pp 359-66.

Friedell, M. and Bryden, C. (2002) 'Editorial', *Dementia*, vol 1, no 2, pp 131-3.

Gibson, M.V. (2002) 'Reawakening the language of the body', *Journal of Dementia Care*, vol 10, no 5, pp 20-2.

Hagen, I., Holthe, T., Duff, P., Cahill, S., Gilliard, J., Orpwood, R., Topo, P. and Bjorneby, S. (2002) 'A systematic assessment of assistive technology', *Journal of Dementia Care*, vol 10, no 1, pp 26-8.

Hall, B.A. (1996) 'The psychiatric model: a critical analysis of its undermining effects on nursing in chronic mental health', *Advances in Nursing* Science, vol 18, pp 16-26.

Handyside, E. and Heyman, B. (1995) 'Mental illness in the community: the role of voluntary and state agencies', in B. Heyman (ed) *Researching user perspectives on community healthcare*, London: Chapman and Hall.

Harding, N. and Palfrey, C. (1997) *The social construction of dementia – confused professionals?*, London: Jessica Kingsley.

Hill, T.M. (1999) 'Western medicine and dementia: a deconstruction', in T. Adams and C.L. Clarke (eds) *Dementia care: Developing partnerships in practice*, London: Baillière Tindall.

Innes, A. (1999) 'A sea-change at Kirklands', *Journal of Dementia Care*, vol 7, no 6, pp 23-4.

Jerrome, D. (1999) 'Circles of the mind', *Journal of Dementia Care*, vol 7, no 3, pp 20-4.

Keady, J. and Gilleard, J. (1999) 'The early experience of Alzheimer's disease: implications for partnership and practice', in T. Adams and C.L. Clarke (eds) *Dementia care: Developing partnerships in practice*, London: Baillière Tindall.

Keady, J. and Nolan, M. (1994) 'Younger onset dementia: developing a longitudinal model as the basis for a research agenda and as a guide to interventions with sufferers and carers', *Journal of Advanced Nursing*, vol 19, pp 659-69.

Kelly, M.P. and Field, D. (1996) 'Medical sociology, chronic illness and the body', *Sociology of Health and Illness*, vol 18, pp 241-57.

Kerr, D. and Innes, M. (2000) *What is dementia?*, Edinburgh: Down's Syndrome Scotland.

Killick, J. (2003) '"Funny and sad and friendly": a drama project in Scotland', *Journal of Dementia Care*, vol 11, no 1, pp 24-6.

Killick, J. and Allan, K. (1999) 'The arts in dementia care: touching the human spirit', *Journal of Dementia Care*, vol 7, no 5, pp 33-7.

Kitwood, T. (1990) 'The dialectics of dementia: with particular reference to Alzheimer's disease', *Ageing and Society*, vol 10, pp 177-96.

Kitwood, T. (1993) 'Towards a theory of dementia care: the interpersonal process', *Ageing and Society*, vol 13, pp 51-67.

Kitwood, T. and Bredin, K. (1992) 'Towards a theory of dementia care: personhood and wellbeing', *Ageing and Society*, vol 12, pp 269-87.

McKee, K.J. (1999) 'This is your life: research paradigms in dementia care', in T. Adams and C.L. Clarke (eds) *Dementia care: Developing partnerships in practice*, London: Baillière Tindall.

McKeith, I. and Fairbairn, A. (2001) 'Biomedical and clinical perspectives', in C. Cantley (ed) *A handbook of dementia care*, Buckingham: Open University Press.

Marshall, M. (2000) 'Homely: the guiding principle of design for dementia', in J. O'Brien, D. Ames and A. Burns (eds) *Dementia* (2nd edn), London: Arnold.

Nolan, M., Ryan, T., Enderby, P. and Reid, D. (2002) 'Towards a more inclusive vision of dementia care practice and research', *Dementia*, vol 1, no 2, pp 193-211.

Oakley, R. (2003) *Health and geriatric care in Namaqualand: Focus on health across the life course of migrant workers*, Cape Town: GeriatrixAfrica '03, March.

Orona, C.J. (1990) 'Temporality and identity loss due to Alzheimer's disease', *Social Science in Medicine*, vol 30, pp 1247-56.

Patterson, M. and Whitehouse, P. (1990) 'The diagnostic assessment of patients with dementia', in N. Mace (ed) *Dementia care: Patient, family and community*, Baltimore, MD: Johns Hopkins University Press.

Pearce, A., Clare, L. and Pistrang, N. (2002) 'Managing sense of self: coping in the early stages of Alzheimer's disease', *Dementia*, vol 1, no 2, pp 173-92.

Phair, L. and Good, V. (1995) *Dementia: A positive approach*, London: Scutari Press.

Pollock, R., Bonner, S. and Gibbons, K. (2000) 'This is the house that JAD built', *Journal of Dementia Care*, vol 8, no 4, pp 20-2.

Reed, J. (1999) 'Keeping a distance: the reactions of older people in care homes to confused fellow residents', in T. Adams and C.L. Clarke (eds) *Dementia care: Developing partnerships in practice*, London: Baillière Tindall, pp 165-86.

Richards, S. (1994) 'Making sense of needs assessment', *Research Policy and Planning*, vol 12, pp 5-9.

Robinson, P., Ekman, S.-L., Meleis, A.I., Winbald, B. and Wahlund, L.-O. (1997) 'Suffering in silence: the experience of early memory loss', *Healthcare in Later Life*, vol 2, pp 107-20.

Sabat, S.R. and Harre, R. (1992) 'The construction and deconstruction of self in Alzheimer's disease', *Ageing and Society*, vol 12, pp 443-61.

Shomaker, D.J. (1989) 'Age disorientation, liminality and reality: the case of the Alzheimer's patient', *Medical Anthropology*, vol 12, pp 91-101.

Sweeting, H. and Gilhooly, M. (1997) 'Dementia and the phenomenon of social death', *Sociology of Health and Illness*, vol 19, pp 93-117.

Webb, D. (2002) 'Sweet memories of the M and Ms', *Conference abstract book*, Barcelona: 18th International Conference of Alzheimer's Disease International, p 79.

Wilkinson, H., Kerr, D. and Rae, C. (2003) 'People with a learning disability: their concerns about dementia', *Journal of Dementia Care*, vol 11, no 1, pp 27-9.

SIX

Older people, sexuality and intimacy

Contents	
Introduction	95
Sexuality and the quality of life across ages	97
Images of older people and sexuality	97
Distaste	99
Changes in attitudes	100
Sexual activity	101
Physical changes over time	101
Psychological factors	102
Social contexts	103
Sexuality and intimacy: the views of older people	103
Professional support	106

Key points

- Older people are assumed to have lost interest in sex, but this is an assumption that is not supported by evidence.
- Some physical changes occur when ageing that may change sexual activity, but these are not inevitable.
- Sexual activity and intimacy can be important contributors to quality of life for older people.

Introduction

"It's about being close, it makes you feel alive."

The comment above, made by an older woman in the course of a conversation about older people and sexuality, sums up several key points about possible meanings of sexuality for older people. First, there is a link between sexuality and intimacy – sexual activity is one way of communicating and getting to know someone else. Second, a connection is made between sexuality and feelings of pleasure, excitement, vigour and self-affirmation.

Sexuality, therefore, is not the only topic covered in this chapter. It broadens out to discuss other relationships that older people might value, and the support that they may need to make and maintain these relationships. Sexuality, however, is a good starting point for a discussion of intimacy and older people for a number of reasons. First, a sexual relationship is an easily and widely recognised form of intimacy, indeed being referred to euphemistically in previous decades as 'intimacy'. A sexual relationship may, of course, be impersonal, and involve no exchange of confidences or personal information, and indeed demonstrate no interpersonal intimacy, but it will always involve physical intimacy, the experience of a body – one's own and perhaps another person's. This physicality is at once the subject of anxiety and distaste in societies where the body and sexuality has been taboo, and paradoxically the source of fascination, as societies become ever more prurient in their curiosity about what people do with their bodies as expressions of sexuality. It must be pointed out, however, that this open curiosity is a fairly recent phenomena, and that some older people may have lived through periods when such discussion was regarded as shocking – this may have some implications for their current discussions of sexuality.

This leads to the second reason why sexuality is a good starting point for examining intimacy in older people – the way in which the idea of sexually active older people challenges some of the stereotypes we have of older people, and what is 'proper' and acceptable behaviour for them, in the eyes of others. As this chapter will go on to explore, the invisibility of older people's sexuality mirrors their invisibility in other areas, and when their sexuality does become visible, the reaction is often negative, as it is to many other activities that they may be discovered doing. As the quote at the beginning of the chapter indicates, sexuality can make people 'feel alive', and it may be that this feeling alive is in sharp contrast to the way in which older people can sometimes be made to feel marginalised and excluded from everyday life that others enjoy.

The social and political dimensions of a discussion of older people and sexuality, however, must take place in the context of changes in physical functioning, and the consequent changes in the way that some older people experience their sexuality. The physical side of sexual activity, however, is not just purely governed by levels of hormones or levels of fitness. As the development of Viagra use has shown, and will be discussed in this chapter, taking tablets to restore functioning is only part of a complex picture, and for some not even the most important part.

Other important dimensions of sexuality are the emotional dimensions of intimacy, closeness and caring. The discussion of these wider dimensions leads from sexuality to other types of relationships that older people may have with friends and peers, and with family. Notions of intimacy and the way in which it maintains and develops a sense of self are explored, alongside the research knowledge that we have about the ways in which people maintain supportive networks.

Sexuality and the quality of life across ages

The notion of sexuality has expanded over the course of debates and discussions beyond the narrow definitions of sexual activity to encompass sensuality, self-esteem, self-image and intimacy. The World Health Organisation definition, cited by Larsen et al (1996), describes sexuality as "the integration of the somatic, emotional, intellectual, and social aspects of sexual being, in ways that are positive, enriching and that enhance personality, community and love" (p 300). As Pangman and Seguire (2000) argue, this type of holistic definition is one in which "the concept of sexuality is articulated in terms beyond sexual activity in sexual relationships" (p 51).

The importance of sexuality to well-being is fundamental, with the opportunities it offers for intimacy and closeness. As Pangman and Seguire (2000) argue, "sexuality provides the individual with the opportunity to express affection, admiration and affirmation of one's body and its functioning" (p 51). With this wider conceptualisation of sexuality, it loses its separate and distant character as only sexual activity, and becomes more a part of everyday life – or, as Simon (1996) has put it, we are moving to:

> ... broaden our concerns for the sexual, to deny it its traditional position of privileged isolation, and to try to understand how the sexual helps to shape the totality of experience and how the larger context of social life may shape the sexual experience at its most fundamental level. (p 19)

This idea of sexuality as integral to life experience, rather than a distinct part of it, has led some to argue that it is also integral to a sense of well-being. For example, Pangman and Seguire (2000) have argued that "sexual healthcare is an essential component of overall wellness during one's developmental lifespan" (p 49), going on to say that "all individuals, especially those who are ageing and those who have been chronically ill need to express their sexuality in alternative ways in order to maintain and enhance their quality of life" (p 51).

In addition, there is some research that indicates that sexuality can have a measurable impact on lifespan. Palmore (1981) found, in a longitudinal survey in the US, that older people who were sexually active also lived longer. Walz and Blum (1987) also found that sexuality was a key factor that contributed to continued health and perceptions of well-being in later life.

Images of older people and sexuality

While sexuality may be pervasive and important for well-being, the sexuality of older people is not necessarily encouraged or acknowledged by those younger than them. As Pangman and Seguire (2000) have argued:

Society falls short on two counts. First, society fails to recognize the importance of sexuality to the well-being of the elderly. Secondly, society helps to impose barriers, which results in the sexuality of older adults being devalued. (p 50)

The images of the sexuality of older people are therefore important in the way that they shape and are shaped by our attitudes to sexuality in later life, and the ways in which we support, discourage or ignore it.

Invisibility

Pangman and Seguire (2000) have argued that one way in which we view the sexuality of older people is that it does not exist, that it is made invisible. The images we have of sweet old grannies, knitting in their rocking chairs, or grandpas playing bowls do not include ideas about them being sexually active – indeed their role as kindly, helpful elders, who are above all of the messiness and confusion of sexual relationships, depends on this. Karlen and Moglia (1995), for example, have argued that until only a few decades ago there was a society-wide denial of older people's sexuality, and Drench and Losee (1996) point out that this is compounded by the presence (assumed or actual) of chronic illness or health problems. As Tilley (1996) has identified, people with disabilities are also assumed to be asexual – the combination of older age and potential health problems plays to stereotypes of both older people and people with chronic illnesses as not being interested in sex.

On television, for example, Bell (1992) has found that sexuality is usually absent from the portrayal of older people, and that if there is an element of sexuality apparent it is "the erotics of the gaze and desire and not the erotics of touch and the satisfied body" (p 309). Willert and Semans (2000) have argued that these 'Victorian values', as they describe them, are connected to the idea that sexual activity is about procreation, and so older people, especially women, who are past child rearing would have no justifiable interest in it. This same connection between sex and procreation also renders homosexual relationships as invalid and therefore invisible – especially so when older people are also viewed as traditionalists with any sexual activity in the past being heterosexual. The idea that anything other than heterosexual within-marriage sexual activity would be anathema to older people is an idea that pays only cursory attention to the sexuality of older people and relies on stereotypes rather than consideration of possibilities that we would perhaps rather not think about.

There are also indications that this invisibility permeates professionals' interactions and care for older people. Matocha and Waterhouse (1993), for example, have argued in their review of research on nurses' attitudes that most studies have found that nurses tend to ignore the sexual needs of older people. Eckland and McBride (1997) argue that this is the case for health professionals generally, with patients concerns' and questions remaining unexplored.

Correspondingly, Ebersole and Hess (1998) have pointed out that older clients do not often confide in professionals about their sexual needs or difficulties. It would seem that the invisibility of the sexuality of older people leads to a conspiracy of silence, where everyone ignores what, for other age groups, is regarded as a legitimate and important part of life.

Distaste

While the sexuality of older people may be invisible to us, the process of denial and hiding is based on a strong unease or distaste that we have for the idea of older people having sex. Walz (2002), for example, has described how sexually active older people are thought of as "crones" or "dirty old men", concluding that "sexuality of old people, like the sexuality of adolescents, frightens most adults in between" (p 99). Walz connects this distaste to the link between sexuality and attractiveness – the idea that sex is only for beautiful people. As beauty is most often defined as being young, slim, lithe and perfectly toned, older people can find themselves excluded from the ranks of those whose sexual activity is approved. Transgressors, who insist on enjoying their sexuality, run the risk of public censure and disapproval and, in the case of those who depend on services and facilities to enable them to enjoy sexual activity, withdrawal of this support and the imposition of barriers.

Where older people are portrayed as sexual, therefore, they are the "dirty old men" (there is an equivalent if less prevalent image for women) whose behaviour is inappropriate, unnatural and disgusting. Furthermore, Walz (2002) argues, where sexual relationships of older people are portrayed in the media, frequently only one partner is old; the other is younger. These stories often have unhappy endings, with the older partner becoming more frail, dying or being rejected, while the younger partner goes on to find another relationship with someone closer to their own age. Where there are media portrayals of older people in sexual relationships, these are restricted to healthy people in their fifties or sixties, who are well preserved and 'young looking'. There are few portrayals of much older people, who may have physical limitations and display clear signs of ageing.

Bildtegård (2000) has analysed one portrayal of older people's sexuality on film, and the 'rules' or conventions observed to make this portrayal credible. These were that the relationship had to be affectionate, the older people had to be 'well preserved', they had to be lively, they had to conform to gendered expectations, and finally that they had to be single. This last rule, Bildtegård conjectures, seems to be based on the assumption that sexual attraction in a long-standing relationship must inevitably decline, and that a plot is more interesting if it involves rejuvenation through a new love. Despite observing these rules, however, Bildtegård notes that there is no depiction of sex on screen; it is hinted at rather than shown directly.

Changes in attitudes

The views, images and attitudes discussed above, that older people do not have sexual feelings, or if they do it is disgusting, may be changing. Pangman and Seguire (2000), for example, follow their discussion of the Victorian values that deny older people's sexuality with the observation that, as sexuality becomes more overt generally, then this may pave the way for recognition of older people's sexuality. Adams (1997) similarly argues that older people are defying stereotypes, and this is supported by Eliopoulos (1997) who argues that current cohorts of older people have been accustomed to more openness about their sexuality than previous generations, as barriers to discussing sexuality have diminished over the course of their lifetimes. Any older person today will have lived much of their life after the 'sexual revolution' of the 1960s and the birth of the permissive society, where contraception became more available, and rules about sex outside marriage were relaxed. They will also have lived in a society that bombards us with sexual images and discussions, from advertising with suggestive and sometimes quite explicit images, and media items about the intimate sexual lives of the famous. While older people may not approve or feel comfortable about this (nor indeed may people of all ages), nonetheless they will have been accustomed to it. It becomes incongruous then to place an age limit on openness about sexuality, or the freedom to enjoy it. As Walz (2002) has argued:

> Yet 'times are a'changin'. A new cohort of late baby boomers is about to make demographic history. They are different. Their lifestyles are different. Their attitudes about their own sexuality are different. They will be the first generation to view sexuality more from a companionate perspective than from a reproductive point of view. It is doubtful whether they will choose to hide or disguise their sexual interests and needs. They can be expected to challenge the existing representations and forge new ones. (Walz, 2002, p 111)

Kingsberg (2002) gives some examples of ways in which images are changing for women: "cultural stereotypes of the middle-aged women as gray-haired, frail and asexual, have given way to images of strong, active and sexual women" (p 431). Kingsberg gives the examples of Sigourney Weaver and Tina Turner, who are respectively in their early fifties and early sixties. Boylan (2000), in a newspaper article, gives the example of the actress Honor Blackman, who is in her mid-seventies, and quotes her as saying, "I've always been told that I'm sexy". These positive images, and corresponding images of sexually active older men, may be breaking some stereotypes, and opening up possibilities for regarding older people as sexual. These positive images, however, are of people who are fit, attractive and not very old – perhaps the real breakthrough will come when role models of positive sexuality in older people incorporate very old people who have physical limitations and are not beautiful in the convention of the stage and screen star.

Sexual activity

Against this background of attitudes, assumptions and stereotypes, there is evidence that older people are getting on with their sex lives. Walz (2002) comments on this body of knowledge, pointing out that most studies, at least in the US, were carried out between 1965 and 1985, and there has been a reduction in research since, with only a small rise in studies based around the introduction of Viagra onto the pharmaceutical market in the 1990s. Some of the earliest studies that asked questions about older people's sexual activity were the Duke Longitudinal Studies, which began in 1955. Analysis of the data showed that most older adults with partners continued to have sex, although this gradually got less frequent over time (Newman and Nichols, 1970). In the second Duke Longitudinal Study, Palmore (1981) reported that no respondents claimed a total absence of sexual activity, and also found that people who were sexually active lived longer. Cross-cultural studies have confirmed these findings in other cultures too – overall, older people are sexually active despite differences in societal attitudes and contexts.

Later studies have confirmed this early work, and perhaps have benefited from the loosening of the boundaries that constrained the earlier work and made it more difficult to discuss sexuality. Mulligan and Palguta (1991), Hodson and Skeen (1994) and Kennedy et al (1997), for example, have all concluded that people are sexually active well into old age. Willert and Semans (2000) argue that people, therefore, "are not likely to cease having sex due to an arbitrary chronological age or because health industry professionals believe that they have or should become asexual" (p 416).

There are, however, some limitations on sexual activity, perhaps most significantly illness and lack of opportunity (Walz, 2002, p 104). People who have physical difficulties may find sexual activity difficult because of lack of flexibility, stamina or sensitivity. People who have lost their partners, through death or divorce, may feel frustrated because the opportunities for sexual activity with a partner have gone, and finding a new partner may feel too onerous to contemplate.

There is also some evidence that changes to the body through the ageing process may cause some difficulties. As Levine (1992) has commented, "many people are finally able to act in a consistently loving fashion only when their bodies are gradually losing their previously smoothly functioning sexual capacities" (p 89). While anxieties about pregnancy and demands of work and child rearing may have disappeared and afford more time for relaxed sexual activity, some ageing changes in bodily function may present other challenges to enjoyment of sexual activity.

Physical changes over time

Willert and Semans (2000) describe the changes in sexual functioning that can occur as people grow older. Changes in blood supply, muscle function and connective tissue may make orgasms and arousal more difficult. For men there may be a loss of libido, as testosterone declines, and penile erectile function declines. This can lead to diminished force of ejaculation and delayed ejaculation. Older men, therefore, may be slower to become aroused and ejaculate, and this can cause anxiety about performance. For women there is a decline in oestrogen and testosterone production after menopause, which may lead to a lowering of libido and decrease in vaginal lubrication, which can make intercourse uncomfortable. Kingsberg (2002) argues, however, that the menopause is often linked to sexual dysfunction in women, but that recent research suggests that this may be more generally age-related than specifically menopause-related.

In addition to life-cycle changes, there may also be some disease-related changes in sexual function. Disease processes that are more evident in older people can make sexual activity more difficult. Arthritis, for example, can reduce flexibility because of stiffness and pain, which can restrict and inhibit sexual activity. Diabetes can lead to neuropathy, which reduces sensation, and may reduce desire for sex, and thyroid problems may lower energy levels. More generally, Laumann et al (1994) found that levels of overall health correlated with sexual activity – the healthier a person was, in the researchers' assessment, the more frequently they engaged in sexual activity.

Disease and illness also carry the risk of iatrogenic effects on sexual activity. Some medications and treatments for chronic diseases have been found to suppress libido or adversely affect sexual functioning in older people. While these drugs may have less effect on younger people, the increased sensitivity of older people to some drugs, and the longer time it can take them to break down and excrete drugs, means that the effects on them can be significant (Leiblum and Segraves, 1989).

Psychological factors

The discussion of physical factors in sexual functioning obscures the most important element of sexuality at all ages, and that is the psychological aspect. While there may be some age-related changes, which make arousal and orgasm slower as people get older, the greatest impact they may have is on the confidence and self-perception of the older person. Uncertainty and anxiety about sexual capacity, whether related to health problems, treatment or just growing older, may hinder sexual activity, making older people less likely to engage in it, or more anxious and enjoying it less when they do (Levine, 1992).

Some of this anxiety and discomfort may be connected to feelings and attitudes that people have acquired throughout their lives, such as family views, teachings and beliefs (Croft, 1982). Some of it may be a response to wider societal views, and the awareness that many younger people disapprove of sexual activity for older people anyway. Sexual activity is not just physical, but psychological and emotional too, bound up with feelings about the self and others. Viewing oneself as a desirable sexual being, and seeing this in others, is a foundation for activity, and if stereotypes and anxieties overwhelm these perceptions, then older people's interest in being sexual can decline (Kingsberg, 2002). Levine (1992) makes a further distinction between three components of desire (one's interest in being sexual): drive, the biologic component of sexuality, manifested in sexual thoughts and feelings; beliefs and values, whether the person sees sexuality positively or not; and motivation, the willingness to behave sexually. The last component, motivation, is, Kingsberg (2002) argues, the one that has the greatest impact on sexual behaviour and is the most complex.

Social contexts

In addition to the biological and psychological factors affecting the sexuality of older people, there are also a number of social factors that can influence behaviour. The attitudes of the rest of society have been discussed above, and these can lead to inhibitions and anxieties about sexual activity, which may restrict activity, but there are also more practical issues that arise from the social context of growing older.

One of these is the longevity of sexual relationships for some older people. Some marriages or partnerships may be many years long – some people who married in their twenties may be with the same spouse 70 years later, for example. This places a different set of advantages and disadvantages on sexual activity. On the one hand, there is the advantage of support and acceptance, as well as love and affection, which can be found in long-standing relationships (Schnarch, 1997). On the other hand, there may be an absence of excitement in a relationship, which may reduce desire. In a society where discussion of sex focuses on those in relationships that are comparatively new, or indeed not in a relationship at all, the dynamics of a long-term sexual relationship are not often addressed or discussed.

In addition, older people may well be in a social context where support for sexual activity is not forthcoming. As older people become reliant on their children to provide care and support, their sexual activity may be inhibited by the expressed or assumed views of their children towards sexuality in older people in general, and their parents in particular. Some older people may be reliant on other types of carers for support, such as professional staff or carers in care homes. The inhibitory effects of this dependence, which brings along with it increased scrutiny by others and decreased privacy and autonomy, may restrict and discourage sexual activity or even discussion of it.

Sexuality and intimacy: the views of older people

The literature about the sexual activity of older people is limited and, as Walz (2002) has suggested, after the recent pharmaceutical interests of companies developing commercial drugs like Viagra, it has died down. There is an additional body of literature about our views about older people and sexuality, although again this is limited. There is, furthermore, an almost complete dearth of research asking older people what their views of their sexuality are. Whether this is because of the lack of interest of researchers and funding bodies or whether it is because of the constraints we assume will be in play if we tried to talk to older people about sexuality is unclear.

Walz (2002) has written about conversations that he has had with clients in a geriatric clinic in the US. As a clinical teaching social worker he was asked to talk to clients who seemed depressed or suicidal, and one meeting with an 82-year-old woman sparked off an interest in older people's views and experiences of sexuality. Presenting the stories of two clients, he recounts what they felt about their sexuality and how they talked about it. What is striking about the two accounts is that, if details about age were omitted, we would be unlikely to suspect that these were older people. Their descriptions of the pleasure and joy they have in sex, and their desires and fantasies, seem as likely to have come from a younger person as an older person. There are some biographical details, however, which frame the storytellers as people who had grown up in a time when sexuality was not openly talked about and remained a covert side of life. Walz, however, comments that, "It would seem that growing old sexually is simply living out life as a sexual being, taking into account some surprises that occur when illnesses and losses become episodes in daily living" (p 109).

One report that did explicitly explore sexuality in older people is one conducted through 'A Better Life in Later Life' in Newcastle, a development from the Better Government for Older People government-supported initiative. The report developed from a whole systems event, which had led to the formation of a sexuality and sexual health action group who organised the research (Swinburne et al, 1997). One interesting feature of the study was that one researcher was an older person, which she felt was significant in the way that older people responded in the group and individual interviews that the study was based on:

> "What was very interesting when I went out with the (younger) researcher, was that the older people were answering me and the eye contact was made with me." (personal conversation)

This observation may point to some of the limitations of research with older people conducted by younger people – that a shared understanding of generational experiences, based on similarities of age, may overcome some of the difficulties of tackling sensitive topics. Even with an older person as researcher, one participant declined to take part, stating: "I think that this research is such a private matter ... I'm not going to discuss it" (personal conversation).

There were also some issues about finding language that was acceptable to participants – as the authors state: "'Romantic involvements' and 'French letters' were more acceptable than 'sexual relationships' and 'condoms'" (Swinburne et al, 1997).

Swinburne et al (1997) summarise their findings by pointing to the contextual and relationship issues that surround sexuality, and the wide range of experiences that older people had. While there was little detailed talk of sexual activity (perhaps because of the group interview strategy which may have precluded discussing intimate personal facts), there was some expression of a degree of 'putting up' with sex, as part of the duties of marriage. As one participant put it:

> "Sex was for men. Women had a duty to do it."

And another:

> "Only good thing I got out of sex is my daughter."

Sex could also be subject to a number of moral codes of conduct:

> "Sex outside marriage, if you got caught, brought disgrace and fear."

Alongside these negative images, there was also talk about the positive aspects of sex, mainly connected with the intimacy and closeness that it involved, and for some this affection was more important than sexual activity. As one woman said:

> "In the last three years of my husband's life we had no sex life. I loved him and that was enough for me."

And another participant:

> "If you have a genuine love for somebody and you enjoy their company at any time for any length of time, that's what love is. It's not necessarily to do with a bodily function."

These comments should not be taken as evidence that the older people speaking do not value sex, simply that they place it in the context of relationships and intimacy. This is also echoed in the comments made about the media discussions about sex. While some participants argued that there should be more openness about sex, in that people could learn more, in general the feeling was that it should not be divorced from intimacy.

> "Sex must be linked with relationships – feelings, experience. To talk about sex is good – better to have the opportunity to talk to others, whatever the discussion."

And another participant:

> "Sex is as important as intimacy – they must go side by side."

These comments suggest other interpretations of the disapproving comments about sex in the media. It is not simply that older people are prudish, but that they feel that sex is not just a 'bodily function' and that media discussions of sex miss out the relationship factor.

Professional support

Older people, then, have an interest in sex, which does not diminish in the ways that younger people expect. How, then, does this impact on the way that professionals support and help older people? Willert and Semans (2000) argue that professionals first of all need education and information to help them to understand the processes of sexual response and activity in older people, including the understanding that older people are sexual beings. This is not simply a matter of giving professionals information – as the discussion above has indicated, widespread attitudes towards older people and their sexuality are powerful and pervasive, and professionals may share them. There is, therefore, likely to be work to be done on these attitudes, exploring and challenging them.

The exercise below may help this process.

Exercises

Case I

You meet a client for the first time, a woman in her eighties whose husband died in the previous year. In the course of a general conversation, asking about various aspects of her life, you ask her about her bereavement. She replies:

"I miss him terribly. I miss having someone to share jokes with, and to talk to. I miss cuddling up to him, especially in bed. That side of our life was very active, and we both enjoyed it a lot. Since he died I haven't had any sex, and I really miss it. I don't know whether there are any alternatives, and sometimes I think I'll just have to put up with the frustration until I die."

Think about the following points:

- Are you shocked? If so, why?
- Do you support this woman's desire to find some source of sexual satisfaction?
- What strategies could she use?
- Can you support her? This may involve giving advice or information, or referring her to a specialist service. What information could you give her? What service could you refer her to?

> ### Case 2
>
> A man and a woman in their seventies attend a lunch club. They are not married, each having lost their partners, but are good friends. Both have severe arthritis, and very limited mobility. During a meeting to review their support, they both request some advice about coping with their physical problems, and beginning sexual activity together. They suggest that because they have problems in meeting each other, and think that the single beds that they have at home would not be suitable for sex, they could use a side room at the lunch club, which has two beds in it that could be pushed together.
>
> Think about the following points:
>
> - Are you shocked, and why?
> - If they had been married, would it have made any difference to your response?
> - Do you think that their request could be accommodated?
> - If so, how do you think that the rest of the people attending the lunch club might respond?
> - If you decide to support the couple, how would you evaluate and monitor this support?

> The two cases above are about fairly traditional older people – who are heterosexual and have (or have had) stable relationships. While the couple in Case 2 may need some help in moving furniture, this is not hugely difficult, and the woman in Case 1 may only need some advice (although this may be intimate and personal). We need, then, to think about our reactions to these cases, and also about how we would respond to requests for help from people whose sexual practices are not as orthodox as the cases above. At what point would requests go beyond what we are comfortable in offering, and what are the reasons for the lines we might draw?
>
> To quote one participant from the Newcastle study: "Professionals have an 'us and them' attitude which assumes that sex isn't an issue for disabled or elderly people". Again, then, we need to reflect on our own sexuality and challenge the assumption that what is appropriate or important for younger people is not for older people.

References

Adams, M. (1997) *Sex in the snow: Canadian social value at the end of the millennium*, Toronto: Penguin.

Bell, J. (1992) 'In search of a discourse on aging: the elderly on television', *The Gerontologist*, vol 32, no 3, pp 305-11.

Bildtegård, T. (2000) 'The sexuality of elderly people on film – visual limitations', *Journal of Aging and Identity*, vol 5, no 3, pp 169-83.

Boylan, C. (2000) 'Love in an older climate', *The Guardian*: online edition, 20 July (www.guardianunlimited.co.uk/archive/article0,4273,4042209,00.html).

Croft, L. (1982) *Sexuality in later life: A counselling guide for physicians*, Boston, MA: PSG Inc.

Drench, M. and Losee, R. (1996) 'Sexuality and sexual capacities of elderly people', *Rehabilitation Nurse*, vol 21, no 3, pp 118-23.

Ebersole, P. and Hess, P. (1998) *Toward healthy aging: Human needs and nursing response* (5th edn), St Louis, MO: Mosby.

Eckland, M. and McBride, K. (1997) 'Sexual healthcare: the role of the nurse', *Canadian Nurse*, vol 93, no 7, pp 34-7.

Eliopoulos, C. (1997) *Gerontological nursing* (4th edn), Philadelphia, PA: Lippincott.

Hodson, D. and Skeen, P. (1994) 'Sexuality and aging: the hammerlock of myths', *Journal of Applied Gerontology*, vol 13, no 3, pp 219-35.

Karlen, A. and Moglia, R. (1995) 'Sexuality, aging and the education of health professionals', *Sex Disability*, vol 13, no 3, pp 191-9.

Kennedy, G., Haque, M. and Zarankow, B. (1997) 'Human sexuality in later life', *International Journal of Mental Health*, vol 26, no 1, pp 35-46.

Kingsberg, S. (2002) 'The impact of aging on sexual function in women and their partners', *Archives of Sexual Behaviour*, vol 31, no 5, pp 431-7.

Larsen, P., Miller-Kahn, A. and Ostrow Flodberg, S. (1996) 'Sexuality', in I.M. Lubkin (ed) *Chronic illness impact and interventions* (4th edn), London: Jones Bartlett, pp 299-323.

Laumann, E., Gagnon, J., Michael, R. and Michaels, S. (1994) *The social organisation of sexuality*, Chicago, IL: University of Chicago Press.

Leiblum, S. and Segraves, T. (1989) 'Sex therapy with aging adults', in S. Leiblum and R. Rosen (eds) *Principles and practice of sex therapy, update for the 1990s*, New York, NY: Guilford Press, pp 352-81.

Levine, S.B. (1992) *Sexual life*, New York, NY: Plenum.

Matocha, L. and Waterhouse, J. (1993) 'Current nursing practice related to sexuality', *Research in Nursing and Health*, vol 16, pp 118-23.

Mulligan, T. and Palguta, R. (1991) 'Sexual interest, activity and satisfaction among male nursing home residents', *Archives of Sexual Behaviour*, vol 20, no 2, pp 199-204.

Newman, G. and Nichols, C.R. (1970) 'Sexual activities and attitudes in older persons', in E. Palmore (ed) *Normal aging*, vol 1, Durham, NC: Duke University Press.

Palmore, E. (1981) *Social patterns in normal ageing: Findings from the Duke Longitudinal Study*, Durham, NC: Duke University Press.

Pangman, V.C. and Seguire, M. (2000) 'Sexuality and the chronically ill older adult', *A Social Justice Issue*, vol 18, no 1, pp 49-59.

Schiavi, R.C. (1997) *Aging and male sexuality*, Cambridge: Cambridge University Press.

Schnarch, D. (1997) *Passionate marriage*, New York, NY: Henry Holt.

Simon, W. (1996) *Postmodern sexualities*, London: Routledge.

Swinburne, S., Williams, F. and Ford, C. (1997) *Relationships and intimacy in later life*, Newcastle: A Better Life in Later Life.

Tilley, C. (1996) 'Sexuality in women with physical disabilities: a social justice or health issue?' *Sexual Disability*, vol 14, no 2, pp 139-51.

Walz, T. (2002) 'Crones, dirty old men, sexy seniors: representations of the sexuality of older persons', *Journal of Aging and Identity*, vol 7, no 2, p 99-112.

Walz, T.H. and Blum, N.S. (1987) *Sexual health in later life*, Lexington, MA: DC Health.

Willert, A. and Semans, M. (2000) 'Knowledge and attitudes about later life sexuality: what clinicians need to know about helping the elderly', *Contemporary Family Therapy*, vol 22, no 4, pp 415-35.

SEVEN

Living in families and communities

Contents

Older people and their families   115
Friendship and socialising   119
Activities   122

Key points

- Older people have a range of social networks, which include family, friends and communities.
- We can often focus only on families, without appreciating the existence of wider networks.
- We can assume that older people are passive recipients of support, without understanding the contributions that they make.

While it is important to recognise the uniqueness of individuals, it is also important to understand their place in social networks, such as families, circles of friends and neighbours, and in communities. This is particularly the case for older people who, over a lifetime, have built up these networks. One of the dangers of thinking about older people as being connected to social networks is that we often see them only as dependent within them – older people being cared for by their families, for example, or receiving community care services.

The place of older people in social networks, however, is much more complex than this. While they may be dependent on others, they also do things for others – there is interdependence, not just dependence. Appreciating this point, then, leads us to thinking about the contributions they make.

A second danger of thinking of older people and their social engagement is to think of them as being involved in traditional activities. Thus older people are thought of as being engaged in whist drives and tea dances, rather than flying to Las Vegas or learning to line dance. The activities that older people are involved in are not limited by our assumptions about what they might want to do, although they may, in a very practical way, be limited by what society is prepared to offer and support.

These points were demonstrated by several speakers at an event hosted by the Centre for Care of Older People at Northumbria University in 1999. In this year, Age Concern began a campaign, the 'Debate of the Age', which aimed to raise awareness of the changes in the population, with the proportions of older people growing over the next millennium. The campaign presented this change as a start to debates about provision for older people, including healthcare, housing and pensions, and the policy changes that might be needed to address issues of funding and quality. In this national campaign, different organisations and groups were invited to host events and debates. One event was hosted by the Centre for Care of Older People, with the theme of 'Involvement and Participation'. Older people whom we had worked with in various different projects and activities were invited to begin the day by talking about some of the activities that they had been involved in, and their ideas about how this type of activity could be encouraged and facilitated. Their accounts give us some indication of the way in which older people can contribute to the communities in which they live.

The first speaker was Billie Cummings, who summarised some of the activities that she had been involved with in her community since retiring in 1983. This has included being a member of the group Action for Health for Senior Citizens in Newcastle (AHSCIN), and participating in a number of whole systems events, including a three-day workshop on improving life for older people in Newcastle.

At an informal level, Billie also talked about her role as a 'good neighbour' to whom people came for help and advice. She also showed us her 'Benwell Oscar', which had been presented to her in recognition of her community activity (Benwell is an area in Newcastle). She gave the example of two women who lived on her estate, and who had Alzheimer's disease. She had contacted social services about them, but nothing had happened. Her contacts through the whole systems events, however, meant that she could talk through things face-to-face with people who could help, with the result that the two women moved into care homes, where they could be looked after. She still visits these women, and has made some observations about the lack of mental or physical stimulation in the care homes – with people sitting around "like zombies".

She has also been involved in a 'Going Home from Hospital' research group (Reed et al, 2002). This had begun with the observation that there was little communication between patients, hospitals and community services – an example was where a hospital would send a patient home on a Friday, when most care workers would have finished work for the week, so no one would visit until Monday, and people would have to rely on friends and family for help. The Going Home group, however, had helped to improve this situation by identifying a number of different strategies that providers can adopt.

Billie then talked about recent experiences of involvement with the Better Government for Older People programme, which has included going to Wolverhampton and Ruskin College, with the Old Spice drama group, doing sketches, poems and songs that highlight the attitudes most younger people have towards 'oldies'.

The next speaker was Keith Pimm, who talked about a particular project that he had been involved in, regenerating Exhibition Park in Newcastle. Keith has been an appreciative user of the park for many years – a personal experience that strengthened his desire to see the park developed as a resource for the city and its people. Keith has received a Millennium Award from the local community, which has enabled him to undertake training and research that has enhanced the contribution he had been able to make to the redevelopment of the park. The project has made considerable progress, helped by the support of organisations like the Newcastle Healthy City Project which provides practical support, such as an accommodation address and meeting space. Keith also discussed the value of the support of a group of people with shared values, which include a commitment to social justice and an enthusiasm for new ideas and developments.

There were several older people in the core group, working on the regeneration of the park, who made important contributions. For example, a practical project was underway developing a sensory garden with the advice of older people with sensory impairment. The awareness of the social isolation of some older people had prompted discussions about designs that are easily accessible and welcoming, and places to sit and talk and meet people.

The thinking that went into the project was also informed by other experiences that some of the older people had had – for example, on Better Government for Older People activities and whole systems events. This made networking much easier and ensured that the project was informed by a broad perspective that took in the whole community. In addition, Keith made the point that the Better Government experience had had a "capacity-building" result, in that it had encouraged older people to get involved with a range of activities, and had developed their skills and confidence in doing so.

Bob Weiner was the third older person to talk about experiences with Better Government, but he also talked about his role as a North East Pre-Retirement Association (NEPRA) liaison officer. This organisation runs workshops for people who are about to retire, and Bob had observed that one problem was that many people did not know how they were to use the extra hours of leisure that they would have each week. When the Leisure, Pleasure and Learning (LPL) group started as a development from the whole systems event held in 1995, there was an obvious connection with the NEPRA work.

The LPL group was made up of people from the local authority, health services and voluntary agencies with good representation from older people. There was an emphasis on health to start with, and one of the early discussions the group had was about exercise. The group realised that keep-fit classes were usually run by younger people, and that this would be discouraging to older people. The group decided to see if they could arrange for some older people to receive training in running keep-fit classes, and they managed to get some funding from the Further Education Finance Council. Fifteen places were advertised, the only restriction being that applicants had to be over 50. There was a substantial response – more than the places available – but the 15 candidates selected underwent a one-year training package, leading to an NVQ (National Vocational Qualification) level III. They are now running exercise groups across Newcastle.

The LPL group also recognised that walking was a very healthy activity, and one that was acceptable to older people. The group developed a guide for people wanting to take up walking, about building up stamina, choosing the right clothing, and a programme for increasing fitness. They have also produced a booklet on walks that are accessible for older people, and a video. They have also highlighted the lack of guided walks around Newcastle for less mobile people, and such walks have now been included in the programme.

The LPL group have also identified the need for computer training for older people. While computer training programmes do exist, these are often highly technical, and are designed for people who will use computers as part of their work. Older people need some basic information about how to use a computer, and might want to use it for fun – for example, playing games with their grandchildren. They need to know how to switch the computer on, use a mouse, run the programs they want, and access the Internet. In response to the group's request, the Centre for Lifelong Learning and the Workers' Educational Association (WEA) are now looking at the development of a programme training older people to train their peers in the use of computers.

The aims and objectives of the LPL group included:

* building a database of leisure and learning opportunities for older people;
* encouraging the development of more facilities, and encouraging more use of them;
* gathering views of older people and their groups and organisations about activities and preferences;
* coordinating activities;
* providing a forum for debate;
* combating ageism by monitoring access and opportunities for older people;
* combating ageism by encouraging older people not to regard age as a barrier to trying out new forms of leisure or learning activity.

Barbara Douglas from Better Government for Older People concluded the presentations by reciting a poem that one older person had written as part of a creative writing exercise, which had asked participants to write a poem on the theme of 'I'm not a burden', in which every line had to mention a weather condition:

> "I'm old
> but able to weather any storm
> Give me a chance
> I'll turn your drab lives into sunshine."

The presentations by Billie, Keith, Bob and Barbara were well received, and the debate that followed was long and enthusiastic. The audience – which consisted of older people, service providers, policy makers, researchers and educationalists

– were impressed by the range of activities that had been described, with one participant writing on the feedback sheet:

> "I'd expected to get caught up in a debate about what we could do for older people. I was very pleasantly surprised to have my assumptions overturned, and to learn what they could do for me!"

This is a key message of this chapter. While it will give an overview of the research and policy about how older people can be helped, the emphasis is much more on reciprocity – the account of how older people live in social networks of family, friends and community makes their contributions central to the discussion. Older people are active in their networks, exercising choice, thoughtfulness and commitment, but this can often be overshadowed by accounts of isolation and need.

Older people and their families

One place to start the discussion of older people and their networks is to start with a discussion of family relationships. Starting here makes sense for a number of reasons. First, we assume that older people place great importance on family, to the extent that these relationships are the most important to them. This assumption may be based on our own personal experiences of older people – if the most important or significant older people in our lives are our grandparents or parents, then we may be tempted to assume that every older person has a similar family network, and if our grandparents have always made a fuss of us, we may assume that we are the most important people to them. These ideas are supported by images in the media that present older people as doting grandparents, looking forward to visits from family, waiting for their phone calls, and receiving their presents with gratitude.

The presentations summarised at the beginning of this chapter suggest that older people can be engaged in networks that are a lot bigger than their immediate families. Nevertheless there is a substantial amount of research indicating that families are important to older people (see, for example, Philipson et al, 2000). Families, for example, provide a great deal of support and care, although this varies with circumstances and needs. Families who live nearby can obviously provide more day-to-day practical support, but even families who live some distance away can still provide important input.

Families are changing as patterns of work, marriage and residence change. This does not necessarily mean, however, that families are not caring and supporting their members, even though they may do this in different ways. Thompson (1999) has argued against the 'myth' of the decline of the family, pointing to the trends in sociological thinking over the years that have swung from bemoaning the destruction of the family because of divorce, lowered birth rates, geographical mobility and limitations on housing, to discovery that the family still plays an important part in everyday life, although in different ways. Families may not see each other as much as they did when they lived in the same house or street, but they stay in touch through telephone calls, and potentially through the Internet.

Thompson (1999) points to research that shows that family networks are not confined to particular sections of society, but are found in people from different social classes, including the middle classes who might, according to current expectations, live further away from family members. This may be because people move to retirement homes when they get older, or because their children move away in search of jobs, or to take up educational opportunities. Both of these moves, according to stereotypes, are things that the middle classes might be likely to do, with a negative effect on their families. Changes in family structure that are evident across all groups in society, such as increasing divorce rates, women's increasing participation in paid work outside the home after they have children and escalating costs of housing, again have been seen as indicators that families are disintegrating.

This bleak picture is seen to have particular relevance for older people, because of the assumption that they need their families most. Many of the negative images surrounding care services (for example, care homes) are connected to the notion that what older people want most is family care and, by extension, any other care will be less welcome and lower in quality. These ideas rest on a number of assumptions, which can be challenged. First, there is the assumption that older people are only beneficiaries in family systems and that they do not contribute anything themselves. Second, there is the assumption that the care and support they receive from families is uniformly beneficial. Third, there is an assumption that families are unable to adapt to changes in society, and are in decline.

The first assumption, that older people are only beneficiaries from family networks, ignores the contributions that older people make. First, there is their bringing up of their own children, a task which, for many, can go on beyond the point where children officially become adults. Support, financial or emotional, through the stages of adulthood may be just as important and just as willingly provided as support in childhood. Helping a child through their first experiences of school may be very immediate, but help through the first experiences of work or university can also be important. Even the process of leaving home and setting up an independent home does not necessarily mean the end of parental support – advice on choosing and equipping a home, along with financial and practical help, may be ways in which parental support continues.

Perhaps the most striking contribution of older people to family networks comes through their role as grandparents – striking because, as pointed out above, this may be our first experience of older people. Research and policy on grandparenting, however, is less prevalent, with an increasing interest only becoming more evident in recent years. Part of this neglect may be, as Thompson (1999) points out, because researchers and policy makers have only just realised how grandparenting is increasing. As people live longer, they are more likely to be around when their grandchildren are born. If they are still fit and active when they become grandparents, this may lead to an active role in caring for grandchildren, taking on responsibilities and roles in playing with, entertaining and sharing new experiences with their grandchildren. Thus the grandparenting experience becomes more common and potentially more diverse – Granny may not just sit in her rocking chair, but might go skateboarding with her grandchildren.

Studies of grandparenting have focused variously on the incidence and frequency of contact, the particular nature of the relationship (Waldrop et al, 1999), the issues of grandparenting in a changing society, with 'step-grandparents' becoming increasingly common (Thompson, 1999), and grandparenting not just through the infancy of the grandchild but through adolescence and adulthood (Mills, 1999). These studies have shown that grandparenting is an important part of family life, and while the common perception might be that it benefits the grandparent, and possibly provides some instrumental support for working parents, there is also research that argues that the benefits are also felt by grandchildren. Not only does a relationship with a grandparent provide love and security, but it can also satisfy children's needs to understand their own origins. A link with family history, developed through a grandparent, can give children an idea of where they came from, what part they have in family history, and a sense of identity within the family context (Waldrop et al, 1999).

The second assumption about older people and their families outlined above was that care by family members would be preferable to care by others. To some extent this seems to be supported, with studies finding that families do provide support and care. Qureshi and Walker (1989), for example, found that families made considerable efforts to provide care for older parents, including moving house or changing jobs to make this easier. This support is variable, however, and depends on a number of factors. Family traditions and histories play a role in care-giving practice, with experiences in the past setting expectations for the present. This is seen in different ethnic groups who have cultural traditions about care for elders, but can also be more immediate and personal – if children grow up in families where elders are cared for, then this can establish their ideas about their duties to others, and others' duties to them.

These ideas and expectations can affect not just whether care is offered and accepted, but also what limits are observed. Care can range from non-personal help, such as help with transport or home maintenance, to carrying out very intimate tasks. Qureshi and Walker's (1989) study suggested that, in the population they studied, there was a common pattern, with daughters being expected to care for parents when tasks became more intimate. If daughters were not available, then sons may become involved, but often the next choice would be a daughter-in-law, unless the older person was male and the care needed was intimate, in which case a daughter-in-law would not usually be expected to provide care. These patterns reflect social mores and customs about the roles of men and women as carers, but also about boundaries and intimacy. Intimate care may be given by women to women, but not men to women, or by non-related women to men. The existence of these patterns, then, suggests that family care can be a negotiated rather than automatic process, and that one of the parameters of negotiation may be issues of privacy and intimacy. Where these boundaries are fiercely protected or threatened, then care by people outside the family may be preferable.

Other research has also suggested that family care is not always preferable, and that is the work on elder abuse. While abuse – that is, neglect or cruelty – towards older people is being found in a range of care settings, and perpetrators can be strangers or professionals, the incidence of abuse by family members may be significant. A report in *The Lancet* (Nelson, 2002) cited the 1996 US National Abuse Study, which found that two thirds of perpetrators were adult children or spouses. Similarly a study carried out by the Community and District Nursing Association in the UK found in 2003 that nine out of ten community nurses had come across incidents of elder abuse, with family members being the perpetrators in most cases (reported in *Nursing Standard*, 2003).

The dynamics of elder abuse are complex and are only just being explored. Part of the problem facing research, however, is the confusion over definition and therefore over incidence. As Biggs et al (1995) have argued, elder abuse could be defined in terms of physical or mental harm, deliberately or accidentally caused, and can range in severity from mild discomfort to serious harm and death. These ambiguities and difficulties of definition make elder abuse difficult to identify even if we are prepared to acknowledge that it happens at all. Hugman (1995), for example, argued that the emergence of elder abuse as an increasingly recognised problem is one that has been led by professionals, who have had to confront the reluctance of societies to admit that it occurs.

In addition to these problems, there are some indications that family support may not be good for older people in other ways. The MacArthur (Glass et al, 1995) study of successful ageing found that those who had high levels of instrumental support from family had a higher risk of functional problems – the possible explanation given being that too much instrumental support may undermine independence and lead to dependency.

The third assumption identified at the beginning of this chapter was that families have been unable to adapt to changing circumstances, and that their capacity to provide support for members has decreased because of factors such as moving to find work and the breakdown of marriage and partnerships. As Thompson (1999) has argued, however, this reflects more about our nostalgia for the 'golden age' of family life than any observable changes in the way families live. The idea of the close family, who live near to each other and are always helping and supporting each other, is perhaps more an invention of fiction and advertising than a reality. Similarly, Thompson argues, the contrary myth, that the happy family is a modern development, and that further back in history family life was governed by practical considerations rather than affection, is again another unsupported idea. Thompson talks about cycles of family myths, but points to the myth of family decline as being one of the most persistent.

There is some evidence, however, that family relationships and interactions with older members are relatively robust and are maintained despite family change. The discussion of grandparenting earlier indicated that there is evidence that grandparents remain important to grandchildren in the face of recent demographic developments. Thompson's study (1999) has shown that when parents divorce or die, for example, grandparenting continues despite the difficulties involved, and that grandparents provided the most common resource for children when their parents divorced or died. Similarly the 'generation gap' that commentators have observed between children and their parents, and which could be expected to be even greater between children and grandparents, may not be the barrier to support that might be assumed. The differences between generations, in lifestyles, goals and values, have been bemoaned by many as either evidence for or causes of family disintegration. Mills (1999), however, has found that the role transitions of adolescence and early adulthood do not seem to affect relationships with grandparents, suggesting that these changes in family dynamics may not be as disruptive as feared, at least not in relationships between grandparents and grandchildren.

Wider societal changes in gender roles could also be assumed to affect intergenerational relationships, as traditional practices change, but research indicates that this is not necessarily the case. A study of grandfathers carried out by Waldrop et al (1999) showed how grandfathering contributed positively to the lives of grandchildren, but also to grandfathers, who were able to build on increasing flexibility of gender roles to develop nurturing and mentoring in ways which had, perhaps, not been regarded as masculine.

Some societal changes, therefore, have been met with adaptive responses which have meant that intergenerational relationships continue to play an important role in people's lives. Other changes or pressures, however, have been resisted, and family networks have remained relatively stable. This perhaps can be seen most obviously in groups that have strong traditions, such as some ethnic communities with strong traditions of family support. Cylwik (2002), for example, carried out a study of intergenerational relationships in Greek-Cypriot families living in London. The study found that family support was expected from all the generations in a family, and that family ties were extremely important to the older Greek-Cypriots in the study. This study suggests that traditions of family support may persist for some time despite relocation and emigration.

Friendship and socialising

Returning to the accounts given by Billie, Keith and Bob at the beginning of this chapter, it is clear that the activities they described did not involve family networks, but were social activities which involved friends, acquaintances and people with mutual interests. Again these activities involved reciprocity – people sharing ideas and work, making contributions based on their skills and talents. Some of the activities and people involved support, which ranged from funding for expenses, provision of materials and places to meet, to advice and information. Others were independent, in the sense that the people involved provided their own resources, certainly in terms of time and sometimes in terms of costs and facilities. The question that these differences raise, of course, is whether spontaneous activity has an energy and involves commitment and reward that 'provided' activities cannot, or whether spontaneous activities run the risk of running out of steam if they are not recognised and supported.

Finding out information to help answer this question is, however, very difficult. The literature that reports on evaluations and descriptions of activity is often very narrow, concentrating on one specific activity. This type of report is difficult to apply to other activities because of the specific groups, contexts or histories involved. Nonetheless there are some lessons that can be drawn from these reports.

One more general and abstract discussion about social activity is the discussion about continuity in activities, relationships and lifestyles. The notion of continuity is discussed in relation to a range of different aspects of growing older – for example, in relation to housing and geographical residence, where preferences and decisions are seen as ways in which older people strive to maintain continuity between their younger and older selves. The same analysis has also been applied to social activity, where these are seen as being long-term features of the way in which people have lived their lives. An example is Finchum and Weber (2000) who have applied continuity theory to older people's friendships. They argue that older people can choose to maintain friendships, and that these friendships go through different phases, from beginnings to endings. The process of developing friendships is an active one, however, and Finchum and Weber argue that the decision to embark on friendship making or maintaining is made in the context of lifelong social preferences and experiences, including geographical location, class, race and gender backgrounds, and interpersonal styles. Another factor in making friends is peer-group similarity, another way in which friendship can be seen as part of life continuity. Choosing friends from those who have had similar generational experiences, have shared memories and understandings, and are experiencing the same age-related changes, allows people to identify and build on commonalities with others.

This does not mean, however, that friendships in later life are not new experiences – evidence suggests that older people do not just stick with the friends that they have had for years, but continue to make new friends (Jerrome and Wenger, 1999). As peers die, become less active or relocate, there is a risk that older people may lose friends, but Jerrome and Wenger have shown that they continue to develop new relationships. In Jerrome and Wenger's study, a follow-up of older people noted that the friends that older people identified could change significantly, with some names disappearing, new ones being included, and friendship patterns and priorities changing.

The meaning and definition of friendship in later life have been explored by some researchers. Adams (1986), in one of the earlier studies of friendship, found that the women in this study defined friendships in terms of affective characteristics, and further detail has been offered by Roberto and Kimboko (1989) who found that older people in their study categorised friends according to whether they were 'likeables', 'confiders' or 'trustables'. Further work has elaborated the complexity of friendships among older people, a complexity which is not unique to older people, with friendships involving help and support, shared activities, trust, loyalty and commitment, to name but a few potential elements.

Emotional closeness and intimacy may be a feature of some friendships, but not all. Older people can and do have a range of relationships, some of which may be quite casual. Cheang (2002), for example, found that older people observed meeting in a fast-food restaurant defined their meetings as 'fun' and did not seek or welcome any further intimacy. Cheang's study explored the notion of 'play' in older adults' activities, noting that this is usually associated with children's activities, and arguing that it is a feature of older people's activities too.

The idea of older people's social activities as taking different forms, as do the social activities of all other age groups, challenges ideas that the only activities of value are those that involve close emotional connections. It also may go some way towards explaining findings of some studies that report that older people do not necessarily report themselves as lonely, even though they may have lifestyles and interaction patterns which could suggest that this would be the case. Victor et al (2002), for example, found that although 90% of the British population felt that loneliness was associated with old age, a historical analysis of survey data found that reported loneliness ranged from 5% to 9% of older people, and for those living alone had decreased from 32% in 1945 to 14% in 1999.

This suggests that older people may be engaging in social interaction more, or are thinking about it differently as opportunities beyond the family open up. These opportunities can include developments in lifelong learning – such as the University of the Third Age, which provides courses and programmes designed for older people – or, less formally, it can involve groups based around activities such as walking, dancing, music or history. Indeed, the options are innumerable, as they are for other age groups.

In this way older people can and do continue to be engaged in communities: either communities based around localities, or communities based around interests and activities. As technology develops, including computer and Internet technology, this engagement is likely to take different forms. The 'Silver Surfers' awards, organised by City and Guilds, demonstrate how older people are engaging in information technology (IT) and developing virtual communities. Chapter Four discussed issues of security and accessibility in public spaces, which can encourage or discourage community activity.

The message of this chapter, however, is not only on what older people get out of their families and communities, but also what they contribute – the notion of reciprocity. This may need some support to help it happen – training and access issues may need to be addressed. This is likely to be an investment that will pay substantial dividends, however, as older people remain engaged and active in their communities. The evidence suggests that within families they can make a huge contribution, most obviously through their grandparenting role, but the way in which they do this, based on energy, experience and the ability to take a long-term view, are ways in which they can make a contribution in wider communities.

Activities

The beginning of this chapter gave examples of different sorts of activities that older people have been engaged in, from community action to advisory roles. These examples challenge our ideas of older people as being inactive or confined to very traditional pursuits. The scope of activities that older people have been involved in is huge – examples from the groups that we have worked with have included exercise groups, outdoor pursuits (including abseiling), poetry and drama groups, advisory and campaigning groups and many more. What we need to think about, however, are the features or activities that make these successful, what older people like about them, what they contribute to them and what they get out of them.

Activities have different features – they can be spontaneous or organised, traditional or innovative, provided for or by older people, and diversionary or developmental, to name just a few dimensions. In all this variety, we can do little but think through the possible consequences and effects of these characteristics, moving to thinking through broad principles.

First, there are the characteristics of the origin of the activity – whether it is spontaneous or organised. Spontaneous activities, which may arise from people accidentally coming together and deciding to do things, have the virtue of being supported and desired by older people, rather than being imposed on them. These activities may include, for example, people meeting up and deciding to go to see a film, or to go and visit a local beauty spot. The spontaneity, however, depends on several things, including the capacity and resources being available to participants to do these things. Where people have good ideas, but not the resources, then activities cannot happen. Spontaneous activities also, by definition, are not regular or routinised, so they may lack the place and structure in people's lives that ensure that they happen often. While the joy of a spontaneous activity is that it is a surprise, if it is to be sustained then it needs to become more planned and scheduled.

What a spontaneous activity can do, however, is give people a sense of possibility, that there are choices and decisions they can make. The activity may develop into something more organised, but there is an important feature of the activity as being something chosen on the spur of the moment because of interest, curiosity and enthusiasm, rather than something that is routine and predictable.

Routine and organised activities, however, have the virtue of having many of the problems of access and availability ironed out. Deciding spontaneously to go to the theatre is easy if everyone has the resources to do it, tickets and transport are available, and the theatre can meet the needs of an audience who may have some health and physical difficulties. If everything comes together at the right time, then spontaneous activity can take place. In other circumstances some planning needs to happen, to make sure that everything goes as smoothly as possible. The downside of this planning is that the thinking that has to go into an activity makes it a more formal activity. Planning also comes with responsibility, and this may become onerous for whoever has taken it on. Activities that are organised by others, perhaps services or voluntary agencies, relieve some of the burden of organisation from older people, but also some of the control – it becomes more difficult to choose if the limitations are constantly emphasised in discussions about planning.

Another dimension of activity is whether it is traditional or innovatory. Traditional activities (such as gardening, bowling or ballroom dancing) have many positive aspects. Because they are traditional, people will have some understanding of them, and can weigh up whether to get involved or not. They may undergo a process of gradual involvement, where past interests and networks gradually become more important in their lives, rather than have the daunting prospect of taking a step into the unknown. In many ways, traditional activities match up with some of the debates about continuity in growing older, that an important part of enjoyment and quality of life as you grow older is the ability to build on existing lifestyles, rather than have an abrupt change. Engaging in traditional activities may, then, be an extension of lifelong interests and roles.

Traditional activities, however, may serve only to trap older people in the stereotypes of age, gender and ethnicity that they may find irksome. If many traditional activities are built around what is expected of older people, then these may become limiting rather than empowering, with people finding themselves involved in activities which are, for them, boring, however 'suitable' others may think. Activities that challenge expectation of older people, such as ideas about acceptable and gender-appropriate behaviour, may well be activities that are most liberating and enjoyable. Strenuous and adventurous activities, such as rock-climbing and abseiling, for example, can be tremendously powerful experiences for older people, partly because of the challenges involved. A scheme in the North East, for example, which took older people on abseiling courses, had been very much enjoyed by participants, who have remarked on how it challenged their expectations of themselves. Comments include some about how people had never thought that they would be able to do this, and how they had surprised themselves because they had completed the course, and how this had given them a sense of achievement and satisfaction. Not thinking that you could do or enjoy non-traditional activities, then, can be as much of a barrier as any physical difficulty.

The abseiling course was, of course, very carefully planned and organised, and led by a skilled group leader who was able to motivate people and increase their confidence. The discussion we have had elsewhere in this book about self-efficacy suggested that confidence in your ability to do things increases the likelihood of you becoming more active and involved generally, so supporting someone through tackling a physical challenge may lead to many other benefits in the way you approach other things in life. Challenges can be mental as well as physical, such as performing or public speaking, creative writing or learning a new language. Again these activities challenge stereotypes of later life as being a period of withdrawal and disengagement.

As mentioned above, in the description of the abseiling course, support and encouragement from a skilled instructor was needed before people felt able to take part. Other, less physically frightening activities may need similar levels of support, despite being relatively safe. In one Newcastle-based initiative, for example, exercise classes for older people were offered, but there was some reluctance among older people to take part. Investigating this reluctance, the organisers found that many were discouraged by the prospect of being taught by younger, fitter and thinner people who would not understand what it was like to be older, with possible physical problems and a dislike of the usual aerobic class music. In the end the group decided to train older people as fitness instructors, so that they could lead the classes. The result was greater recruitment and, in the words of one instructor, "a more comfortable and less competitive environment". Support for non-traditional activities may come in many forms, then, and may not just be about making the activity practical, but about making it accessible.

Exercise

Keep a diary for a week or review your past week, recording:

- interactions you have with your family and/or partner;
- interactions you have with friends;
- interactions you have with colleagues (this may be through formal work or other activities);
- interactions you have with people that you don't know.

At the end of this, answer the following questions:

1. How much help and support did you get from other people? What form did this take? What effect did it have?
2. How much help and support did you give to others? What form did this take? What effect did this have?

Now imagine that you are older – say 75 years old. You aren't working in paid employment, so money is a bit tight, and you're less mobile than you used to be. What engagement would you like to maintain? What adaptations and changes might you need to make? What engagement would you like to stop?

References

Adams, R.G. (1986) 'A look at friendship and aging', *Generations*, vol 10, pp 40-3.

Biggs, S., Philipson, C. and Kingston, P. (1995) *Elder abuse in perspective*, Buckingham and Philadelphia, PA: Open University Press.

Cheang, M. (2002) 'Older adults' frequent visits to a fast-food restaurant', *Journal of Aging Studies*, vol 16, no 3, pp 303-21.

Cylwik, H. (2002) 'Expectations of inter-generational reciprocity among older Greek Cypriot migrants in London', *Ageing and Society*, vol 22, no 5, pp 599-614.

Finchum, T. and Weber, J.A. (2000) 'Applying continuity theory to older adult friendships', *Journal of Aging and Identity*, vol 5, no 3, pp 159-68.

Glass, T.A., Seeman, T.E., Herzog, A.R., Kahn, R. and Berkmann, L.F. (1995) 'Change in productive: MacArthur studies of successful ageing', *Journal of Gerontology: Social Sciences*, 50B S65-S76.

Hugman, R. (1995) 'The implications of the term "elder abuse" for problem definition and response in health and social welfare', *Journal of Social Policy*, vol 24, no 4, pp 493-507.

Jerrome, D. and Wenger, G.C. (1999) 'Stability and change in late-life friendships', *Ageing and Society*, vol 19, pp 661-76.

Mills, T.L. (1999) 'When grandchildren grow up: role transition and family solidarity among baby boomer grandchildren and their grandparents', *Journal of Aging Studies*, vol 13, no 2, pp 219-39.

Nelson, D. (2002) 'Violence against elderly people: a neglected problem', *The Lancet*, 5 October, vol 360, p 1094.

Nursing Standard (2003) February, vol 17, no 22, p 7.

Philipson, C., Bernard, M., Philips, J. and Ogg, J. (2000) *The family and community life of older people: Social networks and social support in three urban areas*, London: Routledge.

Qureshi, H. and Walker, A. (1989) *The caring relationship*, London: Tavistock.

Reed, J., Pearson, P., Douglas, B., Swinburne, S. and Wilding, H. (2002) 'Going home from hospital – an appreciative inquiry study', *Health and Social Care and the Community*, vol 10, no 1, pp 36-45.

Roberto, K.A. and Kimboko, P.J. (1989) 'Friendship patterns in later life: definitions and maintenance patterns', *International Journal of Aging and Human Development*, vol 28, pp 9-19.

Thompson, P. (1999) 'The role of grandparents when parents part or die: some reflections on the mythical decline of the extended family', *Ageing and Society*, vol 19, no 4, pp 471-504.

Victor, C.R., Scambler, S.J., Shah, S., Cook, D.G., Harrisã, T., Rinkã, E. and De Wildeã, S. (2002) 'Has loneliness amongst older people increased? An investigation into variations between cohorts', *Ageing and Society*, vol 22, pp 585-97.

Waldrop, D.P., Weber, J.A., Herald, S.L., Pruett, J., Cooper, K., Juozapavicius, K. (1999) 'Wisdom and life experience: how grandfathers mentor their grandchildren', *Journal of Aging and Identity*, vol 4, no 1, pp 33-46.

EIGHT

Money and financial resources in later life

Glenda Cook

Contents

Introduction	128
Key issues that concern older people regarding money	129
The impact of income on the quality of later life	130
A time to spend money that has accrued throughout life	130
Income: only one of many resources	131
Harsh times: life on a low income	132
Poor benefit take-up	134
Inappropriate housing leading to liquidity problems	136
Financial literacy	137
Money, disability, ill-health and frailty	139
Direct payments and brokerage schemes	140
A national asset: older people's contribution to society	141
Conclusion	143

Key points

- Financial resources are important in determining the quality of older peoples' lives.
- While their everyday expenses may be modest, they are vulnerable to sudden demands on their pockets.
- Financial literacy is increasingly important for older people managing their finances.

"I've got enough to live on, I mean compared to some I'm well off, but it could all go to pot tomorrow, if I had some expenses, and I don't know how I'd get back on an even keel."

"I'm not going to go on a cruise, that's for sure. But I don't mind that much – I probably wouldn't like it anyway." (Comments made by older people in a discussion of finances in older age)

Introduction

Reading the comments above, the importance of money and financial resources for older people becomes immediately apparent, both in the opportunities they offer and the security they afford. Living costs money, even the most basic level of keeping warm and fed, and more if living involves maintaining and developing activities and relationships. Discussions elsewhere in this book, about quality of life, engagement and activity, show that well-being is about much more than just keeping warm and fed.

The material for this chapter has been drawn in part from a commissioned literature review that also involved some discussion groups with panels of experts, including older people (Reed et al, 2003). In the course of this review we talked to various other groups of older people in a range of circumstances, to find out their concerns and experiences.

There has been considerable discussion, during the past decade, about older people's monetary resources. How much income older people have and the plight of those on low incomes are the key issues that have concerned those who have campaigned to improve the financial circumstances of older people. These are important concerns in modern western societies, where there are strong associations between notions of citizenship and choice and control. In such societies consumer spending power is seen as a vehicle for exercising choice and control. Although there is evidence that there is rising affluence among those over 65, a significant proportion of older people continue to experience the poorest economic circumstances in the population. For this reason these issues will continue to dominate the discussion about older people's financial circumstances. In this chapter we want to move beyond the reporting of these important discussions to explore the impact that money has on the quality of life of older people. We were prompted to do this by the following comment that was made by an older man during a discussion about this topic:

> "The importance of money rests not in its monetary value, but in what it enables you to do and in the sense of financial security that it gives."

He suggested that money is a commodity that affects every aspect of life and its value is far more than its economic worth. Money is a vehicle that enables individuals to experience a sense of control over what happens in their life and to make decisions about how they wish to live their life. In this sense, money is not an end in itself, but it is a means to an end whereby financial resources provide the means to consider possibilities and the resource to pursue goals and aspirations.

The topics covered in this chapter will address those issues that concern older people about their economic circumstances and will discuss the literature that has developed about these issues. To do this we have drawn on discussions with older people. In this way the topics that are covered address those issues that concern older people rather than the issues that dominate the literature. All too often the priorities of older people have been overshadowed by those of younger people in public and academic debates about money and we intend to avoid this in the following discussion.

Key issues that concern older people regarding money

The people whom we spoke to indicated that older people have major concerns about their income and how they spend their money. Following retirement the majority of people experience a decrease in their income and they have little opportunity to increase it. As age advances, the ability to earn continues to decrease. Hence, financial assets and income must provide the monetary resources for an unpredictable and perhaps lengthy period of time.

In addition, some people face the prospect that the real value of their income will decrease as a result of poor indexation (Johnson et al, 1998). Evandrou and Falkingham (1993) have argued that the changes that were made to the annual process of pension adjustments, which were introduced in 1980, subsequently led to a decrease in the relative value of the state pension. Their calculations led them to conclude that, if the system remained unchanged, the state pension would only be worth 10% of average earnings by 2020.

Uncertainties about the value of a relatively fixed income, and the period of time that this money must cover, contribute to older people experiencing anxiety about their financial situation and how they will manage in advanced old age. Well-publicised scandals concerning pension fraud only serve to enhance this anxiety and to highlight the vulnerable financial situation of older people. The difficulty in understanding finances in later life has emerged as a recognised problem from the scandals that have been reported in recent years. This has led many people to make inappropriate financial decisions in their retirement plans and has contributed to people living on incomes lower than they had anticipated.

Another key factor that changes as chronological age advances is spending priorities. The priorities of earlier years – mortgages and bringing up children – no longer exist. These are replaced by different and more unpredictable financial commitments. Although there is a general trend for the older population to incur expenditure for payment for care, aids, equipment and adaptations to the home, it is difficult for an individual to know in advance what their particular needs will be and to plan accordingly.

The combination of these factors, stable or reduced income and paying for care and housing, have an impact on the way that older people experience financial security or insecurity in later life. Let us explore these issues first by taking a glance at the lives of those who are living in contrasting financial circumstances – the lives of those who consider themselves to be financially well off and those living on low incomes. This will be followed by a discussion of the factors that contribute to older people existing on incomes lower than they need. The final part of this chapter will focus on paying for care and how the arrangements for this have changed in recent years.

The impact of income on the quality of later life

At the turn of the 21st century an increasing proportion of those entering retirement have diverse financial resources including savings, financial assets, money tied up in housing, and private/stakeholder/occupational pensions. In 2001, 40% of pensioners had incomes high enough to make them liable for income tax and 2% were liable for the higher rate of tax (United Kingdom Parliament, House of Commons, 2001). This situation contrasts sharply with previous generations of pensioners who entered retirement with little other monetary resources than their state pension. It is generally acknowledged that the younger generation of pensioners have more disposable capital and they tend to better off financially than older pensioners (Gnich and Gilhooly, 2001; Villa et al, 2001).

Those entering retirement in recent years do so with relatively good physical health and many will live to an advanced age. In addition, one of the consequences of the major organisational downsizing that has taken place during the last decade in many industries has been an increase in people in their mid to late fifties taking early retirement. These factors have changed the face of retirement in the UK. Retirement is a time when older people with disposable income are able to take advantage of the increasing range of leisure and educational opportunities that have developed in response to demand.

A time to spend money that has accrued throughout life

Those entering retirement are no longer bound by the constraints of work commitments and many have buying power to realise personal objectives and aspirations. Some of the items that the older people that we spoke to spent their money on were:

- personal items such as clothing and mobile phones;
- leisure and learning activities;
- long-standing and new interests;
- travel;
- maintaining their home;
- renewing household items;
- gifts for family and friends;
- intergenerational transfers of money (such as paying for their children's mortgages and grandchildren's education);
- services (such as domestic help) and equipment;
- private healthcare.

According to George (1993) the value of income rests with its potential to be "an empowering resource that fosters a sense of control" or "an illusion of control" over one's circumstances (George, 1993, pp 19-20). With enough money and good health it is possible to make decisions and to carry those decisions out. In this way independence is maintained. Perhaps independence is enhanced as individuals make the transition from asset accrual, which dominates the efforts of many people in their earlier years, to experiencing the freedom to spend the money that they have earned. Having disposable income, money left over after necessary expenditure, enables older people to do what they want to do and when they want to do it. A quick glance at the above list suggests that money is used to provide the means to engage in meaningful, personal activity and to take part in reciprocal activities in their relationships.

The final two points on the list refer to the use of money to provide the means to pay for support and care. With money, older people can reduce their vulnerability to possible limitations of what is provided by the state by reducing their reliance on public services. Paying for support and care gives control to the older person over the type of service that they use and when and how they use them. Having the finances to pay for these items has become increasingly important. As a result of health and social care policy changes, provision by state services in the UK has become increasingly restricted. Also, the boundary between the NHS and social care has moved, with some of the services that were previously provided by health now provided by social care agencies. This is important because the services that are provided by health in the UK are paid for by central taxation and are free at the point of delivery. Those services that are provided by social care agencies are means tested and the service user is required to pay a contribution for the services that they receive. For these reasons, having the financial means to pay for support and care provides a sense of security that they will have the resources to enable them to cope with the circumstances that they may face in their later years.

Income: only one of many resources

There is no doubt that income has a significant impact on the lives of older people. Danigelis and McIntosh (2001) argue, however, that there is an overemphasis on the importance of income in modern western society. They draw on the work of Arber and Ginn (1991) who suggested that income was only one of the many types of material resources that older people possess. Other material resources include financial assets, housing and car ownership. They also take the view that caring resources (supportive and healthcare resources) and health resources (physical well-being and optimal functional abilities) are of equal importance to monetary resources in determining the quality of life of an older person. At the level of personal experience, these resources complement each other and can be used interchangeably. Monetary resources, as discussed above, can be used to purchase caring resources when health resources deteriorate (see Clarke et al, 1998). Non-monetary resources can also be perceived as functional equivalents to monetary resources. This is illustrated through a situation where family members provide informal care or assistance with house maintenance and no financial transaction takes place.

The nature of the interchange between these different resources means that the impact of deteriorating health can be mediated by material and caring resources. Also the effects of having a low income can be lessened by health and caring resources. Conversely, those who have limited caring and health resources experience the greatest vulnerability if they also have minimal monetary resources.

Harsh times: life on a low income

From our discussions with people who were living on a low income, it was evident that they experienced a harsh existence as they struggled to meet their day-to-day needs. Their lives were dominated by making compromises to manage within their limited budget. For example, if they wanted to take part in inexpensive activities they had to make decisions about buying "cheaper, out of date and poor quality food" rather than fresh and nutritious food that would contribute to their health. They also had to adopt other ways of economising to set money aside to pay for bills. They were unable to budget for new clothing and had to request clothing as gifts or had to shop in second-hand stores. Consequently, they described their lives as "living on the breadline". They were not able to afford "a little bit of entertainment" or to take part in activities that would be fulfilling.

Similar circumstances were described by Whetstone (2002) when reporting on an ethnographic study of the lives of 50 people, aged 70 and over, who were living in a deprived area of central London. She noted that the key money management strategies that the participants adopted were to cut back on non-essential items such as clothing or reduce their social activities. She concluded that these strategies diminished the social life of older people and contributed to other problems including poor physical and mental health, loneliness and isolation.

Cost-cutting strategies have been found to extend to commodities that are generally considered as essential. For example, Palmer et al (2002), when assembling the indicators of income poverty, identified that those who were dependent on a state pension as their main source of income spent a quarter less on food than other pensioners. In a report by the Citizens Advice Bureaux, *The fuel picture*, older people are identified as suffering from inadequate heating of their homes in order to reduce fuel costs (Monroe and Marks, 2002). Many older people live in poor, energy-inefficient homes and they have inadequate household incomes to enable them to heat their houses. Although the winter fuel payment is made to older people as a way of addressing the problem of fuel poverty, this has not resolved the problem because annual incidents of hypothermia persist.

In a study by Humphrey and Calder (1990) it was identified that having a telephone was a luxury that many older people could not afford. For many people living in the UK, having a phone in a house is an essential commodity as it enables easy and quick communication with others (Gordon et al, 2000). For older people, access to a telephone also offers the security that they can maintain contact with others and they can contact the emergency services when the need arises. In Humphrey and Calder's study, other unaffordable items included clothes, redecorating and repairing the house, replacing worn out or broken furniture and renewing bedding. These findings contribute to the evidence that suggests that older people who live on low incomes experience relative deprivation and social exclusion, as they are unable to purchase socially perceived necessities (Howarth et al, 2001). Whetstone (2002) summed this up by stating that inclusion in wider society requires an "individual to have access to the range of resources that a majority of their fellow citizens have" (p 17).

In addition to living with the reality of social exclusion, this group of older people also experience the effects of doing without and restriction in their day-to-day life, year after year. They live with the reality that they can make little provision for a 'rainy day' (Kempson et al, 2002). Financial insecurity, diminished control over circumstances, financial dependency, constant stress and anxiety, lower life satisfaction and diminished feelings of self-worth are therefore common experiences (George, 1993; Gnich and Gilhooly, 2001). It can be concluded from this that the impact of living on a low income in later life has wide-ranging and serious effects on the quality of an older person's life.

Factors that contribute to low income

While the earlier discussion in this chapter alluded to the changing financial circumstances of retired people, low incomes continue to be expected and accepted as being part of old age in Britain (Evans and Falkingham, 1997; Mein et al, 2000). This sector of the population continues to be disproportionately represented in the lower income bracket with approximately 2.75 million pensioners, a quarter of all pensioners, occupying the bottom quintile of income distribution (DWP, 2001). The evidence suggests that women, immigrants, the very old and those with broken work records or a long history of low-paid work are over-represented in this group (Bartlett, 2001; Bardasi and Jenkins, 2002).

Low income status in old age also affects many people who have attempted to accumulate assets and contribute to pension schemes in the belief that they are working toward financial security for their later years. Those at the lower end of the salary scales, however, generate moderate investments and perhaps a small pension that is enough to bring their income above the point that they would qualify for Income Support and means-tested benefits. In comparison to those qualifying for minimum income guarantee and means-tested benefits, they are little better off, if not in a worse financial situation in some cases (Hedges, 1998; Parker, 2000; Whetstone, 2000). This situation has come to be known as the 'poverty trap' – a situation that does not reward hard work and savings (Parker, 2000).

Poor benefit take-up

The previous discussion suggests that many older people are living in financial circumstances where they are eligible for a range of benefits. Yet there is considerable evidence that benefit eligibility in the elderly population exceeds actual take-up (Corden, 1995; Flately, 1999; Bramley et al, 2000; Parker, 2000).

The implications of this for older people who are living on lower incomes than necessary has focused researchers' and policy makers' attention on understanding the barriers to benefit take-up (see, for example, Costigan et al, 1999; Bramley et al, 2000; Kempson et al, 2002). The barriers to benefit take-up reported in the literature can be broadly categorised as attitudinal, knowledge and skills, physical, and process barriers.

Attitudinal barriers include the following:

• the belief that there is stigma associated with claiming many benefits;
• negative images of claimants as 'spongers' or 'scroungers';
• the threat that benefit claims present to personal pride and independence;
• a dislike of the procedures that benefit claiming involves;
• an objection to means-testing procedures.

Knowledge and skills barriers include:

• lack of information about eligibility to claim and receive benefits;
• lack of understanding of what to apply for, who to approach and what information should be disclosed when making a claim;
• lack of understanding of the system, leading to fear that they may lose the little income that they have when applying for other benefits;
• those who have poor literacy skills have real difficulties in negotiating the processes for claiming;
• situations where English is the second language, communication with benefit agency staff is problematic and completion of the necessary forms is difficult.

Physical barriers present difficulties in:

• accessing the benefit claim office – this may be particularly problematic for those with mobility problems: the location and opening times of the claims office may impede access;
• using available services – those with hearing impairments face difficulties using telephone helpline services;

- fulfilling the claim process – those with visual impairments are unable to complete forms without the necessary assistance.

Process barriers concern:

- limited or user-unfriendly information;
- complex benefit claim processes;
- complex language associated with claim processes – for example, the term 'gateway benefit', which refers to benefits that lead to others;
- the existence of faceless information services;
- the perception that benefit agency offices lack privacy.

There has been a transition from developing knowledge of the factors that contribute to poor benefit take-up, to the development of approaches to improve older people's awareness of the benefits that they are eligible for and to encourage them to claim. Some strategies are directed at specific problems known to reduce benefit take-up. For example, the Better Government for Older People programme has piloted a range of personal approaches to encourage older people to take up benefits rather than to continue to live in poverty. These initiatives included ways to alert older people to their eligibility for benefits, establishing information surgeries situated in convenient locations such as high streets, and creating home visiting and dedicated telephone helpline services (Chang et al, 2001; Kempson et al, 2002).

Other initiatives have addressed problems concerning the complexity of the claim process. There is no doubt that specialist knowledge and well-developed literacy skills are needed to complete the claims forms. In response to this, Citizens Advice Bureaux in the UK have developed services to guide and support people in their claims.

Alternatively there has been the development of strategies that promote benefit take-up through system-wide approaches that address many of the known barriers to accessing this type of income. This is illustrated through the way that the winter fuel allowance is paid to pensioners who are living in the UK. This is an annual universal benefit that is paid to every woman over the age of 60 and every man over the age of 65 regardless of their financial circumstances. The direct payment of this allowance minimises the physical and process barriers to take-up. Although people's perceptions of benefits are highly negative, in this situation the benefit is regarded as an entitlement arising from citizenship. This results in little or no stigma being associated with receipt of this benefit. The difficulty with this approach to the distribution of benefits is that it may not be the most effective nor the best use of public money with respect to the objective of reducing pensioner poverty.

Reorganisation of the benefit claim process to a system where only a single claim is required for all benefits has been discussed in policy and academic literature (see, for example, Costigan et al,1999). This would reduce the complexity of the current claim system and ensure that the claimant would be assessed for a range of benefits – those that they do know about and also those that they are unaware of. These examples highlight the range of efforts that have been made to improve the situation that has resulted in older people living on incomes lower than they need to.

The changes to the payment of benefits via automatic credit transfer, planned for 2003, will present new challenges and perhaps new barriers to the take-up of benefits. Older people are concerned that these changes have been introduced with no consultation. The changes to the payment of benefits and pensions have been introduced to give people a wider choice over where to access their benefit cash as part of the government's social and financial inclusion agenda. From an organisational perspective this is a cost-effective way of managing the system of benefit payments as administration costs will be reduced. For some older people, these changes will have social and health implications. To those who live alone, going to the post office is a weekly social event and an opportunity to be with other people. When they no longer do this they may become further isolated, lonely and depressed. There will also be a cost implication for the individual, as people tend to live nearer to a post office than to a bank. By contrast, those with high levels of disability who experience difficulty in accessing post offices and who rely on someone else to collect their pension and benefits may be helped by the pending changes (Kempson and Whyley, 2001).

The changes will create the need to develop new skills to manage bank accounts and use modern banking technologies (Rooney, 2002). Some older people who have bypassed the computer society will be directly launched into it, and they will be challenged to develop computer skills. In response to these difficulties, telephone support lines and guidance documents are available to support people with the new payment systems. Help the Aged is concerned that older people require additional support to cope with these changes and they are developing an information leaflet that provides advice and guidance specifically aimed at this population.

Whatever changes take place, they need to take into consideration the views of older people about what is appropriate and most acceptable to them. If this does not happen, the lives of older people will be negatively affected and the problems that have been widely reported, of pensioner poverty and poor benefit take-up, will persist.

Inappropriate housing leading to liquidity problems

A large proportion of older people have their wealth held in the form of housing equity. Some live in large, old properties that are costly to run and maintain. For those who have a high income following retirement, remaining in their property and meeting the housing cost is a matter of personal choice. There are many older people, however, who live in circumstances where housing costs are high and their income is low. Feinstein and McFadden (1989) describe the situation that is experienced by older people as excess or inappropriate housing wealth. Downsizing from a large, expensive property to a smaller, more cost-efficient one is one way of responding to this situation although, as Chapter Four has pointed out, reducing available space might not be a good decision in the long term. Disney et al (1978) discuss this and they conclude that there is little evidence that older people are more likely to move than any other sector of the population in order to downsize housing wealth to release capital.

From a purely economic perspective this is perplexing. Older people continue to struggle to meet rising housing costs and to economise in other ways, when they have housing wealth that they could use to lessen their financial burdens. Considering this situation from a different perspective does shed light on this situation. In recent years there has been an increasing body of literature in the field of social gerontology concerning the meaning of home. In this literature it is argued that a house is more than merely a building where personal capital is tied up. A house is an individual's home that is composed of memories and represents a lifetime of achievement (Golant, 1998; Heywood et al, 2002). From this perspective it is not surprising that decisions about relocation to release capital are difficult.

One response to this situation has been the development of equity release schemes. These schemes enable older people to continue to live in their property and to release some of the capital that is tied up in the building. The people that we spoke to indicated that these schemes provided a wider range of options in later life. For some, the process of equity release reduced some of the burden of living in expensive housing, and for others they were able to access money to finance activities, such as travel, that they had planned for their later years.

Financial literacy

Every source of income in later life has complex rules and processes to negotiate (Hedges, 1998). This is evident if you take a few moments to reflect on the processes that are associated with accessing money from state/occupational/private pensions, investments and savings, state benefits and tax credits. By suggesting that you undertake this simple task, we were making the assumption that you had knowledge of these various sources of income and this may not be the case. Indeed, many people do not know what they are entitled to; consequently they do not access or claim their money. One person that we spoke to told the following story, which illustrates how lack of knowledge has the effect of unnecessarily reducing income:

> "The pension department in the place I worked in write out every year in April to say that the cost of living has gone up so much, so you are going to get that much more money. They got back a letter from a widow saying 'well that's not really good for me' and could she please have the money. She did not want this rise – could she

please have the money. The pensions department looked into this to see what was going on. In fact her husband had died two years previously. There was something like £10,000 in his bank account and that money was actually hers, from her widow's pension. She didn't think that she was entitled to it so she had been living off the state pension for the last few years. They had to explain to her that that was a widow's pension and the money was hers."

The bewildering range of financial choices, poor quality information, poor advice, changes to taxation rules, hybridisation of financial services, and the development of e-commerce compound the difficulty that older people experience in understanding their financial resources (Lord, 2001).

There is evidence that people are generally not financially literate, and therefore are not able to competently manage their monetary resources (Cutler, 1997; FSA, 1998; Walker and Davies, 2001). Older people have particular difficulties in understanding their finances with respect to banking, credit cards and bills (NIACE, 2001). They are also challenged by the necessity to make well-informed decisions about their relatively fixed income. Sometimes this takes place when physical and mental abilities are declining and this may affect their ability to make sound judgements.

Older women, in particular, who experience an end to their relationship or are widowed have been identified as experiencing particular problems. Although they may have been responsible for making short-term financial decisions throughout their marriage, the responsibility for longer-term financial decisions may have rested with their partner. When their circumstances change they need to acquire new skills and knowledge to manage their finances (Bartlett, 2001).

According to NIACE (2001) older people tend to rely on those who support them to obtain information and advice about their financial decisions because there is a general mistrust of financial suppliers and their advisors. As the problems of financial literacy pervade the entire population, this may not lead to the best financial decisions for the older person. They need support to make sense of all the financial information that they confront and in recent years many initiatives have been developed with the aim of increasing financial competency of older people to help them to manage their own finances. Examples of these initiatives include the development of pre-retirement courses (Pre-Retirement Association, 2000), financial training programmes that are tailored to the needs of older people ('Financial literacy and older people' project and 'It doesn't add up' project, undertaken by NIACE) and campaigns for all financial information to be 'financially literacy proofed' (Lord, 2001). The key objective of these initiatives is to raise general awareness of the need for financial literacy and for older people to develop competencies to manage money. These approaches may result in a situation whereby those entering retirement are better prepared to face the challenges of financial decisions in later life.

Money, disability, ill-health and frailty

Levels of disability, ill-health and functional dependence on others to meet personal needs, as a consequence of frailty, increase with increasing age. Around four million adults aged 65 and over report long-standing sickness or disability (Jarvis and Tinker, 1999; Palmer et al, 2002). The direct and indirect costs associated with this for the individual and their family/carers are well reported. For example, Argyle's study of poverty, disability and older carers highlights the material costs of meeting living and caring expenses. These include the payment of substitute care, purchase of domestic help, aids and adaptations to the home, special furniture, and specialised food and equipment (Argyle, 2001). Spending money on these items takes up much of the household income and erodes the older person's financial assets. In response to this, Argyle found that many people exercised financial caution when making decisions about what to spend their money on, often doing without those things that would have improved their day-to-day lives.

Local authorities are required to provide aids, adaptations and services to disabled people to enable them to live independent lives. It could be argued that the direct costs of disability and chronic ill-health will not be borne by the older person and their carers. There is evidence, however, that the processes of assessment of need (to determine eligibility for aids, equipment and adaptations to the home) are not responsive to the needs of older people and their carers. For example, a review of complaints by the Commission for Local Administration in England (1993) identified that there were unacceptable waiting times for the very items older people require to enable them to live in their own home. One consequence of this situation is that older people, if they have the money to do so, finance these items themselves (Age Concern England, 1996). Those living in low-income households are unlikely to have sufficient money to pay for necessary equipment and assistance, resulting in the practical demands that are made on the informal carer increasing (Argyle, 2001). As one in four carers of older people are over retirement age themselves, this increases the physical, social and emotional burden of caring, which has an impact on the carer's health (Howard, 2001).

Older people who are living on modest incomes experience difficulties and worries about meeting the cost of care and assistance because they are required to make a contribution to their package of care. While this financial commitment may be problematic, other difficulties arise when the package of care exceeds the funding ceiling that is set by the local authority. In this situation, the older person can pay the full cost of additional care, which may outstrip their income, investments and assets. When they cannot meet the cost of the additional care, they face the decision to move to a care home.

These issues surface in the debate about payment for long-term care that has been a highly contentious topic in recent years. During the early 1990s there were numerous reports in the press that the older generation was being subjected to asset stripping. Older people experienced great concern, not only about the move to care and what life would be like in a care home, but also whether long-term care would be available to them if they were unable to pay for it. This culminated in the setting up of the Royal Commission on Long Term Care (United Kingdom Parliament, 1999), which set the background for changes to the regulations for the payment of long-term care. Concessions have been made in that healthcare is now differentiated from social care, but there remain many discussions about means testing and the payment of long-term care.

It is clear from the above discussion that monetary resources are used by older people to pay for the direct and indirect costs of frailty, ill-health and disability. For those who are able to pay for care, assistance, equipment and housing adaptations, money has an additional value – it gives control to the older person over what is provided and when it is provided. They are able to retain some independence in circumstances when they are increasingly reliant on others for help. While they may no longer be able to respond to their own personal needs, they are able to make choices about how their needs are addressed in ways that are most acceptable to them.

Older people with low incomes find themselves in situations where they are reliant on the services that are provided by the state. Consequently, they experience limited control over their circumstances and this has the potential to threaten self-respect and to erode their dignity. In acknowledgement of this, direct payment and brokerage schemes have been developed to create a way of increasing service users' involvement in decisions about their life (United Kingdom Parliament, 1997; Hasler et al, 1999).

Direct payments and brokerage schemes

Direct payments allow service users to be given direct funding to enable them to purchase help and support, as they need it, rather than having care packages imposed on them. As such, direct payment provides a means by which service users can be empowered in making decisions and having more control over the help that they receive. Clarke and Spafford (2001), in their evaluation of a pilot of the direct payment scheme, found that, while the scheme generally provided a high level of service, there were some barriers and problems, including:

- People did not take up the scheme because they had limited social networks and could not find people to do the caring. Some also found it a daunting prospect.
- Care managers found it difficult to take ownership of the scheme and did not have a support scheme.
- Minority ethnic groups had a low take-up.
- There were tensions between empowerment and protection – while the social services department (SSD) wanted to promote choice and control for older people, they also wanted to ensure that they were not exploited or put at risk.

• The pilot benefited from proactive support from the SSD involved, and from a proactive policy of offering the scheme to service users.

Clarke and Spafford (2001) concluded that the pilot offered much to service users and potentially enhanced their choice and control over services. For some older people, the responsibilities of direct payment may be onerous and unwelcome, particularly in respect of accounting and employment responsibilities. In response to this, brokerage schemes have developed. These schemes attempt to reduce the service users' responsibilities, while maintaining their involvement in decisions about their care.

The brokerage scheme provided by Age Concern, Newcastle upon Tyne, for example, offers support and advice for people wanting to use direct payments to employ carers. The workers in this scheme offer support in drafting advertisements and job descriptions, managing the interview process, and providing a 24-hour on-call service to address issues as they arise (for example, gaps in care resulting from carers' sickness). The older person determines how much support they require from the brokerage service, which can range from simply giving advice to carrying out the entire process on behalf of the service user. In this way the older person is involved in managing the services that they receive in ways that suit them.

These schemes provide mechanisms to involve older people in the decisions that affect their lives and to have choices. Although there are real benefits to direct payment and brokerage schemes, there are risks and responsibilities for the older person. Prior to embarking on what may be a better system for organising and managing care, the older person and their supporters need to understand the challenges that they will face and to develop the skills and knowledge to address problems that may arise.

A national asset: older people's contribution to society

It would be neglectful to leave a discussion about monetary resources in later life without mentioning the contribution that older people make to society. Some older people continue to participate in the workforce while others make a non-monetary contribution to society. For example, many older people provide childcare for grandchildren, domestic work, voluntary work, informal care, and learning activities, while also helping friends and neighbours. In addition, many older people participate in government committees set up specifically to involve them in priority-setting decisions for public spending (Barnes et al, 2002).

It is beyond the remit of this chapter to explore all of the different types of contributions that older people make. As our discussions with older people particularly highlighted their continuing contribution to society as grandparents, volunteers, unpaid work in committees and care giving, we will discuss each of these topics briefly.

Harper (2000) highlighted the way that increasing longevity has had an impact on ties across the generations. Children are now more likely to have surviving grandparents who are more likely to occupy this position for a longer proportion of their lives. An increasing number of older people provide childcare for their grandchildren, to enable their own children to work. In these situations there may or may not be monetary exchanges, and the activity serves to increase the interdependence between older and younger members of the family (Smith et al, 2001). There is evidence that grandchildren benefit emotionally and cognitively from having a close relationship with a grandparent (Adkins, 1999) and this may contribute to the older person's sense of well-being. Excessive demands to provide childcare, however, can have negative consequences, such as decreased social networking, and increases in stress for the grandparent (Davidhizar et al, 2000).

It is estimated that 50% of the adult population of the UK do voluntry work at least once a year (Lynn and Davis Smith, 1991) and a significant proportion are older people. The motivation behind volunteering is not just altruism, personal interest or merely a response to direct requests. Volunteering also involves social benefits, wider social networks, physical and mental fitness, meaningful activity, a sense of purpose, and new skills and experience (Dean and Morton, 1995; Krause and Shaw, 2000; Wardell et al, 2000; Reed et al, 2002). Volunteering, therefore, serves multiple purposes that meet the needs of those using and providing services. In recent years, policy makers have had high expectations of volunteers and voluntary organisations (Volunteering Unit, 1995) to increase their range of activity and contribution to service provision. Nonetheless there are policy and contracting practices that present organisational barriers to the extended involvement of older volunteers. As the policy and regulatory framework for the voluntary sector is developing, careful consideration needs to be given to support and value the contribution of older volunteers to maintain their commitment to this type of activity.

Another form of volunteering has developed in recent years – participating in committees to give the views of older people. There has been considerable emphasis on the involvement of older people in priority-setting and service-planning groups in recent government policy. From the perspective of the volunteers this type of involvement is important, although it can equate to unpaid work. It is generally accepted that expenses will be met, but there are real hidden costs to participation, such as purchasing suitable clothing. If this type of activity is to be maintained and encouraged, it needs to be fully funded as a valuable and recognised activity.

The contribution of older people to the provision of unpaid care is significant. Older people are more likely to be spouse carers in contrast to younger carers and they are likely to spend long periods of time caring (Howard, 2001). For these reasons the physical and emotional burden of care is considerable. The financial cost of care poses additional burdens, as there are additional care-related costs to meet, such as heating, clothing and laundry. In situations where alternative personal care is required, the older person may have to make a contribution to the package of care or to pay for this out of their savings. In situations where the older carer perceives that their financial situation has deteriorated, this has been attributed to the charges for services that they have faced (Holzausen and Pearlman, 2000).

This discussion has been an attempt to give illustrations of the way that older people make an important contribution to society. Often the contribution is unrecognised, unpaid and unrewarded. This poses a major challenge: to rethink the way that making a contribution to society is conceptualised, to include both monetary and non-monetary contributions as valued resources.

Conclusion

The overriding conclusion that can be drawn from the conversations that we have had with older people is that money is valued, not as an end in itself, but as a means to an end. The value of money rests in what it enables you to do and in the sense of financial security that it gives. An enjoyable and satisfying later life is one where there are possibilities to pursue goals and aspirations, and to have enough money to be able to meet the costs of living in modern society. These costs include more than being able to pay for the essentials of food, heating and clothing. The cost of living refers to having the money to access the range of resources that fellow citizens accept as essential commodities and the activities that others enjoy. Without the monetary resources to do this, older people experience exclusion from a society that is dominated by notions of consumerism.

There has been extensive research and campaigning about the plight of older people who are living on low incomes. There is no doubt that the lives of older people living in these circumstances are harsh and impoverished. This is a grinding and never-ending experience. State benefits and pension credits have been made available to improve the financial circumstances of those who are living in these circumstances. Older people, however, have a general dislike of the means-testing processes used to determine eligibility for welfare benefits, resulting in problems with benefit take-up. These issues are well recognised and there is no doubt that campaigns will continue in the future to alter the plight of so many older people.

Exercise

Find out how much the basic state pension is for a single person or a couple. Now make a list of your expenditure over the last month. This should include food, heating and fuel bills, Council Tax, telephone bills, clothing and entertainment. It should not include hire purchase payments or credit card bills, because if you were living on a pension, you would be unlikely to be given credit. You should, however, make a note of the total sum you owe and what you have spent the money on.

Now compare your expenditure over the last month with the pension (applying the single or the couple rate depending on your personal circumstances). How do they compare?

If you had to live on a basic pension, would your lifestyle have to change? What could you economise on? Would your spending priorities change? Would you have been able to afford the things that you are paying for on hire purchase schemes or credit cards?

Now think through the cost implications of getting more frail. If your mobility decreased and you were unable to drive, how much could you afford for taxis? If you needed to keep warm, how much could you increase your heating bill or expenditure on warm clothing? If you needed help with housework, how much could you afford to pay (and how much would it cost – check with your local social services department for costs and charges, and any means testing that might affect the amount you would have to pay). Might there be any other cost implications of getting more frail (for example, in modifying your house, buying services or help)? Are there any sources of help with these? How could you access them, and what are the eligibility criteria?

Now think about how you would cope with an emergency. Imagine that your roof started to leak, or your house or flat needed rewiring. How much might this cost? Imagine that the washing machine or cooker stopped working. What would be the minimum charge to get someone to see if it could be repaired? Would it be worth paying, or should you just get a new one? If you need another one, what would be the cheapest? Are there any places locally where you can buy cheap, perhaps reconditioned appliances? Do they have a guarantee? What would be the delivery charge?

What other possible sources of income might you have? What are the restrictions on income – how much could you earn without losing benefits?

Can you afford to grow older?

References

Adkins, V.K. (1999) 'Grandparents as a national asset: a brief note', *Activities, Adaptation and Aging*, vol 24, no 1, pp 13-18.

Age Concern England (1996) *Stuck on the waiting list: Older people and equipment for independent living*, Age Concern National Campaign, London: Age Concern.

Arber, S. and Ginn, J. (1991) *Gender and later life: A sociological analysis of resources and constraints*, London: Sage Publications.

Argyle, E. (2001) 'Poverty, disability and the role of older carers', *Disability and Society*, vol 16, no 4, pp 585-95.

Bardasi, E. and Jenkins, S.P. (2002) *Income in later life: Work history matters*, Bristol/York: The Policy Press/Joseph Rowntree Foundation.

Barnes, H., Parry, J. and Lakey, J. (2002) *Forging a new future: The experiences and expectations of people leaving paid work over 50*, Bristol/York: The Policy Press/Joseph Rowntree Foundation.

Bartlett, A. (2001) *Financial planning: An examination of women's special needs*, PRA research seminar, September, London, PRA occasional paper, Guildford: Pre-Retirement Association.

Bramley, G., Lancaster, S. and Gordon, D. (2000) 'Benefit take-up and the geography of poverty in Scotland', *Regional Studies*, vol 34, no 6, pp 507-19.

Chang, D., Spicer, N., Irving, A., Sparham, I. and Neeve, L. (2001) *Modernising service delivery: The better government for older people prototypes*, DWP Research Report No 136, London: DWP.

Clarke, H. and Spafford, J. (2001) *Piloting choice and control for older people: An evaluation*, Bristol/York: The Policy Press/Joseph Rowntree Foundation.

Clarke, H., Dyer, S. and Horwood, J. (1998) *That bit of help: The high value of low level preventative services for older people*, Bristol/York: The Policy Press/Joseph Rowntree Foundation.

Commission for Local Administration in England (Local Government Ombudsman) (1993) *Report on investigation no 9\A\1173 into a complaint against the London Borough of Redbridge 9\12\93*, London: Commission for Local Administration in England (Local Government Ombudsman).

Corden, A. (1995) *Changing perspectives on benefit take-up*, SPRU (Social Policy Research Unit), University of York, London: HMSO.

Costigan, P., Finch, H., Jackson, B., Legard, R. and Ritchie, J. (1999) *Overcoming barriers: Older people and Income Support*, DWP Research Report No 100, London: DWP.

Cutler, N.E. (1997) 'Introduction: financial dimensions of aging – and middle-aging', *Generations*, vol 21, no 2, pp 5-8.

Danigelis, N.L. and McIntosh, B.R. (2001) 'Gender's effect on the relationships linking older Americans' resources and financial satisfaction', *Research on Aging*, vol 23, no 4, pp 410-28.

Davidhizar, R., Bechtel, G.A. and Woodring, B.C. (2000) 'The changing role of grandparenthood', *Journal of Gerontological Nursing*, vol 26, no 1, pp 24-9.

Dean, J. and Morton, M. (1995) *A chance to help: Survey of later life volunteers in Scotland*, Stirling: Volunteer Development Scotland.

Disney, R., Grundy, E. and Johnson, P. (eds) (1978) *The dynamics of retirement: Analyses of the retirement surveys*, DWP Research Report No 72, London: DWP.

DWP (Department for Work and Pensions) (2001) *The pensioners' income series 1999/00*, London: Analytical Services Division, DWP.

Evandrou, M. and Falkingham, J. (1993) 'Social security and the life course: developing sensitive policy alternatives', in S. Arber and M. Evandrou (eds) *Ageing, independence and the life course*, London: Jessica Kingsley Publishers.

Evans, M. and Falkingham, J. (1997) *Minimum pensions and safety nets in old age: A comparative analysis*, London: The Suntory and Toyota International Centres for Economics and Related Disciplines, London School of Economics and Political Science.

Feinstein, J. and McFadden, D. (1989) 'The dynamics of housing demand by the elderly: wealth, cash flow and demographic effects', in D. Wise (ed) *The economics of aging*, Chicago, IL: Chicago University Press for the National Bureau of Economic Research.

Flately, J. (1999) *Helping pensioners: Contextual survey of the Income Support pilots*, DWP In-House Report No 60, London: DWP.

FSA (Financial Services Authority) (1998) *Promoting public understanding of financial services: A strategy for consumer education*, London: FSA.

George, L.K. (1993) *Financial security in later life: The subjective side*, Philadelphia, PA: Boettner Institute of Financial Gerontology.

Gnich, W. and Gilhooly, M. (2001) 'Planning for financial well-being in old age: an investigation of baby boomers and older adults in Scotland' [abstract], *Gerontologist*, vol 41, no 1, p 143.

Golant, S.M. (1998) 'Changing an older person's shelter and care setting: a model to explain personal and environmental outcomes', in R.J. Scheidt and P.G. Windley (eds) *Environment and ageing territory: A focus on housing*, Westport, CT: Greenwood Press, pp 33-60.

Gordon, D., Adelman, L., Ashworth, K., Bradshaw, J., Levitas, R., Middleton, S., Pantazis, C., Patsios, D., Payne, S., Townsend. P. and Williams, J. (2000) *Poverty and social exclusion in Britain*, York: Joseph Rowntree Foundation.

Harper, S. (2000) 'Locating grandparents', in A. Dickinson, H. Bartlett and S. Wade (eds) *Old age in a new age. Proceedings of the British Society of Gerontology Annual Conference, 8-10 September 2000, Keble College, Oxford*, Oxford: Oxford Brookes University, p 12.

Hasler, F., Campbell, J. and Zarb, G. (1999) *Direct routes to independence: A guide to local authority implementation and management of direct payments*, London: Policy Studies Institute.

Hedges, A. (1998) *Pensions and retirement planning*, DWP Research Report No 83, London: DWP.

Heywood, F., Oldman, C. and Means, R. (2002) *Housing and home in later life*, Buckingham: Open University Press.

Holzausen, E. and Pearlman, V. (2000) *Caring on the breadline: The financial implications of caring*, London: Carers National Association.

Howard, M. (2001) *Paying the price: Carers, poverty and social exclusion*, Child Poverty Action Group in association with Carers UK, London: Russell Press.

Howarth, C., Kenway, P. and Palmer, C. (2001) *Responsibility for all: A national strategy for social inclusion*, New Policy Institute, London: Fabian Society.

Humphrey, R. and Calder, J. (1990) *Resilience or resignation? Retirement and unmet need in the West End of Newcastle*, Newcastle upon Tyne: Search Project.

Jarvis, C. and Tinker, A. (1999) 'Trends in old age morbidity and disability in Britain', *Aging and Society*, vol 19, pp 603-27.

Johnson, P., Stears, G. and Webb, S. (1998) 'The dynamics of incomes and occupational pensions after retirement', *Fiscal Studies*, vol 19, no 2, pp 197-215.

Kempson, E. and Whyley, C. (2001) *Payment of pensions and benefits: A survey of social security recipients paid by order book or girocheque*, DWP Research Report No 146, London: DWP.

Kempson, E., Collard, S. and Taylor, S. (2002) *Social Fund use among older people in Britain*, DWP Research Report No 172, London: DWP.

Krause, N. and Shaw, B.A. (2000) 'Giving social support to others, socioeconomic status, and changes in self-esteem in late life', *Journals of Gerontology Series B – Psychological Sciences and Social Sciences*, vol 55B, no 6, pp S323-33.

Lord, N. (2001) *Summing up: Bridging the financial literacy divide. A CAB evidence report*, London: National Association of Citizens Advice Bureaux.

Lynn, P. and Davis Smith, J. (1991) *The 1991 national survey of voluntary activity in the UK*, Berkhamsted: The Volunteer Centre UK.

Mein, G., Martikainen, P., Stansfeld, S.A., Brunner, E.J., Fuhrer, R. and Marmot, M.G. (2000) 'Predictors of early retirement in British civil servants', *Age and Ageing*, vol 29, no 6, pp 529-36.

Monroe, F. and Marks, S. (2002) *The fuel picture: CAB clients' experiences of dealing with fuel suppliers*, CAB Evidence Report, London: National Association of Citizens Advice Bureaux.

NIACE (National Institute of Adult Continuing Education) (2001) *Adult Financial Literacy Advisory Group (AdFLAG) Report. A response from NIACE on the AdFLAG Report to the Secretary of State for Education and Employment*, Leicester: NIACE.

Palmer, G., Rahman, M. and Kenway, P. (2002) *Monitoring poverty and social exclusion*, York: Joseph Rowntree Foundation.

Parker, H. (ed) (2000) *Low cost but acceptable incomes for older people: A minimum income standard for households aged 65-74 years in the UK*, Bristol: The Policy Press.

Pre-Retirement Association (2000) *Financial education project: A report from the Pre-Retirement Association*, Guildford: Pre-Retirement Association.

Reed, J., Cook, G. and Stanley, D. (2002) *Help the Aged – Good practice report*, Newcastle upon Tyne: Centre for Care of Older People, Northumbria University.

Reed, J., Cook, G., Childs, S. and Hall, A. (2003) *Does money matter?*, York: Joseph Rowntree Foundation.

Rooney, S. (2002) *Payment of tax credit and benefits via bank accounts: A review of availability and access in Washington*, Washington, England: Washington Citizens Advice Bureau.

Smith, C.J., Beltran, A., Butts, D.M. and Kingson, E.R. (2001) 'Grandparents raising grandchildren: emerging program and policy issues for the 21st century', *Journal of Gerontological Social Work*, vol 35, no 1, pp 33-45.

United Kingdom Parliament (1997) Statutory Instrument 1997 No 734, The Community Care (Direct Payments) Regulations 1997, London: The Stationery Office.

United Kingdom Parliament (1999) *With respect to old age: Long term care – rights and responsibilities. A report by the Royal Commission on Long Term Care*, Chairman: Professor Sir Stewart Sutherland, Cm 4192-I, London: The Stationery Office.

United Kingdom Parliament, House of Commons (2001) 'Written answers to questions, Pensioners (Tax) [26 February 2001], col 518W', in *Hansard*, vol 363 (House of Commons Debates).

Villa, V.M., Wallace, S.P. and Markides, K. (1997) 'Economic diversity and an aging population: the impact of public policy and economic trends', *Generations*, vol 21, pp 13-18.

Volunteering Unit (1995) *Make a difference: An outline volunteering strategy for the UK*, London: HMSO.

Walker, J. and Davies, M. (2001) *Financial literacy in later life*, PRA research seminar, September, London, PRA occasional paper, Guildford: Pre-Retirement Association.

Wardell, F., Lishman, J. and Whalley, L.J. (2000) 'Who volunteers?', *British Journal of Social Work*, vol 30, pp 227-48.

Whetstone, M. (2002) *Hard times: A study of pensioner poverty*, Centre for Policy on Ageing (CPA) Report 31, London: CPA.

NINE

Safety and risk

Contents

Introduction	149
Safety and living	150
Safety, risk and professional practice	152
Risk taking and risk management	156
Organisational risk management	162
Conclusion	164

Key points

- There is a tension between living a life and maximising safety.
- The experience of risk is mediated and sometimes amplified by personal experience and social and political processes.
- Professional practice with older people is full of ethical dilemmas that concern risk identification and management.
- There is a shift from individual practitioners only to also organisations being responsible and accountable for risk management.

Introduction

There are two main points to this chapter: that there is a tension between maintaining safety and being surrounded by the artefacts of one's life; and the other point concerns the difficulties of understanding risk and risk management – because it is so bound to the cultural and social background of each person and group, each brings a different understanding of a situation to decision making. Both points are made very eloquently through scripts written and performed by Old Spice, the group of older people based in Newcastle upon Tyne, UK, who work with a range of community groups, older people and professional care staff to convey through drama some of the key issues faced by older people. These scripts are reproduced in large part in this chapter with their kind permission, although you do have to see the full performance by older people to experience the full effect of their messages!

Safety and living

Some points about the lived environment and security have been made in Chapter Four, where the preferences of older people for home and street design were discussed. Here, however, we turn to a very vivid dramatisation, which explores the details of safety and security for older people. The extract from the first Old Spice script is delivered while a room full of older people are invited to complete a safety checklist of their own homes. Throughout this performance the message is that there is a tension between maintaining safety and the artefacts of an individual's life.

It is these very artefacts of life that both create the increased risk of accident but also chart the life course of the person and in so doing serve perhaps to define that person. These are not irrelevant, threatening artefacts but are crucial to that person's sense of who they are, much as a photograph of a family member serves to remind and define the person who places the photograph in view. Note, for example, one older person who resists getting rid of a loose mat: "I can't do that – it was made by my Granny".

Note, also, the references to the consequences of accidents for older people. One older person described having slipped getting out of the bath: "I'm not going in the bath again – I'm too frightened now". It is this heightened sensitivity to safety and risk that pervades the literature base of this field.

We join the first extract of an Old Spice script ('Older and safer') at the point at which a Health and Safety Advisor (HSA) enters a room of older people who are attending a workshop on home safety, facilitated by the 'speaker'.

SPEAKER	Did you find that most people need to make some changes?
HSA	Yes I did, and I've been telling them what they should do – but old people are so stubborn they don't want to change anything even if it's dangerous.
SPEAKER	I'm just telling this audience about the information we have here today – if they want to know what to do they've only to ask *(at the information stalls)*.
HSA	I've brought some people with me – can I bring them in now?
SPEAKER	Yes, bring them in. *(HSA brings forward Older Person 1 [OP1])*
SPEAKER	Oh dear, what happened to you?
OP1	*(Limping forward)* I fell down the stairs and broke my leg – it's taking ages to mend. *(Speaker shows to chair)*
HSA	You've still got those old slippers on – I told you to throw them away – that's what tripped you up.

OP1	There's plenty of wear in these yet – and they're very comfortable – anyway it wasn't just the slippers – I tripped on some things left on the stairs by somebody.
HSA	Oh – and who was the somebody – you told me you live alone.
OP1	Well, I suppose I left them there myself – but I leave things on the stairs to take them up next time I go up – can't keep running up and down – have to use your head to save your legs.
HSA	Didn't work that time, did it? A week in hospital and your leg's still in plaster.
OP1	All right, I know, anyway what did you bring me here for?
SPEAKER	Just take a seat for now – then you'll be able to get some more information.
OP2	*(Approaching, holding arm in plaster/bandage)*
HSA	*(Helping OP2 forward)* Oh, you've made it, come and sit down.
SPEAKER	What happened to you?
OP2	I fell in the sitting room – tripped over the mat and then caught my foot in the lamp flex.
SPEAKER	So what was the damage?
OP2	I'll have to get a new lamp – it was all smashed.
SPEAKER	But what about your arm?
OP2	It's not so bad now I've got a lighter plaster, but I wish it would mend properly.
HSA	And have you got rid of that loose mat yet?
OP2	I can't do that – it was made by my Granny – it's lovely, you see proggy mats like that in museums now.
HSA	Aye, a museum's the best place for it – it's a death trap in your house.
SPEAKER	You must have a good look round – and get some advice about plugs – you don't want a lot of trailing wires across your sitting room.
	(OP2 moves to another seat)
OP3	*(Approaches, head bandaged)*
SPEAKER	Oh dear, another casualty – what's been happening to you?
OP3	It's my head. It's all his fault, not mine. I keep telling him to shut the cupboard doors in the kitchen, but he will leave them open. I'd bent down to the bottom cupboard and when I stood up again I caught the back of my head, such a crack.
HSA	What about the wobbly chair as well?
OP3	I was so mad. I decided to move things to a lower shelf so he wouldn't need to go in the top cupboard, but the kitchen

	chair's gone a bit wonky – it gave way when I stood on it – I knocked myself right out when my head hit the sink.
SPEAKER	Kitchens are the most dangerous places in the house you know – so you'll be looking for ideas to make it safer.
OP3	Yes and I'll be telling him outdoors to do what I tell him. *(Moves to another seat)*
SPEAKER	*(To HSA)* Have you found a lot more people who need advice about safety in the home?
HSA	There's one more still to come. You'd think after an accident they'd be rushing to make things safer – but old people don't like to change anything.
SPEAKER	They don't think about the cost to the NHS – just think of all the time they've taken at the hospital.
HSA	And the older you are the longer it takes to recover, they don't think about that.
OP4	*(Has been approaching – arm in bandage and holding his ribs. Has been listening and getting indignant.)*
OP4	Excuse me, I can hear what you're saying – have I come to the right place for the 'Older and Safer Day'?
HSA	Come along – we were just talking about the cost of accidents.
OP4	I'm not staying if you're going to blame me for having an accident – I didn't do it on purpose – and I'm the one suffering, not you.
SPEAKER	Tell us what happened – come and sit down here.
OP4	I scalded myself in the bath – I always run the hot water first just to make sure the boiler's working – I forgot to put some cold in – when I got in I couldn't get out again quick enough and I slipped on the floor.
HSA	I've told you before about putting cold water in first – and you need a handrail to grab quickly when you have to get in or out of the bath.
OP4	Well, I've come today to find out about handrails and anything else to help. I don't want any more bruised ribs or scalds in tender places. I'm not going in the bath again – I'm too frightened now.

Safety, risk and professional practice

Concerns about safety and risk also pervade decision making by health and social care practitioners and this is central to professional practice (Alaszewski and Alaszewski, 1998). The value of practice that concerns the need to reduce risk is in inherent conflict with the value that requires the autonomy and self-determination of the older person to be respected.

Risk management has become a dominant feature of contemporary health and social care practice. Although in general it is promoted in legislation, there are critics who feel policy could promote the safety of older people to a greater extent. For example, Cowan (2003) argues that the National Service Framework (NSF) for Older People does not emphasise risk management and safety sufficiently. Always an area for contention, the balance between the management of possible adverse events and self-determination is a constant battleground. Kane and Levin (1998) argue that:

> The social workers, nurses, and others who hold up safety as a goal may be doing so as part of their commitment to do no harm. But such professionals may have lost perspective on the nature of their appropriate role in helping individuals plan their lives; they may be assuming too much responsibility.... Paradoxically, the desire to do no harm and to achieve safety above all other goals may actually result in harm to the consumer. (Kane and Levin, 1998, p 76)

Kaufman (1995), describing uncertainty and dilemmas in the care of older people in care homes, identifies two broad topics: end-of-life decision making in institutional settings and the problems of maintaining autonomy, dignity and choice for the older person. She interviewed 40 physicians and found that they spend a considerable amount of time confronting the following problems:

- how much to intervene in patients' lives in order to balance risk reduction and safety with independence, so that frail and sick old people can continue to direct their lives in the community;
- how to be the best possible advocate for the old person while making demands for medication compliance and behaviour change;
- how to assess vulnerability and quality of life when pondering placement decisions. (Kaufman, 1995, p 481)

Not surprisingly, these issues were seen as multidimensional and complex, there being no 'right' resolution achievable in many cases. In particular, Kaufman (1995) describes the doubts and struggles that the physicians identified as they attempt to reconcile these tensions: "Clinical problems are not conceived or addressed either by isolating their component parts or by invoking abstract principles of bioethical theory such as 'autonomy' or 'justice' in order to make sense of or solve them. Rather they show the irreducible nature of certain complex dilemmas in geriatric care" (Kaufman, 1995, p 48). Indeed, Kane and Levin (1998) describe such complexities of professional practice as 'anguishing situations'. This picture of professional turmoil differs from that identified by Alaszewski and Alaszewski (1998). In describing interview and diary data with 17 community nursing and social work staff, they noted that decisions became problematic where there were differences in perception of what was in the person's best interests between the individual, themselves and others involved in the decision-making process. In this study the professional members defined risk in terms of negative consequences, articulating broader and perhaps more positive aspects of risk only when prompted. In a small action research study about continence care for older people with mental health needs, Clarke and Gardner (2002) identified complexities of clinical decision making arising from conflict between the perceived professional duty of care and the ethical concerns of respecting autonomy. At times, the autonomy of the individual was compromised in the interests of 'the greater good' where actions influence a wider group of people than the individual patient. For example, an incontinent individual's expressed wish to be left alone was accommodated if they were alone in a room but was not tolerated if they were eating a meal with other patients.

There are a number of issues that are considered when attempting to balance safety with autonomy (Kane and Levin, 1998). These include:

- *Severity of consequences.* Clearly when managing risk it is necessary to consider the relative impact of different courses of action. Unfortunately, however, different stakeholders weigh up these risks differently. Most notably, adverse events that have consequences for psychological and social well-being are not taken as seriously as physical risks (for example, the threat of harm as a result of falling downstairs is taken more seriously than the threat of psychological harm from being relocated into a residential home).
- *Likelihood of consequences.* Often the perceived threat of harm outweighs the actual incidence of the adverse event occurring and as a result people can feel more at risk than they are. One example is the anxiety that people may have of being burgled and attacked. The likelihood of this occurrence is small, yet anxiety about such an event can result in someone feeling restricted to their own home with considerable anxiety about leaving their home.
- *Difficulty of predicting risk.* Risks associated with care interventions are a great deal harder to quantify than, say, from a surgical procedure. Indeed, for older people who require long-term assistance, there tends to be a series of decisions rather than one big decision to be made. It is this cumulative effect of decisions to ensure safety that may expose someone to iatrogenic risk (that is, threat of harm as the result of a care action designed to increase safety) just as much as the single large decision to have, for example, heart bypass surgery.
- *Negative effects of avoiding risk.* Risk avoidance, or risk aversion, results in people being 'wrapped in cotton wool' and unable to achieve their full potential (Kane and Levin, 1998). The removal of risk is to remove a key dynamic of living and threatens the well-being of the individual. It is managed risk that is necessary rather than the total abstinence from risk-taking activity.

There are several parallels between these aspects outlined by Kane and Levin (1998) and those highlighted by Cook and Ayris (2001), who argue that for risks to be perceived, they must be identified, must be seen as controllable, and must be judged to have significant consequences.

Falls as an example of threats of harm for older people

Falls are the leading cause of death from accidents for people aged over 75 years (ONS, 2000) and between 5% and 10% of these falls result in injury sufficiently severe that it requires medical care (Nuffield Institute for Health and NHS Reviews and Dissemination, 1996). The prevention of falls is, not unexpectedly, high on the UK government priorities. *Saving lives: Our healthier nation* (DoH, 1999) and the NSF for Older People (DoH, 2001) both place expectations on the NHS to reduce the incidence of falls that require medical attention.

Repeated studies identify two types of factor that contribute to falls of older people. First, the environment is implicated and, second, intrinsic or functional factors that are more directly associated with the actions of the individual (Mackenzie et al, 2002). That the risk of falls may be reduced through management of the environment and/or the individual is supported by Gillespie et al (2002) in a review of the literature. They conclude that the incidence of falls may be reduced by intervention that targets both intrinsic and environmental risk factors for older people living at home, but that there is a lack of evidence to support the effectiveness of such measures in institutional settings. However, Mosley et al (1998) report on an educational programme with staff about falls prevention that resulted in 72% (13) of the units involved in the study experiencing significantly fewer falls.

In describing the development of a screening tool for domestic environments to identify those at high risk of falls, Mackenzie et al (2002) identify that home safety involves aspects of the physical environment, how the person interacts with the environment, and personal or individual factors. Luxton and Riglin (2003) identify a similar screening as the first of the three-level pyramid of assessment for identifying falls risk. Having identified a falls problem through a simple screening tool, level 2 assessment determines risk factors for falling and only a small number of people require third-level assessment from specialist services such as a falls clinic or specialist therapy assessment.

Luxton and Riglin (2003), reviewing a number of other papers, identify the following as risk factors for falls and fractures:

- a history of falls;
- nutritional status;
- environmental hazards (for example, loose carpets, baths without handles or non-slip mats, poor lighting, trailing wires, unsafe stairways, ill-fitting shoes);
- medication (including antidepressants, sedatives, analgesics, diuretics);
- physiological changes associated with normal ageing (for example, loss of joint

range and muscle strength, bone loss, deteriorating gait pattern and exercise tolerance);
- medical conditions (for example, poor eyesight, Parkinson's disease, stroke, postural hypertension);
- reduced confidence, resulting from the fear of a further fall.

While most work on falls has concentrated on falls in domestic or institutional settings, Clemson et al (2003) focused on falls in public places. Through interviews and re-enactments of falls, they identified 10 themes that contributed to the falls: not attending to the route ahead, lack of familiarity, pace, mobility behaviours, environmental influences, eyesight behaviours, health factors affecting physical abilities, lack of confidence, overexertion, and unnoticed environmental hazards.

Risk taking and risk management

The example of falls in relation to safety and risk for older people exemplifies the twin aspects of risk for older people that are identified by Stevenson (1999). First, she describes the "unnecessary or avoidable risk brought about by the failure of society to adapt the environment to the needs of people who are frail" (p 202). Located in the social model of disability, such a position challenges society's response to less able members and the value with which they are held in society. This model postulates that it is society that creates disability and, in this case, unnecessary risk rather than any aspect of the individual's impairment. Second, she highlights the extent and nature of risk, arguing that taking risks is an essential component of life, and that risk assessment requires, therefore, for a distinction to be made between acceptable and unacceptable risk. There is, however, an interrelationship between these two dimensions since defining acceptable risk is unlikely to be consistent across population groups. A risk taken by a younger person is likely to be defined by society as carrying a different level of risk significance than if undertaken by an older person. One example is abseiling or other 'extreme sports'.

This leads to an appreciation of risk as 'ideologically loaded', as described by Lupton (1993). This is an aspect of risk theory, expounded by Douglas (1994) in particular, who argued that health and social care professions tended to discount the social and political dimensions of risk. This interrelationship between risk, care provision and the needs of service users creates a 'complex web of perceived risk, identified need and care' that allows questions to be asked about how and why care is managed (Clarke, 2000). Similarly, Tansey and O'Riordan (1999), referring to cultural theory, argue that risk 'cannot be reduced to concerns about safety', arguing that risk is 'inseparable from issues relating to power, justice and legitimacy'. As a result of these more social and culturally led understandings of risk, Tansey and O'Riordan (1999) argue for a shift away from research that focuses on 'illusionary' notions of objectivity in risk to research that supports "better deliberative processes that create legitimate decision-making structures" (p 88).

These approaches to risk are in some contrast to those that emphasise the negative aspects of risk. Cook and Ayris (2001) describe the negative attributes of risk as including 'chance, possibility, probability, uncertainty, vulnerability, value, danger, hazard and peril', attributes that arise from the Royal Society's (2001) definition of risk as "the probability that a particular adverse event occurs during a stated period of time, or results from a particular challenge" (p 2).

Our second script written and performed by Old Spice ('Accident promotion versus accident prevention') portrays environmental risks and their management as a war zone, and in this case an army has a mission to promote accidents, with soldiers given directions to cause accidents for older people. It is performed for community groups of older people as a means of highlighting some of the things that may increase their chance of falling or having other accidents.

Scene:	Briefing room of special unit to promote accidents
Characters:	Officer and soldiers of a special unit
ACT 1	
	(Soldiers are lounging on their chairs. Officer with cap and stick and clipboard under arm enters and struts across once or twice glaring fiercely at everyone.)
OFFICER	*(Turning to soldiers)* ATTENTION!
	(Soldiers shamble to their feet, adjust caps and shuttle into a line and look at each other and salute)
OFFICER	Squad, number.
SOLDIERS	1, 2, 3, 4, 5.
OFFICER	*(Walking up and down and glaring at them)*
	YOU rotten lot have been chosen as front-line troops in our campaign to PROMOTE accidents. *(Poking Soldier 1 with a stick)*
	What are you?
SOLDIER	We are a rotten lot, Sir!
OFFICER	No, no! Repeat after me – we are front-line troops in a campaign to *promote* accidents.
SOLDIERS	*(Prompting each other)* We are front-line troops in a campaign to *prevent* accidents.
OFFICER	*(Very angry)* NO, NO! To *PROMOTE* accidents, to *CAUSE* accidents, not prevent them! You STUPID lot!
SOLDIER 1	Permission to speak, Sir?
OFFICER	Yes, you stupid boy, what is it?
SOLDIER 1	Sir, we don't know what to do.
OFFICER	That's why you're here for this briefing session – so sit down and I'll tell you what to do.

(Soldiers shuffle about and sit down and prepare to listen. Officer struts about until they settle. Soldiers prepare to write on clipboards produced from under their seats.)

OFFICER   The objective of this unit is to cause as many accidents as possible. This troop will make older people its main target. Now where do most accidents to older people happen?

SOLDIER 1 Sir! Crossing the road – it's easy to mow them down.

SOLDIER 2 Sir! Walking down the street – you can trip them up.

SOLDIER 3 Sir! On the buses – you can jerk them off their feet.
           (Speaking quickly and eagerly one after the other)

OFFICER   Most accidents to older people happen in their homes. Now what are our tactics in this campaign? *(Impressively)* We always attack our target at its weakest point. *(Soldiers nod to each other and look impressed)*
           (Officer turning to map and plan of house) Our first target is older people in *(Town)*. Here are the streets of *(Town)*. *(Pointing to one part of the map)* AND here is a plan of a house *(pointing to drawing on part of the map)*. Now this campaign requires your skills in house-to-house fighting and unarmed combat – you must get into every older person's house.

SOLDIER 1 Permission to speak, Sir!

OFFICER   This stupid boy again, now what?

SOLDIER 1 What if they won't let us in?

OFFICER   You must INFILTRATE – creep in when they're not looking – use your cunning tricks....

SOLDIER 1 *(Unconvinced)* Yes, Sir.

OFFICER   *(Consulting instructions on clipboard)* Now I want some volunteers for important tasks – you, you and you will do *(poking each one with stick)*.
           (To Soldier 1) YOU will be on loose mat and carpet holes duty. *(Soldier 1 stands and salutes)*

SOLDIER 1 What's that, Sir?

OFFICER   You will collect up any loose ragged mats and put them in dangerous places. And if you see any holes in carpets – make them bigger – do you understand?

SOLDIER 1 Yes Sir, yes SIR! *(Sits)*

OFFICER   *(To Soldier 2)* YOU will volunteer for top shelf and wobbly chair duty. *(Soldier 2 stands and salutes)* You will keep moving things to top shelves, out of reach, and loosen the legs on the nearest chairs.

SOLDIER 2 Sir, why do I do that?

OFFICER	Our spies have been out and they tell us that if somebody wants something quickly they'll just use the nearest chair to stand on – then crash! Down they go.
SOLDIER 2	Yes Sir, thank you Sir! *(Sits down)*
OFFICER	*(To Soldier 3)* You are volunteering for very important electric flex duties.
SOLDIER 3	*(Stands and salutes)* What do I do, Sir?
OFFICER	Make sure all flexes are frayed and wires exposed. Make sure all flexes hang down off the kitchen bench – and all wires trail across the floor – so the old people will get shocks – or fall over – there's scope for initiative here.
SOLDIER 3	*(Looking uncertain)* Yes Sir, I'll try Sir. *(Sits down)*
OFFICER	*(To Soldier 4)* You are volunteering for light bulb duty.
SOLDIER 4	*(Standing up and saluting)* Yes Sir, what's that Sir?
OFFICER	You must swap all the light bulbs so there's dim lighting everywhere, especially on the stairs.
SOLDIER 4	Yes Sir. Why on the stairs, Sir?
OFFICER	Because, you stupid boy, that's where the old person is most likely to trip up – in dim light because their eyesight is bad anyway. And if they try to replace a bulb themselves – they'll fall over.
SOLDIER 4	Yes Sir, thank you Sir! *(Sits down)*
SOLDIER 1	Permission to speak, Sir?
OFFICER	Well, what now?
SOLDIER 1	I've got an idea Sir. I want to volunteer for extra duties Sir. *(Other soldiers nudge each other and glare at him)* *(Stands and salutes)* I think we should start fires Sir, but some people have smoke alarms....
OFFICER	*(Crossly)* I'm just coming to that – if a house has a smoke alarm, you must make sure it keeps setting itself off – blow smoke on it when no one's looking – then they'll get fed up and switch it off – then you can start fires.
SOLDIER 1	*(Abashed)* Yes Sir, thank you Sir! *(Sits down)*
OFFICER	*(To Soldier 5)* Now, you are volunteering for slippy slipper duty. Old people shuffle round the house in their old slippers and trip themselves up.
SOLDIER 5	*(Stands and salutes)* Yes Sir, but what if they've got some new slippers?
OFFICER	You must break down the backs, slash the soles, make holes in the toes – make them dangerous again!
SOLDIER 5	Yes Sir! Yes Sir, I'll do that Sir. *(Sits down again)*
OFFICER	Now we come to the most important job of all – and this will involve a team effort.
SOLDIERS	*(All nodding eagerly)* Tell us Sir! Tell us Sir!

OFFICER	*(Impressively)* CHIP PAN FIRES! Now what you have to do is distract their attention when the pan's on so they forget it.
SOLDIERS	What can we do?
OFFICER	You can telephone and keep them talking, ring the bell and get them to come to the door.
SOLDIERS	What if they come back and try to stop the fires spreading?
OFFICER	Let them throw water on it. Don't tell them that's the worst thing to do – if they have a fire blanket in the kitchen, then move it.
SOLDIERS	Why's that?
OFFICER	Because a fire blanket's the best way to put it out. Our job is to make it as BAD as possible – do you understand, you stupid lot?
SOLDIERS	Yes Sir, yes Sir!
OFFICER	*(Checking through his instructions sheets)* Now have you all got your instructions?
SOLDIERS	Yes Sir, yes Sir!
OFFICER	SQUAD ATTENTION! *(Soldiers shamble to their feet again)* You are the front-line troop in the *(Town)* manoeuvres. Off you go into battle. Right turn. Quick march! *(Soldiers shamble round and return to seats at back)*
OFFICER	*(Walking up and down in front and speaking to the audience)* Now my troops go over the top – infiltrating the houses of *(Town)*. Soon the accidents will start to happen. The streets of *(Town)* will resound to the sirens of ambulances *(pauses to listen)* and fire engines *(pauses again)* *(Soldiers make sound effects in wrong order)* – ah, that's music to my ears.

ACT 2

OFFICER	Now my troops will soon be returning for a debriefing session *(brings forward map / diagram / flip chart)*. This will be covered with red dots *(snarling to audience)*. Red for blood. In every street – in the kitchens, the stairs, the bedrooms, the living rooms *(pointing with stick to the relevant points on the map)*. *(Soldiers start to trudge in wearily in a line, hand on shoulder of soldier in front and slump into chairs.)*
OFFICER	*(Preparing to make up flip chart)* Now for your reports. *(To Soldier 1)* What about the loose mats and carpet holes?
SOLDIER 1	Sir, they've all thrown away their loose mats and mended their carpets.... *(barely able to stand).*

OFFICER	Sit down, you useless lily-livered ... *(To Soldier 2)* What about top shelf and wobbly chair duties?
SOLDIER 2	*(Standing wearily)* It was no good Sir, they've all rearranged their shelves and got new steps.... *(sinks back into chair).*
OFFICER	Another useless clot! *(To other soldiers)* So what do you have to report?
SOLDIER 3	*(Staggering to feet)* Sir, I couldn't do anything about the electric flexes, they've all been renewed – no trailing wires anywhere.... *(sinks back into chair).*
	(Officer reels under each blow)
SOLDIER 4	*(Wearily)* Sir, I couldn't do anything, they've all got long-life bulbs and they get help to change them and check the smoke alarms as well.
OFFICER	*(To Soldier 5 sarcastically)* I suppose you're going to say they've all got safe footwear and thrown away their old slippers....
SOLDIER 5	*(Wearily)* Yes Sir, I am Sir!
OFFICER	*(Getting worked up)* Sabotage, SABOTAGE! Our plans have been leaked to the enemy! Ah but what about chip pan fires? How many can you report?
SOLDIERS	*(Humming and hawing)* Well Sir, none Sir ... none Sir! Sir, they've been told about having a fire blanket in the kitchen and never leaving the chip pan....
OFFICER	Who has been doing this? How did they get this information? Who is the TRAITOR among us?
SOLDIER 1	None of us Sir! They really got a secret weapon – Action for Health has given out an information pack which tells people what to do....
OFFICER	*(Contemptuously)* AN INFORMATION LEAFLET – That's no good – the people of *(Town)* won't take any notice of an information leaflet – they're all too stupid ...
SOLDIERS	They will Sir. They will! *(Starting to creep among the audience)*
OFFICER	*(To Soldiers)* The people in *(Town)* ARE not going to throw away their loose mats, are they?
SOLDIERS	Oh yes they are.
OFFICER	*(To audience)* Oh no you're not.
AUDIENCE	*(Encouraged by soldiers)* Oh yes we are.
OFFICER	*(To audience)* You people in *(Town)* are not going to use steps instead of wobbly chairs, check your electric flexes, get long-life bulbs are you?
AUDIENCE	Oh yes we are.
OFFICER	Oh no you're not.
AUDIENCE	Oh yes we are.

OFFICER	You people in *(Town)* are not going to throw away your slippery slippers and wear hard-soled slippers are you?
AUDIENCE	Oh yes we are.
OFFICER	Oh no you're not.
AUDIENCE	Oh yes we are.
OFFICER	*(Brightening up)* But you people in *(Town)* are not going to watch over your chip pans and … you don't know how to put out a chip pan fire?
AUDIENCE	OH YES WE DO.
OFFICER	OH NO YOU DON'T.
AUDIENCE	OH YES WE DO!
OFFICER	*(Disbelief)* So you're going to follow all the advice in this leaflet…. Throw away loose mats.
OFFICER	Use steps not a wobbly chair.
OFFICER	Check your electric flexes and light bulbs.
OFFICER	Remember to watch your chip pan – have a fire blanket in the kitchen.
OFFICER	Throw away your slippery slippers.
AUDIENCE	Yes we are.
OFFICER	Oh, I know you people in *(Town)* you say that now, but you'll go home and forget all about it. You'll still have scalds and burns and falls and we're not going to let you have any more information leaflets. *(To soldiers)* ATTENTION! *(Soldiers shamble to feet).* Now, my men, we may have lost this battle in *(Town)* but the war goes on! *(To audience)* We shall return, we shall fight again another day. *(To soldiers)* About turn, FORWARD MARCH, LEFT RIGHT, LEFT RIGHT, QUICK MARCH … *(All shamble away, officer making final thumbs up to audience)*

Organisational risk management

Kane and Levin (1998) describe 'managed risk contracting' in the US as a multistep process that involves:

- defining risks and provider concerns;
- defining probable consequences of behaviours or conditions;
- identifying the preferences of everyone involved, including the older person, their family members and care providers;
- identifying possible solutions;
- choosing a solution.

This forms a written document in which the search is to find a compromise agreement and a mechanism for clarifying and potentially resolving ethical conflicts of 'safety–freedom tradeoffs'. While not all agree with the use of such a process and documentation, Kane and Levin (1998) have found in their study that identification of issues is an important step that in itself often leads to creative solutions.

Safety–freedom tradeoffs are one dimension of the need to explore what it is that older people value in their lives and how they may therefore prioritise issues in making such a risk analysis. Dabbs (1999) explored this issue in relation to people with dementia and found that it is the social, interpersonal and emotional aspects of life and care, rather than the physical aspects, that are most important. Dabbs proposes a framework of quality of life for people with dementia that is orientated around four key areas: social and interpersonal, emotional, practical, and physical health.

Until recently, in the UK clinical risk management was left to the professional decision making of qualified staff. However, an increasing awareness of the complexities of such decision making (discussed earlier in this chapter) has combined with heightened societal awareness of risk taking and safety and resultant litigation actions. The consequence has been for organisations to assume a greater responsibility for risk management and to place a more transparent level of accountability on professional staff. No longer is competence to practise assumed on qualification but it is required to be demonstrated and assessed in an ongoing, career-long pattern.

Cook and Ayris (2001, p 112) describe the risk management process as "a systematic and comprehensive review of services and systems in an organisation", which includes the interrelated steps of:

- risk assessment and risk identification – the process by which the organisation becomes aware of potential or actual harm to service users and staff;
- risk analysis – the measurement of risk and the impact it has on the organisation;
- risk reduction and control decisions – implementing changes to clinical and organisational practices, so that adverse events are eliminated or made less likely;
- risk funding – recognising that some adverse events will happen, and ensuring that the costs of such events are both minimised and provided for: for example, through good claims management and adequate insurance (from Cook and Ayris, 2001, pp 112-13).

The search for a risk-free environment is paradoxical, however, and such a state can never be achieved since freedom from physical risk carries a high price of other aspects of someone's life and of the actions of practitioners. In relation to dementia care in residential care settings, Stokes (2001) describes the 'standard' design features of secure perimeters and hidden (baffled) exits to buildings, the promotion of surveillance technology such as tagging, and the lingering use of physical and pharmaceutical restraint. He describes these as "features of care that are open to abusive malpractice, driven not by malevolence, but borne out of a loss of regard for the person, a preoccupation with risk and, on occasions, desperation for peace of mind" (p 27).

A chapter on safety and risk would not be complete without at least some consideration of perceptions of risk on a more macro, society level. Perceived risks are, as highlighted earlier, mediated by the values that we place on the consequences of actions and outcomes. For example, Calman et al (1999) identify a number of 'fright factors' that contribute to risks being generally more worrying (and less acceptable). These include:

- being involuntary rather than voluntary (for example, exposure to pollution rather than choosing to smoke);
- inequitably distributed (some benefit while others suffer the consequences);
- inescapable by taking personal precautions;
- arising from novel or unfamiliar sources;
- resulting from man–made rather than natural sources;
- causing hidden and irreversible damage;
- posing particular danger to small children or pregnant women – that is, the future generation;
- threatening a form of death, illness or injury that arouses particular dread;
- damaging identifiable rather than anonymous victims;
- being poorly understood by science;
- subject to contradictory statements from responsible sources.

Thus risk mediation is not wholly an internal individual process, but is shaped by those around us and the ways in which risks are presented, amplified through the media, and debated and discussed by those around us. Our individual understanding of risk, whether as a healthcare consumer or provider, is a product of the way in which risk is communicated and the way in which risk knowledge is moved and shaped in a social system. Calman et al (1999) describe the public not as a homogenous mass or as a collection of individuals with different views, but as typically "a whole range of more-or-less organised groups seeking (quite legitimately) to pursue their own agendas" (p 112).

Conclusion

This chapter has sought to set out some of the dilemmas faced by older people and by practitioners working with them. So often these dilemmas result from differing perceptions of the level of risk that the older person should be exposed to, or should be able to experience in order to have a meaningful and enriched life. This is a multilevel and multisystem issue. A single issue, such as the ability of an older person to keep on their own floor a rug made by their grandmother, is shaped by:

- their own balance of retaining that generational connection with the fear of tripping and falling;
- the communication of 'fright factors' to them, their family and their care practitioners through the media and through conversation with those around them;
- the extent of the practitioner's anxiety about ensuring absolute safety; which is in turn influenced by
- the practitioner's organisational response to risk management.

The challenge in contemporary health and social care is to retain, at the centre of such complex decision making, the views and wishes of the older people themselves.

Exercises

For classes or groups, it may be useful to read or act some of the sketches above, followed by a group discussion. For individual activity, people can ask themselves the following questions:

- List the activities that you have carried out in the past few days, including shopping, cooking, walking, driving and so on.
- Rank these in order of danger – which activities were the most likely to result in the most harm? You may need two lists – one of the likelihood of harm, and one of the seriousness of the harm. For example, you may feel that shopping is only likely to cause mild harm (sore feet and stiff shoulders) while driving a car could be fatal. The harm from shopping, however, is more likely than a fatal car accident.
- For the most dangerous, list the skills and abilities that you need to avoid harm, and the unforeseen factors (such as the acts of others) that you can do little about.
- Decide how safe you are and what could make your life safer.
- One way of making life safer is to not engage in some activities – which ones would you be prepared to stop?
- If you stopped these activities, what would be other untoward consequences?
- What would you advise older people about risk, having gone through this exercise?

References

Alaszewski, H. and Alaszewski, A. (1998) 'Professionals and practice: decision making and risk', in A. Alaszewski, L. Harrison and J. Manthorpe (eds) *Risk, health and welfare*, Buckingham: Open University Press.

Calman, K.C., Bennett, P.G. and Coles, D.G. (1999) 'Risks to health: some key issues in management, regulation and communication', *Health, Risk and Society*, vol 1, no 1, pp 107-16.

Clarke, C.L. (2000) 'Risk: constructing care and care environments in dementia', *Health, Risk and Society*, vol 2, no 1, pp 83-93.

Clarke, C.L. and Gardner, A. (2002) 'Therapeutic and ethical practice: a participatory action research project in old age mental health', *Practice Development in Healthcare*, vol 1, no 1, pp 39-53.

Clemson, L., Manor, D. and Fitzgerald, M.H. (2003) 'Behavioural factors contributing to older adults falling in public places', *Occupational Therapy Journal of Research*, vol 23, no 3, p 107.

Cook, G. and Ayris, W. (2001) 'Concepts of risk in the development of practice', in S. Spencer, J. Unsworth and W. Burke (eds) *Developing community nursing practice*, Buckingham: Open University Press.

Cowan, J. (2003) 'Risk management and the NSF for older people', *Clinical Governance*, vol 8, no 1, pp 92-6.

Dabbs, C. (1999) 'What do people with dementia most value in life?' *Journal of Dementia Care*, vol 7, no 4, pp 16-19.

DoH (Department of Health) (1999) *Saving lives: Our healthier nation*, London: DoH.

DoH (2001) *The National Service Framework for Older People*, London: DoH.

Douglas, M. (1994) *Risk and blame: Essays in cultural theory*, London: Routledge.

Gillespie, L.D., Gillespie, W.J., Robertson, M.C. and Hill, K. (2002) 'Review: intrinsic and environmental risk factor modification reduces falls in elderly people', *Evidence-Based Medicine*, vol 7, no 4, p 116.

Kane, R.A. and Levin, C.A. (1998) 'Who's safe? Who's sorry? The duty to protect the safety of clients in home- and community-based care', *Generations*, vol 22, no 3, pp 76-82.

Kaufman, S.R. (1995) 'Decision making, responsibility, and advocacy in geriatric medicine: physician dilemmas with elderly in the community', *The Gerontologist*, vol 35, no 4, p 481.

Lupton, D. (1993) 'Risk as moral danger: the social and political functions of risk discourse in public health', *International Journal of Health Services*, vol 23, pp 425-34.

Luxton, T. and Riglin, J. (2003) 'Preventing falls in older people: a multi-agency approach', *Nursing Older People*, vol 15, no 2, pp 18-22.

Mackenzie, L., Byles, J. and Higginbotham, N. (2002) 'Professional perceptions about home safety: cross-national validation of the Home Falls and Accidents Screening Tool (Home Fast)', *Journal of Allied Health*, vol 31, no 1, pp 22-9.

Mosley, A., Galindo-Ciocon, D., Peak, N. and West, M.J. (1998) 'Initiation and evaluation of a research-based fall prevention program', *Journal of Nursing Care Quality*, vol 13, no 2, pp 38-45.

Nuffield Institute for Health and NHS Reviews and Dissemination (1996) 'Preventing falls and subsequent injury in older people', *Effective Healthcare*, vol 2, p 4.

ONS (Office for National Statistics) (2000) *Mortality statistics: Injury and poisoning. Review of the Registrar General on deaths attributed to injury and poisoning in England and Wales*, London: Office for National Statistics.

Royal Society, The (2001) *Risk: Analysis, perception and management*, report of a Royal Society study group, London: The Royal Society.

Stevenson, O. (1999) 'Old people at risk', in P. Parsloe (ed) *Risk assessment in social care and social work*, London: Jessica Kingsley Publishers.

Stokes, G. (2001) 'Difficult decisions: what are a person's "best interests"?', *Journal of Dementia Care*, vol 9, no 3, pp 25-8.

Tansey, J. and O'Riordan, T. (1999) 'Cultural theory and risk: a review', *Health Risk and Society*, vol 1, no 1, pp 71-90.

TEN

Services, satisfaction and service-user involvement

Contents

Introduction	169
The policy context	170
Satisfaction with the services	171
Satisfaction and service users	172
Conclusion	182

Key points

- This chapter discusses issues of service use and satisfaction.
- The chapter discusses the differences and similarities between formal and informal services.
- Current policy initiatives for services are summarised.
- Service-user involvement in the planning and shaping of services is discussed.
- Principles for practice are outlined.

Introduction

This chapter considers how stakeholders, especially service users, experience selected aspects of health and social care services and notes that older people take a more holistic view of their health than do individual service providers. It explores the continuum of healthcare and social care: the one often inextricably intertwined with the other, although sometimes poles apart on conceptual grounds and professional cultures. Following a very brief location of services within their policy context, aspects of satisfaction with health and social care services are discussed. Finally, through a detailed presentation of a commissioned study of selected older people's services, good practice principles for service-user satisfaction and involvement are reviewed. In doing so, differentiation between formal (statutory) and informal (voluntary and community) service provision is explored, and the methodology of Appreciative Inquiry is introduced.

The policy context

There can scarcely have been a time when policy interest in the quality of provision of health and social care services for older people has attracted greater interest. In March 2001 the introduction of the National Service Framework (NSF) for Older People (DoH, 2001) was introduced as part of a government 10-year strategy to improve national health and social care services for older people. The NSF for Older People presented an ambitious remit to address eight standards, namely:

1. rooting out age discrimination;
2. person–centred care;
3. intermediate care;
4. general hospital care;
5. stroke;
6. falls;
7. mental health in older people;
8. the promotion of health and active life in older age.

Each of these standards is associated with its own rationale, key interventions and milestones for achieving implementation targets. The government recognised that older people, who are the major users of health services, were not always well served by them. There was evidence of unacceptably discriminatory ageist practices – for example, age-related cut-off points for particular services and procedures – together with a failure to place the service user at the centre of service provision, hence the first two standards of the NSF. This initiative coincided with a more integrated overall approach to health and social care services, led by policy and with an imperative for structural and practice-led change. Central themes to this approach were that continued good health and independent living were increasingly dependent upon effective support, especially support targeted at maintaining community rather than institutionally based living, and that there should be an emphasis on local delivery and accountability.

This was not an initiative that was peculiar to the UK. The demographics of ageing have long been recognised as a Europe-wide issue and the Commission of the European Communities is also active in this arena. Its report *Healthcare and care for the elderly: Supporting national strategies for ensuring a high level of social protection* (2003) was essentially focused on fiscal and policy perspectives concerned with access, quality and sustainability in healthcare and long-term care policies for older people. This report, as a European Union (EU)-wide policy document, was inevitably more concerned to address structural mechanisms for ensuring outcomes such as financial models for 'social protection systems', staff recruitment and training regimes and distribution of services across the EU.

An interesting and significant facet of the report is that it combined in one document rationales for, and benefits of, both healthcare and social care (or, as it phrased it, long-term care for older people). There is a subtle difference between the ways in which the EU document and the NHS use the phrase 'long term'. The EU version differentiates it clearly from healthcare, using it in a way that is more analogous in the UK with 'social care', and also articulates very clearly the importance to maintaining health of meeting long-term care need. It is also worth noting that in a 25-page report the EU devotes substantially more space to differentiating definitions of health and long-term care than do the almost 200 pages of the NSF for Older People document. This is not merely a matter of semantics: the NSF standards are promoted as applying equally to health and social care, but the thrust of the documentation is heavily weighted to health matters and references to social (long-term) care are relatively insubstantial and generally subordinated to health. Such a position is not unexpected, for social work and social care of older people has traditionally operated within a medical model of disease. It is, however, of interest to note the relatively heavy emphasis on the value of long-term care in the EU report.

Satisfaction with the services

The policy position provides the context for service delivery. However, the nature of service experience is perhaps the most important indicator by which consumer satisfaction is expressed. Within, for example, mental health and disability services user groups there has emerged a very powerful voice of user empowerment and involvement in service development. This movement has increasingly both challenged the supremacy of medical, especially biomedical, models of care and developed an enhanced model of social care. There is a range of varying perspectives. In social work and social care the newly developed regulatory and professional bodies have embraced the imperative for user empowerment (see, for example, Beresford and Croft, 2001). In a different vein, Thompson and Thompson (2001) explore the developing acknowledgement that older people will increasingly play an active role in the planning and delivery of care. Evidence from previous chapters in this book demonstrates the impact that movements such as the Better Government for Older People initiative have had in enabling older people to take control of their own interests, in partnership with other stakeholders including health and social care. The introduction to this book has also discussed some of the issues involved in using older people's views and experiences as a knowledge base for practice.

Notwithstanding these developments, Calnan et al (2003), in their study on the relationship between ageing and levels of satisfaction with the health service, demonstrated that there was little support for the view that older patients are becoming more consumer-orientated and critical of health services. The authors argued that this was likely since older people are "because of their structural position ... characterised by passivity, acceptance and dependency" (p 5). They went on to suggest that this may be because older people have been disempowered by the experiences of professional power which have "tended to leave both older patients and their families excluded from discussions concerning medical treatment and can be said to have encouraged an inherently passive approach to health care among older people" (p 5). These issues are precisely the reasons why a biological model of ill-health is often rejected in favour of a social model. The picture is by no means a clear one and the authors cite a previous study (Calnan et al, 1994) to make the proposition that the increasing satisfaction levels of older people associated with healthcare usage may be as a direct result of recent experience of healthcare, together with a changed understanding of what healthcare can and cannot deliver, brought about by the experience of old age itself.

These findings are consistent with those of Hardy et al (1999) who found that older people were less inclined to complain and were likely to report high levels of satisfaction with their care services. These views collectively demonstrate the extent to which there is both diversity and disagreement surrounding the assessment of user satisfaction. However, it is also necessary to take into account the views of those who elect not to use services. One project in the ESRC Growing Older Research Programme (Baldock and Hadlow, 2002) explored the links between identity, self-esteem and the use of care services. Findings concluded that in older people aged over 80 there can be a conflict between one's self-esteem and the acceptance of help and services. Characteristically respondents saw the acceptance of help as demonstrating negative qualities associated in their own minds with failing to manage. However, the study concluded that notwithstanding the respondents' negative perceptions of services, there was evidence to show that service inputs could improve the quality of lives. Conversely, and paradoxically, Tanner (2001), in an examination of decisions made to exclude, through the application of eligibility criteria, older people from services that they felt they needed, found that the respondents directed their efforts at managing the denial of services through maintaining a positive sense of self:

> It is apparent that while the situation of some participants whose needs have remained unmet has deteriorated physically and/or psychologically, others have managed to 'resist' threats to selfhood by finding alternative 'strategies' in practical terms or new ways of 'coping' in terms of psychological readjustment. (Tanner, 2001, pp 273-4)

In order to make sense of these apparent contradictions it would be helpful to look in some detail at examples of what needs older people might have, and how they might perceive them best being met.

Satisfaction and service users

This part of the chapter focuses on selected implications of an evaluation study commissioned by Help the Aged and undertaken by the Centre for Care of

Older People at Northumbria University in 2002 (Stanley, 2003). The purpose of the study was to examine and describe services for older people that were identified as demonstrating good practice in order to gain insight into the ways in which both service users and providers valued those 'good practice' services.

Methodological approach

The study commissioners were interested to establish what was valued about the schemes by both their providers and users and it was agreed to use a methodology known as Appreciative Inquiry (AI). AI is an approach, grounded in qualitative understandings, that emphasises capitalising on organisational assets rather than focusing on problems. It has emerged from work by Cooperrider and Srivastva (1987) who noted that there were situations where organisations were efficient and effective. In these situations exploring problems in order to identify a solution was not appropriate. They therefore changed their approach and began to inquire into the successes to discover, understand and learn from success. This represented a move from a positivistic stance that there is a world that can be described and engineered, toward a social constructionist position in which the social world is created and constructed by the debates that we have about it (Steier, 1991), and the method of inquiry used to explore a social world is part of this debate (Reed et al, 2002). Bushe (1998) suggests that AI is a form of action research that attempts to create new theory and images that facilitate change in a social system. He states, "The key data collection innovation of AI is the collection of people's stories of something at its best … these stories are collectively discussed in order to create new, generative ideas or images that aid in developmental change of the collectivity discussing them" (p 1).

AI is premised in three assumptions. First, organisations are responsive to positive thought and positive knowledge. Second, the image for the future, and the process of creating that image, create the energy to drive change throughout an organisation. Third, affirming and envisioning what we want will increase the possibility that it will happen (Hammond, 1996).

From these assumptions it is evident that AI has an explicit focus on examining positive and productive aspects of a situation, rather than focusing on problems. In its simplest terms, AI suggests that one way to develop practice is to do more of what works, rather than less of what does not. AI argues that by looking at factors that are productive and helpful, it is then possible to think of ways of extending and developing these positive factors. AI does not dismiss problems, or try to underplay their importance – it just offers an alternative way of approaching issues (Johnson and Leavitt, 2001). AI has been criticised for being uncritical in its alleged overemphasis on highlighting the positive, and there are arguments that inquiry and productive discourse can be discouraged through a lack of constructive criticism (Patton, 2002). However, the use of open questioning enables respondents to express anxieties and concerns. Its results identify themes and topics that can become the foundation for positive organisational development and thus AI methodology matched the commissioners' desire to know 'what worked and was valued' in order to allocate its finite funding resources effectively.

The study

There were two strands to the study and it is with the outcomes of Strand 2 that we are principally concerned here.

- Strand 1: Literature review of the relationship between older people and the informal sector.
- Strand 2: Evaluation of 10 informal sector schemes (to listen to the stories of those involved with informal sector schemes about their experiences in order to discover what they valued and identify the factors that enabled this to happen, and find out how it could be developed further). The schemes were identified on a judgement sample basis by regional coordinators: judged impressionistically to be examples of how the informal sector could develop innovative and effective ways of working. Data was collected by a fieldworker spending two days at each scheme.

The schemes

Table 1 provides a brief outline of the schemes included in the study. They ranged from befriending projects to transport provision, with different backgrounds, purposes and structures. Their range and scale were diverse, covering – and sometimes combining – health and social care and social and educational activities. Their common characteristic, however, was the way in which they were valued by those who used or contributed in some way to their services.

Most were set up in the late 1980s to 1990s with only one having been in existence for more than 20 years, although a small number of others had either developed from previously existing organisations or had developed from a gap left by the closure of other services. Structure and size were also extremely variable and it seems that the longer established each scheme became, the wider and more varied became their network of service provision. The particular focus of activity ranged from specialist services for frail older people, including an integrated day centre for people with dementia and those with disabilities and support for carers, to leisure activities for active people over 50, home-visiting support services for people over 65, to a scheme for volunteer peer support for people of all ages and disabilities, to an organisation aimed at promoting well-being and self-empowerment in later life for older people who were mobile.

Most schemes originated from clear identification of need, from the legacies of previous schemes or from meetings of people employed in a service-provider capacity. For example, a day centre for frail older people, people with disabilities and people with dementia arose from an identified lack of supporting services for older people living at home. A leisure, recreation and learning activities facility for people over 50 became established as a result of threat of closure to the range of unconnected previous services, following an independently funded needs analysis. A self-referral organisation aiming to foster self-reliance and social interaction was established following concerns expressed by a community

Table 1: Brief description of the schemes included in the sample (many of the schemes have a wide range of activities and services that are not described in the table)

Scheme	Description
1	This scheme provides day care for frail older people, disabled people and those suffering from dementia. It also includes a befriending service, volunteers support group and transport services. Approximately 65 members use the services of this scheme.
2	This scheme enables people to meet up with and develop relationships with others who have similar interests. Consequently the scheme addresses the loneliness that many members had experienced prior to joining it. There are approximately 800 members of this scheme.
3	This scheme meets the needs of individuals over 60 years of age who are experiencing crisis or change in their lives by providing a range of services such as bereavement counselling, home visiting, a form-filling service and lunch clubs. There are approximately 350 individuals who use this scheme.
4	This scheme is a self-help resource centre, which enables people to support one another while providing services including a lunch club and activity groups. This scheme uses its resources to support other organisations to meet the needs of their users.
5	This scheme is a community care network that provides home care in a rural community. It includes a befriending scheme, home-care provision, a gardening service and an advice service.
6	This scheme provides leisure and educational activities for those aged 50 and over. These activities include tai chi, painting, craft and singing. There are approximately 650 users of this scheme.
7	This is a neighbourhood community-based scheme, which aims to help and support older people to live in the community through the provision of a range of services and activities. These include gardening and decorating, advocacy services, swimming and tea dance activities. There are 1,073 members of this scheme.
8	This scheme aims to assist in the prevention of loneliness, isolation and ill-health and at the same time give basic practical assistance to enable older people to remain independent in their own homes. The main areas of activity are the volunteer visiting services (approximately 7,750 hours) and day-care centres (approximately 180 users).
9	This scheme provides a wide variety and depth of services, ranging from day centres and a transport department through to domiciliary and domestic care. There are 6,000 people registered to use different aspects of the scheme.
10	This scheme centres around the premise that older people have a right to be involved in decisions and events that affect their lives and, by using professional and volunteer advocates, aims to support and enable people in exercising choice.

development officer and clinical psychologist about rising GP referrals for depression.

The size of membership was also variable but, because of the sometimes federal and in other ways quite complex interrelationship between the various services and opportunities provided by each particular scheme, it is not possible to make direct comparisons. However, the range of scale is demonstrated by a writing group of 10 members, albeit a sub-unit of a larger scheme, in contrast to a multiple provision scheme with an overall membership of around 800 older people.

Those schemes with extensive membership tended to be characterised by multiple smaller-scale activity and interest groups. There was also the recognition of a potential paradoxical dilemma in the question of expansion.

Key themes

The following themes emerged from the data.

Managing the organisation

Structural diversity was evident, ranging from forms of the traditional hierarchical structure to the essentially self-managed collective. A generally common pattern was for schemes to have a combination of full-time and part-time paid staff, a manager or coordinator and various forms of committee, although the terminology varied from location to location. One model adopted by an association based on a philosophy of self-help was that of a committee of volunteers with co-opted members: here it was sometimes quite difficult to differentiate between volunteers and members.

It was also evident that the schemes, to a greater or lesser extent, had very active links, which they valued, with health and social care professionals – social workers, health visitors, nurses, community psychiatric nurses (CPNs) and GPs. These links were not restricted to their professional inputs but also involved direct inputs as volunteers, committee members and the like. In some cases the nature of the contractual relationship between a scheme and a funding stakeholder led to the adoption of standards in relation to quality criteria.

The personnel

Membership referral took on a number of forms. For example, one scheme was founded on a basis of self-referral, indicating a level of self-motivation, commitment and mobility on the part of members. One scheme promoted its existence in the local press and libraries, referrals were often made by other agencies or by friends, and sometimes there were self-referrals, often after unhappy experiences with other agencies. Yet another had created a referral committee, which met on a monthly basis. In many respects the referral process reflected the resource implications of membership: in self-help settings there was more scope for recruitment than others where there might be quite finite limitations on space/places available.

The recruitment and retention of good quality volunteer services were important to most schemes and essential to the success of some. In more than one scheme, volunteers' ages ranged from 14 years to 80 years. Within organisations the therapeutic value of volunteering was recognised and many people who joined schemes as members were encouraged to become volunteers themselves to contribute their skills and experience to the scheme. This led to older people becoming actively involved in supporting others and contributing to the community in a positive way, serving also to enhance their sense of being valued by others.

The funding dilemma

While this study was not concerned with finances per se, just below the surface of any of the data collectors' inquiry lay issues of the instability and short-termism of the funding regimes of these schemes. Their relatively recent existences indicate, to a certain extent at least, the central difficulties faced by relatively small-scale, locally based, independent volunteer enterprises. Almost without exception, when asked to envision improved services for the future, funding was identified by respondents as being problematic.

Qualities and characteristics

It is not difficult to establish the underlying principles that informed the provision of these schemes. Almost paradoxically, their prime goal was to do with life-skills acquisition in later life. However simplistic and self-evident a statement this might be, the schemes were essentially concerned with the promotion of well-being and, where at all possible, self-empowerment. Members repeatedly expressed the view that one of the significant gains from association with their schemes was the acquisition of life skills that they had not expected to develop.

Examples cited included increased self-confidence and self-esteem, the capacity to make connections with their local communities, and the creation of caring networks. Another skill was the actual process of learning how to organise activities on behalf of other members. This sense of contributing to their communities, however defined, was highly prized. In addition, many learned new, or developed existing, skills in arts and crafts and other leisure activities. Many members took on multiple roles within their schemes – for example, acting both as a volunteer and as a consumer of activities – and it was frequently reported that skill acquisition was also just as valued an aspect for volunteers as it was for members.

Valued characteristics included perceptions of the schemes as being warm, friendly places that encouraged involvement and the provision of opportunities to learn across a range of dimensions. There was also an explicit appreciation of links with health and social care services, especially the provision of direct services such as chiropody and welfare advice.

Facilities

Reference has already been made to the variety of facilities provided by these schemes. Transport, especially minibuses, and accommodation were both major items in terms of resources. The acquisition of property on either short- or long-term lease or through purchase did much for securing the ongoing future of a scheme, although equally posed a burden of maintenance and associated fundraising. Availability of transport was critical in the provision of appropriate services: volunteer transport was heavily relied upon but had its limitations, while capital and running costs for dedicated transport services seemed to pose constant financial worries. The scale and uptake of services was always dependent upon location and access. There were also major issues to do with shared and short-term accommodation. There is no simple way to categorise these, mostly because of the very varied nature of the schemes, the services that they provided and the members who accessed them.

Range of activities

The spectrum of activities, services and facilities was extensive and complex. Free services – for example, where chiropody or hair care was provided by staff – were particularly valued. Some were found across the range of schemes while others were highly scheme specific. The range of activities can be clustered into four general categories:

- personal and social;
- health and social care;
- fitness and activity based;
- cultural and educational.

Providing services such as a lunch or a tea is a tangible manifestation of care. However, in many schemes the members, staff and volunteers were concerned to use these events as an opportunity to monitor a range of other less tangible issues in relation to health and well-being. This atmosphere of care and concern could frequently become a reciprocal affair, with members feeling a responsibility towards keeping in touch with people from the scheme, and in a circular way promoted a sense of shared values.

The voices of members

The members' voices ran deeply throughout the data, and not just where they were explicitly requested to give their responses. The most striking aspect of these voices was the clarity with which they echoed the common theme that membership of their scheme really had made a substantial difference to the quality of their lives. The language varied from scheme to scheme but in essence the message was that there were two ways in which these differences could be described. First, there was the sheer significance of *the impact*, and second were the very *personal meanings* that impact had for the members in a wide variety of different ways.

The impact

This was variously described as "a lifeline", "a new and fulfilling life", "cornerstone of everything"; imparting the capacity to "derive confidence to do other things eg travel abroad"; "fun, good company, a life saver"; "changed my life for the better"; "feel lucky in relation to others"; "opportunities for new experiences": the voices were unanimous in expressing their views. There was no scheme that did not in some substantive way reflect these sentiments.

Equally important to the nature of the impact was its depth. There was no more telling a phrase than "[it is] nourishment to my soul", a phrase that instantly encapsulated the meaning of the experience for that particular member – and many others besides. The sense of purpose, sense of belonging and encouragement of independence and self-reliance – to the degree possible in the light of members' capacities and potentials – all spoke volubly of how the schemes offered outlets that were not replicated elsewhere and which the members valued to the utmost. It is important to say that members were not blithely uncritical of their schemes. It was not necessary to coax or coach responses: they were spontaneous, voluble and respondents were only too pleased to be able to have the opportunity to express them to the fieldworkers.

The personal meanings: being valued

First among the personal meanings was a strong sense of being valued as an individual and a person. Common themes that emerged from the data included: not being patronised, being respected as an older person in ways not always present in other organisations, and being treated as an individual. Their involvement enhanced a sense of mutuality, ownership and commitment.

Great value was attached to the feeling that their scheme reflected "normal life", in the sense that members did not feel institutionalised, to the fact that there was no feeling of being "forced" to take part in any particular activity and that it was possible to opt out of events without any recrimination.

The personal meanings: personal/social

A major asset was the transformation of members' personal and social lives: the development of a new social network, often where none or very little previously existed, and opportunities for warm, friendly, even animated, conversation. While the actual scheme base was a valued asset, it was equally important for members to feel a sense of normative, rather than institutionalised, activity – such as holding scheduled meetings in everyday places ranging from public libraries to public houses and selecting venues for their appeal, warmth, cheerfulness and brightness.

Being a scheme member made going out without a partner acceptable, provided companionship for those living alone, and offered a forum in which both happiness and worries could be shared.

The theme of the therapeutic value of scheme activities was often repeated. Membership activity served to relieve the boredom and monotony of a previously inactive existence, and broke dull routines. The secondary values of getting out of the house, with consequential opportunities for shopping, visiting the post box, form filling and so on, were identified along with the significant belief that membership activity led to some people remaining in their own homes when, if no facility had existed, they might have been in residential care or elsewhere.

The personal meanings: health

In the sense of ill-health, or pathology, this was not a point that was laboured in the specific member responses. Members were likely to take a more holistic approach in their views on health. References were made to the availability of opportunities for using the full range of one's abilities: physical health, flexibility and stamina. There was a strong belief that the improved quality of life derived from scheme membership led to better health than if no facility existed. In turn a number of respondents felt that there was a considerable, although difficult to measure, consequential saving to the NHS in terms of reduced incidences of depression, accidents and illnesses.

The personal meanings: family/friends

It was not unexpected to hear members' views that the schemes provided means of making friends, or that their associates there were more like a family than friends. Of equal significance was the statement that "You can discuss matters with members and staff that you might not wish to discuss with your family". This view underlines the often under-recognised function of the schemes in providing a context for their members to have space to act, think and relate as people independent of their families: a concept that most adults would take for granted but where there is evidence in old age that quite complex and subtle pressures can be applied in familial situations.

Key findings: principles for good practice

Overall, the data provided an uplifting record of services and activities available to people in later life. In every instance there was a clear message that the schemes offer something substantial and meaningful that is generally outside of members' experiences of the statutory sector provision. The essential characteristics of the schemes are to be found in the ways in which they creatively and caringly address the positive, proactive, quality of life issues. Formal agencies, with their safety-net function in terms of social care and emphasis on ill-health in terms of healthcare, are poorly resourced for such work – even if they had the skills and even if they had the remit – and they tend to focus almost exclusively on a reactive approach. There is also an argument to be made about the relative roles of 'preventive' work in contrast with the provision of 'normative' facilities. The language of health and social care is often more redolent, perhaps inevitably, of a pathological approach to ageing rather than seeing the whole person as an individual.

The aspirations of the NSF for Older People, a major facet of policy for improving services for older people in the UK, have yet to pervade the generality of practice in a substantial way. However, from the evidence we saw, the schemes were fundamentally contributing to key aspirations of the NSF standards. In particular they were making substantial contributions to: Standard 1, in addressing issues of age discrimination; Standard 2, delivering person-centred care; and Standard 8, promoting healthy, active lifestyles. In addition, significant contributions were being made to Standards 3, 5, 6 and 7 in the provision of a variety of services that could be defined as intermediate care, stroke-related services, the prevention of falls, and services for older people with mental health problems, especially dementia. In some instances these are contracted services with commissioning agencies; in others they are services quite outside the scope of the formal health and welfare systems. In all cases they were addressing the key concepts of age discrimination and person-centredness. In other words, the schemes that were visited were, in a very manifest way, making both direct and indirect contributions to delivering government welfare policy. One way in which the informal sector could develop its profile would be to exploit the significance of these assets as a contribution to the development of integrated care services.

Furthermore, the schemes have taken on a number of service provision areas that have been abandoned, in part at least, by the formal sector as a result of shifting social policy and financial regimes initiated by government. Examples include the provision of advocacy, advice, counselling and befriending services, certain types of domiciliary services including light maintenance, window cleaning and gardening.

Conclusions from the study

The study evaluated 10 very different informal sector projects with older people. The evaluation was a focused one, rather than an extended exploration. Nevertheless it identified key themes, which led to a discussion of ways in which these projects work. Perhaps the central message was about the increasing incorporation of informal and user-led initiatives into mainstream service provision. Informal sector projects can offer a different form of service, with a creative energy and responsive development that formal services may not be able to offer. Through mechanisms such as formal contracting, these qualities can become threatened. Restricted formulations about goals and outcomes can discourage organic developments beyond these parameters, and the inflexible implementation of guidelines and regulations can restrict activities and participation.

This suggests that the process of contracting and collaboration needs careful thought, and that strategies have to be developed that will establish relationships between the formal and informal sector in ways which do not compromise the independence and flexibility of the informal sector and which offer some stability of funding and support. The processes of identifying needs, encouraging participation and developing a sense of ownership varied among the projects that were evaluated, and researchers were dependent upon retrospective accounts of members to trace developments. There are two issues in particular which would provide considerable scope for the development of more effective integrated care services: first, through the ways in which engagement and participation among older people is encouraged and supported; and, second, in some of the projects through the evident sense of shared experiences and commonalities between the service providers and service users, to the extent that it was difficult to distinguish between them in some projects.

What became clear in the course of this study was that the informal sector makes an important contribution to the lives of older people, and that it does so in ways that challenge formal sector-based notions of providing integrated care services.

Conclusion

The notion of social enterprise is usually related to informal services that have been established as a result of some motivating force within the communities studied. In this study there was considerable strength of feeling that, notwithstanding the UK government policy drive for 'joined-up' working, there was wide variety in perceptions about how far the formal services – especially health and social care – really responded to the local needs of local people rather than expecting or requiring the local population to fit in with the pattern of provision that was usually defined by the professional and driven by government policy. It must be acknowledged that issues of boundary and continuum were not explored in this study. However, it was found that respondents often had a greater sense of engagement with their informal sector services than they had with the orthodox formal service delivery mechanisms.

No one benefits from complex, disconnected services being pulled in different directions by conflicting policy developments and funding methodologies. While the public sector role is particularly linked to short-term political expediency, there is scope for every stakeholder within a pluralistic welfare system to gain from the better development of integrated services: especially and primarily the service user. The evidence from this study indicated how older people were demanding that their perspectives and needs are responded to by the services that they require, and that their health and social well-being were essentially indivisible and benefited from effective integration. The informal sector gains by doing what it does best and by being more in control of its own destiny, especially through being assured of longer-term, more adequate funding. The professionals involved gain from the undoubted benefits that effective partnership brings. Furthermore, while this is not simply a matter of financial imperative, there were seen to be considerable economic and efficiency benefits too.

This raises questions concerning modes of holistic integrated care in the community. The UK Government Review of September 2002 (Audit Commission, 2002) concluded that policy makers, including local government, should involve the informal sector at an early stage in the design and planning of services and explore the full range of options for their involvement. There were recommendations aimed at recognising the particular strengths of the informal sector: how far these will be addressed in practice will be seen in the outcomes. A strategic document (Audit Commission, 2002) suggests that there are two key components of a whole system of services for older people: first, a comprehensive range of services; and, second, a way of guiding older people through the system. It is quite surprising that it does not add a third imperative: the participation of older people in both. While inclusion is implicit, unless it becomes explicit there is little likelihood of the voices of older people making a substantive contribution to service development.

Exercises

- Make an inventory of services for older people in your neighbourhood.
- Compile a list of characteristics of a successful service for older people.
- Try to arrange a visit to one of the services and check out your list of characteristics.

References

Audit Commission (2002) *Integrated services for older people: Building a whole system approach in England*, London: Audit Commission.

Baldock, J. and Hadlow, J. (2002) *Housebound older people: The links between identity, self-esteem and the use of care services*, GO research findings 4, June, Sheffield: Sheffield University.

Beresford, P. and Croft, S. (2001) 'Service users' knowledges and the social construction of social work', *Journal of Social Work*, vol 1, no 3, pp 295-316.

Bushe, G.R. (1998) 'Appreciative Inquiry with teams', *Organization Development Journal*, vol 16, no 3, pp 41-50.

Calnan, M., Almond, S. and Smith, N. (2003) 'Ageing and public satisfaction with the health service: an analysis of recent trends', *Social Science and Medicine*, vol 57, no 4, pp 757-62(6).

Calnan, M., Coyle, J. and Williams, S. (1994) 'Changing perceptions of general practitioner care', *E Journal of Public Health*, vol 4, pp 108-17.

Commission of the European Communities (2003) *Joint report: Healthcare and care for the elderly: Supporting national strategies for ensuring a high level of social protection*, COM (2002) 774 final, Brussels: Commission of the European Communities.

Cooperrider, D. and Srivastva, S. (1987) 'Appreciative Inquiry in organizational life', *Research in Organizational Change and Development*, vol 1, pp 129-69.

DoH (Department of Health) (2001) *National Service Framework for Older People*, London: DoH.

Flynn, R.J. and Lemay, R.A. (eds) (1999) *A quarter-century of normalization and social role valorization: Evolution and impact*, Ottawa: University of Ottawa Press.

Hammond, S.A. (1996) *The thin book of Appreciative Inquiry* (2nd edn), Thin Book Publishing.

Hardy, B., Young, R. and Wistow, G. (1999) 'Dimensions of choice in the assessment and care management process: the views of older people, carers and managers', *Health and Social Care in the Community*, vol 7, no 6, pp 483-91.

Johnson, G. and Leavitt, W. (2001) 'Building on success: transforming organizations through an Appreciative Inquiry', *Public Personnel Management*, vol 30, no 1, pp 129-36.

Patton, M.Q. (2002) *Qualitative research and evaluation methods* (3rd edn), Thousand Oaks, CA: Sage Publications.

Reed, J., Pearson, P., Douglas, B., Swinburne, S. and Wilding, H. (2002) 'Going home from hospital – an Appreciative Inquiry study', *Health and Social Care in the Community*, vol 10, no 1, pp 36-45.

Stanley, D. (2003) *Social enterprise, service delivery and integrated care for older people in the UK, International Journal of Integrated Care*/World Health Organisation Conference, Barcelona, peer reviewed proceedings: http://www.ijic.org/portal/publish/issues/conf2003/proceedings.html.

Steier, F. (1991) 'Reflexivity and methodology: an ecological constructionism', in F. Steier (ed) *Research and reflexivity*, London: Sage Publications.

Tanner, D. (2001) 'Sustaining the self in later life', *Ageing and Society*, vol 21, no 3, pp 255-75.

Thompson, N. and Thompson, S. (2001) 'Empowering older people: beyond the care model', *Journal of Social Work*, vol 1, no 1, pp 61-76.

persistently kept us informed about their ideas and views, and gently corrected us when our academic experiences and ideas threatened to overshadow theirs. You may not have this opportunity, but we would suggest that you try to create and develop it. This may be a difficult and sometimes frustrating process, as discussions become ever more complex and seemingly contradictory, and the clarity you began with is lost. Nonetheless, we would argue that the ambiguity you may end up with as a result of talking with older people is better than the neat and tidy ideas you had before you did so.

Some of this complexity comes from the diversity and complexity of older people themselves. As with any other group in society, opinions, views and experiences differ, and older people are much more diverse than many other people we label as members of a group, whether the parameters are defined by age, gender, ethnicity, class or any other characteristics. Older people, as we have pointed out elsewhere, can be from a variety of races, and classes, can have different gendered experiences, and may not even be of a similar age if definitions of 'older' range from the mid-fifties up to the current limits of the human lifespan. This means that it is not possible to say that older people feel a certain way about a certain issue, because there will be as many views as there are older people. What we can do, however, is point to the experiences shared by older people, such as ageism, and also to the differences in experiences, such as financial circumstances. Including awareness of this range and diversity in our thinking is a vital step in developing research, policy, education and practice in a responsive and relevant way.

In the introduction to this book, we talked about the values that have informed it, in terms of the view that planning and thinking that takes place *with* older people is better than that which simply takes place *for* older people. Throughout the book we have included what older people have said to us and to others about what they think and feel about their lives and the services and support that they use. Through the chapters on physical ageing, the lived environment, memory, ability, families and communities, money, risk and safety, and using services, the starting point has been statements and views from older people about what they want and need. This notion of partnership and involvement can be traced to a number of ethical positions about the nature of personhood, the exercise and using of power, and the values of justice and equity. These values bear examination and discussion if the implications of this book are to be fully explored.

Personhood

In many cultures importance is placed on the idea of individuality, of every person as a unique person. This uniqueness is something that, it is argued, we must respect when talking about needs, duties and rights. These will vary from person to person, due to their different circumstances and experiences, and this acknowledgement forms the basis of our relations with each other.

ELEVEN

Issues for discussion and practice

Contents

Personhood	188
Sharing and exercising power	189
Justice and equity	190
Practice	191
Policy	192
Research	192
Final comments	193

Readers come to books with a range of different expectations and hopes.
too, have a set of aims when they write. An ideal would be for both r
authors to achieve their aims, or find what they are looking f
ambiguities, confusions or misunderstandings. Writing and r
however, is not always such a straightforward process, and perh
the good. As authors we have certainly found that the views
started off with have changed and developed as we talked t
or saw their work, read the academic literature and tried to
form that did justice to the range of views and ideas tha

For readers, expectations and ideas may also have unde
This may or may not be an entirely positive exper
specific purpose – for example, to find out about p
we do not achieve this purpose, then it feels like v
however, in the course of our reading, come a
and ideas that we were not looking for – a
important. We hope that those of you wh
this book have instead come across ide
contribution to the work that you do v

This final chapter offers some idea
with a summary of the key themes
these ideas may be incorporated
These are, of course, only sugg
experiences of your own th
would ask, however, is that v
critically and with reference to
able to work with experienced, insig

Personho

In western c
human being
should be resp
differ from pers
but their acknow

188

These relations may be subject to dispute, as when rights may conflict, or to different definitions, as we debate the nature of humanity as connected beings rather than completely separate entities, but they will still form the basis of the way we think about each other and about ourselves.

These debates do not, however, always play out in the same way for all people. While we may have some notion of 'common humanity' we can still apply conditions and qualifications to this – we grant or deny rights, for example, based on whether the people we are talking about qualify, in our view, as full human beings. The discussions we had earlier in this book, particularly in the chapter on ageism, point to ways in which older people can be excluded from the state of 'personhood' by attitudes that assume, either covertly or overtly, that because someone is older, then they do not fully qualify as a person, and therefore that we do not need to treat them as full people. We can exclude older people because they do not work in paid employment (and therefore do not qualify as 'taxpayers') or because they have physical limitations and are not as active as others (and are therefore lazy or passive), or because they do not look like younger people (and have 'let themselves go'). Any of these reasons can be used to differentiate between older people and others, and also blame them for their own exclusions. One of the most insidious processes of exclusion comes with memory problems, as Chapter Five has shown. If we think that a prerequisite of personhood is the ability to remember recent events, then the diagnosis of dementia, even in the early stages, can be enough to invalidate any claims we might make.

Sharing and exercising power

A second theme or value running through the book is that of power. While there is a rhetoric about involvement and power sharing with the users of services, this rhetoric tends to gloss over the inequalities in power that involvement strategies are supposed to address. We need to think through these issues very carefully in order to be able to address them thoroughly and effectively.

Older people, like other marginalised groups in society, have limited power to influence the structures and processes of the social worlds in which they live. One of the most obvious areas in which they lack power is in the area of finances and money. As people who are not often wage-earners, and do not anticipate future wage-earning, they are immediately disadvantaged when it comes to 'putting their money where their mouth is' – they may have no money to put anywhere. Whereas other groups may have money to spend, or not spend, depending on their needs and preferences, older people may not have this power, and can be dependent on the benefits and services that society deems appropriate for them.

Interestingly, this form of inequality has been challenged by the image of the affluent retiree, the favourite of advertising campaigns. The idea is that there is a type of older person who has retired at a comparatively young age, on a decent pension and with few financial responsibilities for dependants. This person is the natural customer for luxury cruises, fine wines and expensive cars, and is presented as an object of envy. While this may, indeed, be the situation of some older people, as Chapter Eight shows, it is not the case for many, and the development of this image draws attention away from the real need that they feel.

Power is not all about money, however – money can be seen as symbolic of influence and control, and there are other characteristics that could also be described as constitutive of or contributing to the power that older people can or cannot exercise. The chapter on ageism in this book (Chapter Two) discusses some of these characteristics, which older people are assumed not to have – understanding of contemporary issues, physical attractiveness and robustness, and mental agility are some of them. Ageist assumptions, then, tip the balance of power away from older people – if power is something that is socially negotiated, then anything that weakens the negotiating position of older people limits their power. Returning to our discussion of personhood above, if older people are seen, through an ageist lens, as being less than 'full' people, then they are also not seen as powerful.

In this respect the calls for power sharing are ambitious. Aside from the technical issues that need to be thought through, there needs to be a rethinking and examination of attitudes and assumptions if any change is to happen. Part of this process is, of course, bringing the need to rethink to people's attention, and calls for increased involvement and power sharing in planning for services and policies will go some way towards starting the process off.

Justice and equity

One of the themes in debates about provision and support for older people is the theme of justice – most often expressed in debates about what is the fairest way to treat older people. There is, for example, the debate about what is the fair way to recognise and reward the contributions that older people have made over their lifetimes. A generation who lived through wars, for example, almost inevitably made sacrifices and contributions for the national good. This is a strong argument for younger generations, who have benefited from these sacrifices, to respond with support and aid.

There are, however, as we discussed in Chapter One, some difficulties with this argument. The sacrifices made in the past were also motivated by self-interest, and if thought was given to future generations, the thinking was abstract rather than personal – that generation did not know those who were unborn. This does, as we pointed out in Chapter One, make applying the notion of reciprocity more difficult. The impersonal nature of the sacrifice, however, does not constitute a reason for dismissing it, or not responding with gratitude. In some ways, the impersonality of the sacrifice makes it more powerful.

Aside from the debate about justice for older people, however, is also the debate about equity, both between and within generations. In a world where we are told that resources are limited, we are often posed choices between meeting the needs of older people or younger people. If asked to choose, then, we may feel that younger people should be helped in order to enjoy their life to come, while older people, as the saying goes, 'have had their life'. If this is a crude life-or-death choice, that logic becomes compelling, but often it is not – it is a choice about providing resources to improve quality of life. Then the choice becomes less clear, and the justice arguments become stronger. Calling on justice arguments is very relevant, however, because of what they suggest about the sort of society we want to live in. We do not want to live in a world where we make sacrifices for future generations, just to have these generations turn their backs on us when we need them. To support the reciprocal justice argument, therefore, is to move from thinking 'us' and 'them' to simply thinking about us – what we all want.

The other equity debate is about equity within generations, most often arising when we try to work out what is the fair way to distribute resources throughout the older generation. This question arises when we debate the merits of universal or means-tested benefits, the development of different services, or pensions and savings schemes. Should every older person get the same benefits regardless of their income or assets, or should they be assessed to determine the amount of benefit they will get? Should we fund hip operations or home helps? Should we raise state pensions or encourage people to save for their retirement? All of these questions are about equity within the older generation, and as such are subjects of serious and sometimes furious debate.

These three themes, then, of personhood, empowerment and justice, have informed and shaped the contents and approach of this book. We want to do more than just explore the issues in it, however; we also want it to be useful – we want it to change the way that people think and act. While publication alone may be enough for our CVs, a much better outcome would be if readers did things differently because of what they had read. This is not a case of us believing that we know best, but simply a process of opening up debates. Some people may find that what we have written echoes and supports what they have thought before, while others may find the ideas new and may even be reluctant to engage with them, but the point is to become involved in the debate, the arguing of points and the teasing out of ideas, so that what we do now can be evaluated and developed.

Practice

Throughout this book we have made links between the discussions and practice in health and social care. The implications of the discussions, however, could extend beyond this, to housing and transport, for example. For everybody working with and for older people, then, the key messages are about listening to what older people think and feel about their lives and the support they get. In this book we have drawn on material from some older people, but we would not claim that their views are universally shared by all older people. It is important, therefore, to ask older people about their views, and to listen and act on what they say.

Going back to the discussion in the introduction to this book, finding a place for user knowledge in evidence-based practice is not always an easy matter, given the emphasis on research and science. The views and experiences of older people, therefore, are much more akin to experiential or tacit knowledge, and therefore more difficult to examine and generalise. Moves to provide 'person-centred' services, however, which respond to individuals' needs and which have user satisfaction as the central driving force, open up possibilities of making user views a clear and explicit basis for practice.

Policy

The book has less explicit links to policy development, but they are still there. If policy is to have the support of society (and therefore the governments that make it stay in power) then it has to address the views and experiences of those it is aimed at. This is not, however, just a matter of giving people what they want – the discussion above about justice and equity showed that there are many different needs and wants to be balanced in any policy making. What policy makers can do, however, is engage in debates with older people about how they live their lives and how they want to be helped. This is not simply opening the doors to wild demands – listening exercises can often spend more time encouraging than discouraging demands – but it does mean trying to understand the complexity of people's lives, and how different aspects are interlinked. One of the difficulties we had when writing this book was dividing up the ideas and material into distinct chapters that had their own distinct content, which did not spill over into other chapters. We were not always completely successful in doing this, and so we have had to cross-reference between chapters in the book. This is because life is not neatly divided into compartments, and the message for policy is that it should not be either. This is not just the question of how health and social services work together, although this is a central question, but how they work with housing, transport, pensions, environmental policies and community developments. Older people, like everyone else, have 'joined-up' lives, and need 'joined-up' policies.

Research

Policy and Practice is supported, ideally, by research, and this book has some implications for the ways in which research could be carried out, and the questions it could ask. In 1992 Jerrome pointed out that:

> The methods used to acquire information are such that the subjective experience of ageing is subordinated to the objective accounts provided by youthful researchers. Very little contemporary research addresses the issues of ageing from the elderly person's point of view. (Jerrome, 1992, p 4)

While research may have moved on from this, and more work might be done to elicit the views of older people, there is another stage to go. Having older people not just as subjects in a research study but as partners planning and carrying out the study is this next stage, and as we discussed in the introduction this is beginning to happen. A stage after this would be for older people to entirely take over research – perhaps employing the occasional academic to do the leg work on a study, but taking control of project management themselves. As more older people become involved in research, as members of funding panels, as advisors on projects or data collectors, this stage becomes more realisable. While research carried out by older people will not necessarily be 'better' research (it is likely to vary in quality, as all research does), it will offer a different view from that of the academic researcher.

Final comments

Making final comments at the end of a book that has taken so long to come to fruition feels like an anticlimax – what can we say that will sum up our ideas in a short and snappy way, which readers will take with them when they have closed the covers? It may be safer just to end with the key message of the book: listen to older people – they know more about their lives than anyone else does, and whether you are a practitioner, a policy maker or a researcher, they can shake up your assumptions, challenge your ideas and lead to new ways of thinking, if you only listen carefully.

Reference

Jerrome, D. (1992) *Good company: An anthropological study of old people in groups*, Edinburgh: Edinburgh University Press.

Index

A

accidents *see* safety and risk
Action for Health for Senior Citizens
    (AHSCIN) 112
action research 4, 173
activity and health 57-8, 59, 61-2, 87
activity theory 35-6
    see also 'successful ageing'
Adams, M. 100
Adams, R.G. 121
Age Concern 22, 24-5, 38, 75, 112, 141
age stratification theory 35
'ageing education' 35
ageing process
    acceptance of 47-8, 59, 61-2
    denial of 19-20, 52-3, 60
    experiential knowledge 15-16, 193
    theories of 16, 18-20, 35-6, 59-61
     physical ageing 49-53
    see also physical functioning
ageing society 22
ageist attitudes 17, 18, 31-44
    and empowerment 190
    and health 37-8, 56
    methods to combat 42-3, 170, 181
    and right to personhood 189, 190
    transport providers 76
    see also stereotypes
Alaszewski, A. and H. 153-4
Allen, D. 7
Alzheimer's disease *see* memory loss/
    dementia
Andrews, Molly 18
Antonovsky, A. 58
Appleton, N.J.W. 72, 74
Appreciative Inquiry (AI) 173-4
Arber, S. 18, 131
Argyle, E. 139
artistic therapies and dementia 87
Ashley, Peter 83
assistive technologies 82
Atchley, R.C. 36
autonomy and risk management 153, 154
Ayris, W. 155, 157, 163

B

Baago, S. 88
Baltes, M.M. 60
Becker, L.C. 21
'bed-blockers' 38
Bell, J. 98

benefits 134-7, 143, 191
Bennet, G. 50-1
Berrios, G. 89
'best practice' evaluation 173-83
Better Government for Older People 11,
    104, 112, 113, 135, 171
Beveridge, William 24
Biggs, S. 118
Bildtegård, T. 99
biomedical models of ageing 49-51, 59, 62
Blackman, Honor 100
Blaxter, M. 55-6, 58
Blomfield, R. 4
Blum, N.S. 97
Boden, C. (also Bryden, C.) 83
body
    youthfulness 48-9, 52-3, 60
    see also physical functioning
Boore, J.R.P. 89
Bowling, A. 60
Boylan, C. 100
Brabazon, K. 37
Bradley, H. 35
Brechin, A. 9
Bredin, K. 85
British Gas 73
Brodaty, H. 89
brokerage schemes 141
Brooker, D. 87
Broom, D.H. 85-6
Brush, J. 82
Bryant, L. 57-8
Bryden, C. (also Boden, C.) 79-80, 83
Bury, M. 56
Bushe, G.R. 173
Bytheway, Bill 18, 33, 34, 49

C

Calder, J. 132-3
Calkins, M. 82
Calman, K.C. 164
Calnan, M. 171, 172
campaigning groups 24-5, 171
care environment: knowledge basis 6
care provision *see* informal care; service
    provision
Carstensen, L.L. 60
cell division 51-2
Centre for Care of Older People 111-12
    user satisfaction study 172-83
challenging activities 123-4
Charmaz, K. 56

Cheang, M. 121
childcare: grandparent provision 142
childhood: as construct 34
Cicero 33, 60
Citizens Advice Bureaux 132, 135
Clarke, C.L. 8, 154
Clarke, H. 140-1
Clarke, J.B. 8
Clemson, L. 156
client knowledge 6
clients *see* service users
Coates, V.E. 89
cognition 80-7, 88, 89, 189
Coleman, P.G. 83, 85
Commission of the European Communities 170-1
Commission for Local Administration in England 139
community environment
  safety issues 74-6, 157-62
  social activities 111, 112, 122-4, 142
'compassionate ageism' 18
complementary therapies 56-7
'compression of morbidity' model 59
computer skills 114, 121, 136
'conflictual ageism' 18
consultation *see* participation/partnership
consumerism 10-11, 25-6
  limitations 11, 25
  see also service users
contextualised scientific knowledge 4
continuity theory 120
Cook, G. 155, 157, 163
Cooperrider, D. 173
coping strategies and health 56-7, 59, 60
'corruption of care' 5
Cotterell, V. 89
Cowan, J. 153
creative therapies and dementia 83, 87
Crisp, Jane 84, 87
cultural differences
  and family support 119
  and memory loss 80-1
  and sexual activity 101
  and successful ageing 56, 60
Cumming, E. 19, 35
Cummings, Billie 112
Cylwik, H. 119

D

Dabbs, C. 163
Danigelis, N.L. 131
decision making 5, 8
  and risk management 153-4, 156-7, 163-4
decontextualised scientific knowledge 3-4
Delta Chair 82

dementia *see* memory loss/dementia
Dempsey, M. 88
desire: components of 103
Dick, R. 82
direct payments 140-1
disability
  cognitive disability 81-2
  and financial resources 139
  direct payments 140-1
  prevalence 54-5
  and sexuality 98, 101
  social model and risk 156
Disch, R. 37
discredited people 56
discrimination *see* ageist attitudes
disengagement theory 19, 35-6
Disney, R. 137
disposable soma theory 53
distal knowledge 7, 8, 9
domestic space 68-9
Douglas, Barbara 114
Douglas, M. 156
downsizing 68-9, 137
Doyal, L. 5
drama *see* Old Spice
Drench, M. 98
Duke Longitudinal Studies 101

E

Eastley, R. 88
Ebersole, P. 99
Ebrahim, S. 50-1
Eckland, M. 98
Economic and Social Research Council (ESRC) 76, 172
elder abuse 119
Eliopoulos, C. 100
emotional distance 5
empowerment 42, 171, 189-90, 191
ENABLE project 82
environment *see* lived environment
equity and justice 190-1
equity release schemes 137
ethical dilemmas 5
ethical knowledge *see* moral knowledge
ethnicity 36-7
  see also cultural differences
ethnography 4, 80-1, 132
European Union (EU) 170-1
Evandrou, M. 129
Evers, H.K. 24
evidence-based practice: knowledge basis 3-6, 7-9, 12-13, 191
exercise classes 113, 124, 178
Exhibition Park, Newcastle 112-13
experiential knowledge 4-5, 13

of ageing process 15-16, 193
difficulty of communicating 9-10
Expert Patient initiative 11
extrinsic ageing theories 52-3, 61

F

Fairbairn, A. 80
Falkingham, J. 129
falls: safety issues 150-2, 155-6, 157-62
families
   care provision 117-18
   changing patterns 35, 115-16, 118-19
   and financial assets 132
   intergenerational relations 35, 37, 119
   and social activities 111, 115-19, 122
   value as individual away from 180
Featherstone, M. 48, 49
Feinstein, J. 136-7
feminist theory: on body 49
Field, D. 87
film: images of sexuality 99
financial resources 127-44
   affords security 131
   anxiety over 129
   benefit take-up 134-6, 143
   disposable income 17-18, 32, 130-1
   and empowerment 189-90
   financial literacy 137-8
   health issues 139-41
    direct payments 140-1
   housing equity 136-7
   income and assets 131-2
   key issues 129-30
   and quality of life 130
    low incomes 128, 132-3, 139, 140, 143
   social contribution of older people 141-3,
     190
Finchum, T. 120
Fisher, A. 6
fitness
   obsession with 49
   for older people 113-14, 124, 178
'fortress living' 75
Frank, B.A. 87
Frank Theatre 39-42
Friedell, Morris 79-80, 83, 84, 88
friendship and socialising 119-22, 180
fuel payments 132, 135
Fuller, R.C. 22
furniture: assistive technology 82

G

Gardner, A. 154
gender
   and family care provision 117-18

and financial literacy 138
and health in older age 54
General Household Survey (GHS) 54
genetic theories of ageing 52, 53
George, L.K. 131
geriatric medicine 50-1
germ-line continuation 53
gerontology
   ageing as social construct 34
   intergenerational studies 35
   origins of 51
   see also theories of ageing
gerotranscendence theory 19
Gilleard, C. 11
Gilleard, J. 89
Gillespie, L.D. 155
Ginn, J. 18, 131
'Going Home from Hospital' group 112
Good, V. 82
'good practice' evaluation 173-83
Government Review (2002) 183
grandfathers 119
grandparenting 116-17, 119, 122, 141-2
Green, A. 89
Greenhalgh, T. 4, 8
'grey power/grey pound' 18, 32
'grey vote' 34
Griffin, Andy 39
Ground, I. 5
Growing Older Programme 76

H

Hagen, I. 82
Hall, B.A. 85
Harding, N. 85
Hardy, B. 172
Hardy, S. 4
Harper, S. 141-2
Harre, R. 85, 87
Haslam, R.A. 73-4
Havighurst, R.J. 19, 35-6
health 53-9
   and activity 57-8, 59, 61-2, 87
   and financial resources 139-40
   fitness for older people 113-14, 124, 178
   management of ill-health 56-7, 59, 60
   quality of life issues 59-61
    and low income 132
   self-assessed health 55-6, 57-8, 61
   and sexuality 97, 98, 101, 102
   therapeutic value of informal sector
     schemes 180
   views of older people 57-9
   walking safely in community 75
   see also disability; memory loss/dementia
health care provision

ageist attitudes 37-8, 56
and financial resources 139-41
  direct payments 140-1
  paying for services 131, 132
  informal sector schemes 178
  medicalisation of old age 34, 49, 85, 181
  policy context 170, 171
Health and Lifestyles Survey 54
Health Survey for England 54-5
heating 132
Help the Aged 72, 73
  user satisfaction study 172-83
Henry, W. 19, 35
Hepworth, M. 49
Hess, P. 99
Hewitt, M. 34
Higgs, P. 11
Hill, T.M. 87
Hodson, D. 101
home 137
  see also housing
'home zones' 75-6
homeless older people 72
homosexual relationships 98
House for Life project 69-71, 77
housing 67-74
  adaptation for old age 69-71, 82
  as equity 136-7
  as home 137
  safety and risk 73-4, 150-2, 155-6
  winter survival 72-3
    fuel payments 132, 135
Howell, Dr 51
Hugman, R. 118
humanitarian formulation 23, 24, 25
Humphrey, R. 132-3

I

iatrogenic effects 102
identity
  and diagnosis of dementia 85-6
  see also individuality; selfhood
ill-health *see* health
income inequalities 17-18, 130
  low incomes 128, 132-4, 143
  see also financial resources
independence: social value 56, 60
independent living 170
  see also housing
individuality
  and informal sector schemes 179-80
  personhood 188-9, 190, 191
inequality
  equity and justice 190-1
  in income 17-18, 130
  power sharing 189-90

infant mortality 54
informal care
  by families 117-18
  by older people 142-3
  and costs of care 139, 142-3
informal sector schemes 174-83
  benefits of 177-8, 179-81, 182-3
  funding issues 177, 178, 182, 183
  integration with formal sector 182
  and policy formation 181, 183
  and quality of life 179-81
information technology 121
Innes, A. 82
institutional ageism 37
integrated service provision 183
intergenerational relations 35, 37, 119
Internet 121
intimacy *see* sexuality
intrinsic ageing theories 51-2, 61
intuitive knowledge 4-5
  see also experiential knowledge

J

Jerrome, D. 120, 192-3
Joseph Rowntree Foundation 12, 72
justice 190-1

K

Kahn, R.I. 60
Kane, R.A. 153, 154-5, 162-3
Karlen, A. 98
Kaufman, S.R. 153
Keady, J. 85, 89
keep-fit classes 113, 124, 178
Kelly, M.P. 87
Kennedy, G. 101
Killick, John 87
Kimboko, P.J. 121
Kingsberg, S. 100, 102, 103
Kirkwood, T.B.L. 53
Kitwood, Tom 85, 87
knowledge 1-13
  for evidence-based care 3-6, 7-9, 12-13, 191
  financial literacy 137-8
Koch, T. 37-8

L

Lancet, The 119
language: referring to older people 17
Larsen, P. 97
Laumann, E. 102
learning activities 121, 177-8
leisure activities 113-14, 177

Leisure, Pleasure and Learning (LPL) 113-14
Levin, C.A. 153, 154-5, 162-3
Levine, S.B. 101, 103
Liaschenko, J. 6
life expectancy 53-4, 61
  and sexuality 97, 101
  social impact 141-2
life skills acquisition 177-8
lifelong learning 121
'Lifetime Homes' 72
lived environment 67-77
  community environment 74-6
  housing 67-74, 82
  safety and risk 73-4, 150-2, 155-6, 157-62
loneliness 121
long-term care 139-40, 170-1
long-term relationships: sexual activity 103
longevity *see* life expectancy
Longino, C. 50
Losee, R. 98
low incomes 128, 132-4, 143
  and costs of care 139, 140-1
Lupton, D. 156
Luxton, T. 155-6

M

M and Ms group 83-4
MacArthur study 118
McBride, K. 98
McFadden, D. 136-7
McIntosh, B.R. 131
Macintyre, Sally 22, 23-4, 33
McKee, K.J. 86
McKeith, I. 80
Mackenzie, L. 155
Making Memories Group 83-4
managed risk 162-4
management
  informal sector schemes 176
  of risk *see* risk management
marginalisation 11, 21-2, 189-90
  see also social exclusion
Marshall, M. 82
Martin, P.J. 8
Matocha, L. 98
media images 98, 99, 115
medicalisation of old age 34, 49, 85, 181
Meerabeau, L. 4-5
memories: importance of 83-4
memory clinics 88
memory loss/dementia 79-90
  evolution of 88-9
  experience of 79-80, 81, 82-7, 88
  and quality of life 83-4, 85, 163
  and relationship to self and others 82-7,
    88, 89

right to personhood 189
responses to diagnosis 85-6, 88-9
therapeutic interventions 87-8
menopause and sexual activity 102
mental health *see* memory loss/dementia
Mills, M.A. 83, 85
Mills, T.L. 119
Minichiellio, V. 38
Minois, G. 23, 33
models of ageing 18-20, 35-6, 60
Moglia, R. 98
money issues *see* financial resources
moral knowledge 5-6, 8, 10, 13
morbidity 54, 59
Mosley, A. 155
Mulligan, T. 101
musical therapy and dementia 87
Myers, R.R. 22

N

'narrative reconstruction' 58-9
National Care Standards Agency 26
National Health Service (NHS) 11
National Service Framework (NSF) for
    Older People 11, 153, 170, 171, 181
needs of older people 18
  and informal sector schemes 174-6
  sexual needs 98-9, 106
Nelson, Helen 68-9
New Osbaldwick community 72
Newcastle City Council 69-71
NHS 11
NIACE 138
Nolan, M. 84-5
normalisation
  and dementia 83-4, 86-7
  and ill-health 57
  informal sector schemes 179
  sickness/normality continuum 33
Norman, A. 22
North East Pre-Retirement Association
    (NEPRA) 113
NSF *see* National Service Framework

O

Oakley, R. 80-1
Öberg, P. 27, 48, 52
Office of Population Censuses and Surveys
    (OPCS) 54
Old Spice 39-42, 112, 149, 150-2, 157-62
older people
  demarcation as group 16-17, 18, 188
  historical context 22-4, 33-4
  as preferred term 17
oppression factors 36

optimisation strategies 60
organisational formulation 24, 25
organisational risk management 162-4
organised activities 122-3
O'Riordan, T. 156-7
Orona, C.J. 85

P

Palfrey, C. 85
Palguta, R. 101
Palmer, G. 132
Palmore, E. 97, 101
Pangman, V.C. 97-8, 100
participation/partnership
    costs of 142
    informal and formal sectors 182-3
    and power 171-2, 190
    in research 11-12, 192-3
    see also consumerism
Paterson, L. 55-6
patient knowledge 6
Patterson, M. 86
Pearce, A. 89
pensions 17, 24, 129, 136
    'poverty trap' 133-4
Percival, J. 69, 71
person knowledge 6
person-centred care 11, 84-5, 170, 181, 192
personhood 188-9, 190, 191
    see also selfhood
Phair, L. 82
Phillipson, C. 33, 34
physical functioning 47-62
    biomedical models 49-51, 59, 62
    longevity 53-4, 96, 101, 141-2
    for 'positive ageing' 20
    quality of life issues 59-61
    and sexual activity 101-2
    theories of ageing 51-3, 61
    see also health; memory loss/dementia;
        sexuality
physical theories of ageing 18, 49-53
Pimm, Keith 112-13
Pinchbeck, I. 34
'play' in social activities 121
policy
    historical treatment of older people 22-4,
        33-4
    'joined up' policy 192
    on retirement 17, 130
    and service provision 170-1
    and informal sector 181, 183
    and theories of ageing 20-2, 26
poor laws 22-3, 33
population-based findings 4, 8
poverty indicators 132-3

'poverty trap' 133-4
power
    and knowledge forms 10
    and participation 171-2, 190
    sharing and exercising 189-90, 191
pre-retirement courses 113, 138
professional practitioners
    ageist attitudes 37-8, 39-42
    informal sector schemes 176-7
    and knowledge 7-8
    risk management 152-65
    and sexual needs 98-9, 106
Protestant work ethic 56
proximal knowledge 7-8, 9
psychological functioning 20, 102-3
psychological theories of ageing 18-20, 35-6
public space and safety 75, 156
public transport 76

Q

qualitative research 11-12
    Appreciative Inquiry 173-4
quality of life
    and financial resources 128, 130, 132-3
    and health issues 59-61, 132
    and informal sector schemes 179-81
    and lived environment 67-77
    and memory loss 83-4, 85, 163
    and sexuality 97-8
Qureshi, H. 117

R

Raines, M.L. 5
reciprocity 21-2, 190, 191
    social activities 119-20, 121-2, 142
Reed, J. 5, 86-7
regulation 25-6
relationship-centred care 84-5, 89
research
    participative research 11-12, 192-3
    on views on sexuality 103-5
residential care: risk management 163-4
retirement
    policy on 17, 130
    pre-retirement courses 113, 138
Richards, S. 85
Riglin, J. 155-6
risk 73-4, 149-65
    risk avoidance 154
    risk management 152-65
    risk taking 156-62
    managed risk 162-4
    see also safety
Roberto, K.A. 121
Rolfe, G. 8

Roman Empire: old age in 23, 33-4, 60
Rowe, J.W. 60
Royal Commission on Long-Term Care 140
Royal Commission on the Poor Law 22
Royal Society 157

S

Sabat, S.R. 85, 87
safety and risk 149-65
  in community environment 74-6, 157-62
  in the home 73-4, 150-2, 155-6, 157-62
  risk management 152-65
'safety–freedom tradeoffs' 163
Salvation Army 72
Schon, D. 8-9
Schulz, R. 89
scientific knowledge 3-4, 9, 10, 13
Scottish Down's Syndrome Association 83,
  84
Seedhouse, D. 5
Seeman, T.E. 58
Seguire, M. 97-8, 100
self-assessed health 55-6, 57-8, 61
self-efficacy 58, 59, 61, 124
self-esteem of service users 172, 177
self-help literature 19, 20
selfhood
  and dementia 83-7, 88, 89
  and user satisfaction 172
Semans, M. 98, 101-2, 106
'sense of coherence' and health 58
service provision
  costs of 24, 131, 139, 142-3
  policy context 170-1, 181
  regulation 25-6
  satisfaction of users 171-83
    informal sector schemes 174-83
  see also health care provision; professional
    practitioners; social care
service users 169-83
  campaigning groups 24-5, 171
  consumerism 10-11, 25-6
  knowledge chains 8
  satisfaction with services 171-83
    study of 172-83
  see also participation/partnership
service-context knowledge 6
sexuality 95-107
  definition 97
  images of older people 97-100
  and quality of life 97-8
  sexual activity 19, 101-6
    limitations 101-3
    views of older people 103-6
Shakespeare, William 49
Shomaker, D.J. 87

sickness *see* health
sickness/normality continuum 33
Sidell, M. 54, 58, 59
Silver Surfers 121
Simon, W. 97
Skeen, P. 101
smart houses 69-71, 77, 81-2
social activities 111-15, 122-4
  financial constraints 132
  informal sector schemes 177-8
  voluntary work 142
social care
  costs of 24, 131, 139-40, 142-3
  European policy on 170-1
  informal sector schemes 178
  medical model 181
  paying for services 131, 132
    direct payments 140-1
  see also informal sector schemes
social care practitioners *see* professional
  practitioners
social constructivism 173
social costs of older people 24, 25
social exclusion 32-3, 132-3, 143
  see also ageist attitudes; marginalisation
social knowledge 6
social model of disability 156
social networks 111-24
  families 115-19
  friendship and socialising 119-22, 180
  and informal sector schemes 177, 180
social security
  benefit take-up 134-7, 143
  European policy 170
social value
  of cognitive skills 80-1, 82-3, 86-7
  contribution of older people 141-2, 190
  of independence 56
  of knowledge 10
  social exclusion 32-3, 132-3, 143
  of youthfulness 21-2, 48-9, 60
socio-psychological theories of ageing 18-
  20, 35-6, 59
Spafford, J. 140-1
spirituality and dementia 82-3, 85
spontaneous activities 122, 123
Srivastva, S. 173
stages of old age 36
stairs and risk 73-4
stereotypes 33-4, 37
  and sexuality 96, 97-100
  traditional activities 123
Stevenson, O. 156
Stokes, G. 163-4
Stoppard, Miriam 72-3
stratification of age 35
Strawbridge, W. 20, 60, 62

Strehler, B.L. 51
'structured dependency' 25-6
subjective ages 27
subjective well-being 55-6, 57-8, 61
'successful ageing' 19, 20, 36, 56, 60-1
  and family support 118
Surging Ahead 83
Swinburne, S. 104-5

T

Tanner, D. 172
Tansey, J. 156-7
tasks in old age 36
telephone ownership 132-3
theories of ageing 16, 18-20, 59-61
  ageing as social construct 34
  and ageist attitudes 35-6
  physical ageing process 49-53
  policy implications 20-2
  socio-psychological theories 18-20, 35-6,
    59
therapeutic interventions 56-7, 87-8, 180
Thomas Pocklington Trust 74
Thompson, N. 171-2
Thompson, P. 115-17, 118-19
Thompson, S. 171-2
Tilley, C. 98
Tinetti, M.E. 58
Tinker, A. 36-7
Tornstam, L. 19, 27, 48, 52
Torres, S. 60
traditional activities 123
transport provision 76, 178
Trinder, L. 8

U

unpaid care *see* informal care
users *see* service users

V

Viagra 96, 101
Victor, C.R. 121
visual impairment: support in home 74
voluntary sector *see* informal sector schemes
voluntary work 141, 142, 177

W

Waldrop, D.P. 119
Walker, A. 117
walking 75, 114
Walz, T.H. 97, 99, 100, 101, 103, 104
'warehousing' 24
Warren, Marjorie 51

Waterhouse, J. 98
Webb, C. 37-8
Weber, J.A. 120
Weiner, Bob 113
Weiner, C. 57
welfare policy 20-2, 24
well-being
  subjective well-being 55-6, 57-8, 61
  see also health; quality of life
Wenger, G.C. 120
Whetstone, M. 132, 133
Whitehouse, P. 86
'whole journey' strategy 76
whole systems events 112, 113, 183
Wilcock, G. 88
Wilcockson, J. 8
Wilkinson, H. 83
Willert, A. 98, 101-2, 106
Williams, G. 58
winter survival 72-3
  fuel payments 132, 135
Woodward, R.V. 85-6
work ethic 56
World Health Organisation (WHO) 97

Y

youthfulness: desire for 21-2, 48-9, 52-3, 60